Y0-ELL-430

Loring
A Trustee's Handbook

Loring
A Trustee's Handbook

Seventh Edition revised by

Charles E. Rounds, Jr.

Professor of Law
Suffolk University Law School
Member, Massachusetts Bar

and

Eric P. Hayes

Vice President and Senior Trust Counsel
State Street Bank and Trust Company
Member, Massachusetts Bar

Little, Brown and Company
Boston   New York   Toronto   London

Copyright © 1994 by Estate of James F. Farr

All rights reserved. No part of this book may be reproduced in any form or by any electronic or mechanical means including information storage and retrieval systems without permission in writing from the publisher, except by a reviewer who may quote brief passages in a review.

Library of Congress Catalog Card No. 94-75308

ISBN 0-316-35073-7

Third Printing

KP

Published simultaneously in Canada by
Little, Brown & Company (Canada) Limited

Printed in the United States of America

Summary of Contents

Contents

Preface

The first edition of *A Trustee's Handbook*, by Augustus Peabody Loring, appeared in 1898. Mr. Loring, who saw his brainchild through its fourth edition, was a practicing lawyer and a Boston trustee. In the 40 years that passed before his death, his small, compact Handbook played an important role in the dramatic growth of trust administration in this country. It quickly became the trustee's text of first resort. In 1940 Professor Scott wrote that for more than three decades the Handbook had been on his desk or near at hand. Mayo Adams Shattuck, Esq. and James F. Farr, Esq. prepared the Handbook's fifth and sixth revisions respectively.

The Handbook was last updated in 1962. Like Rip Van Winkle it awakens into a very different world where the state dispenses many more entitlements and regulates commercial activity far more intensely than it did then. In the late 1960s — perhaps in response to these developments — law schools set about the process of downgrading courses in the law of trusts from required to elective status, so that today, while almost all law schools have made courses on state regulation mandatory, only a few (most notably Suffolk University Law School in Boston) continue to afford the law of trusts the status that it enjoyed in Mr. Loring's time. In most law schools, the law of trusts is now an afterthought, buried somewhere in an elective course on estate planning. The current authors, therefore, may not assume — as Mr. Loring could and surely did — that the lawyers who read the Handbook have received formal instruction in the law of trusts.

Moreover, much has happened in the field of trusts since the last revision. The years since 1962 have seen major developments in the area of creditors' rights, spousal rights, and Medicaid eligibility and recoupment. ERISA would not arrive on the scene until 1974. There was no such thing as an IRA or Keogh plan. RICO, CERCLA, and the consumer protection statutes had yet to be enacted. It would be many years before the social investment movement would come into its own. These are just some of the recent developments that have been worked into this edition.

Our challenge, as the authors of the seventh edition, was to produce a modern handbook that is convenient, practical, and also "user friendly" in the Loring tradition, but that can also serve as a guide to the fundamental principles of trust law that are no longer standard fare in American law schools today. It is a tall order. The taxation of trusts has been given only passing mention, because to cover this subject would unnecessarily duplicate the work of others and thwart efforts to return the Handbook to "pocket size."

A Trustee's Handbook is not — nor was it ever — intended to be a treatise. We designed this seventh edition to be a handy, ready reference: a gateway, as it were, to the treatises, restatements, law review articles, uniform statutes, and seminal cases. In 1898 Mr. Loring succeeded in producing just such a book. On the eve of the twenty-first century we endeavor to revive and carry on the Loring tradition.

Charles E. Rounds, Jr.
Eric P. Hayes

March 1994

Acknowledgments

Without the support of Suffolk University Law School this project could not have gotten off the ground. A research "boiler-room," for example, was set up in the Law School's Pallot Library with Professor Michael Slinger, or someone from his dedicated library staff, available seven days a week to help move things along. Over the years a number of third-year students who had successfully completed Suffolk Law School's intensive Trusts course served tours of duty as the authors' research assistants. They are, in alphabetical order: Christopher J. Akeley, Jessica E. Coccoli, Ann Graglia-Kostos, Ernst Guerrier, Michael F. Hogan, W. Todd Huston, Celia H. Ketley, Cynthia A. Korhonen, John P. Larochelle, Emanuel J. Markis, Colleen J. McHugh, James A. Miller, Salina Millora, Paul J. Moura, Suzanne Marie Murray, Robert S. Nedder, Jr., Melanie Ann Patenaude, Michael J. Riley, Randall Pratt, Gwendolyn Ann Rotter, Anthony Sciaraffa, Mark L. Seiden, John D. Tuerck, James Patrick Winston, and John J. Yered.

The authors wish to extend their special thanks to George McElroy, Esq., once a research assistant and now a promising Boston attorney, who stayed with the project to the very end processing chapter drafts and footnotes and maintaining the project's institutional memory.

The authors wish to recognize Sandborn Vincent, Esq., Trust Counsel (Retired), The First National Bank of Boston, who introduced Charles E. Rounds, Jr. to the world of the trust and endeavored to furnish him with the skills he would need to confront its challenges. The authors wish to pay their respects to the late Frederick W. Clapp, Esq., Senior Trust Officer, Bank of New England, whose quiet wisdom, competence, and guidance will never be forgotten by Eric P. Hayes and countless others. These men were emissaries from a golden age.

And finally the authors wish to express their gratitude to Alicia S. Rounds and Dorothy M. Hayes, as well as Masters Chad and Mark Rounds, for their unstinting cheerfulness and support during the many weekends, evenings, and holidays sacrificed in the cause of the seventh edition.

Special Notice

The citations to the following books are thus abbreviated:

A. W. Scott & W. F. Fratcher, Scott on Trusts (4th ed. 1987), is cited as "Scott on Trusts."

G. G. Bogert & G. T. Bogert, The Law of Trusts and Trustees (2d ed. 1984), is cited as "Bogert, Trusts and Trustees."

Loring
A Trustee's Handbook

CHAPTER *1*
Introduction

A trustee holds title to property for the benefit of another. That is the essence of the trust, whose development from century to century is, in the opinion of Professor Maitland, the greatest achievement of English jurisprudence[1] and the largest and most important of equity's exploits.[2] Title is the key to unlocking the secret of the trust. To the person who does not know this, the trust is a vague, elusive, somewhat mysterious concept. Title is what makes the trust work. Title is what gives the trust its utility.

Let us take, for example, the matter of probate avoidance. As title is not in the beneficiary per se, the beneficiary's incapacity or death usually will not interrupt the continuity of the trust's administration. Thus a single trust can substitute for the durable power of attorney, the property guardianship, and the will.

To the lawyer, the trust is a "fiduciary relationship with respect to property, subjecting the person by whom the title to the property is held to equitable duties to deal with the property for the benefit of another person, which arises as a result of a manifes-

---

[1]Maitland, Selected Essays 129 (1936), *quoted in* 1 Scott on Trusts §1.
[2]Maitland, Equity 23 (1936), *quoted in* 1 Scott on Trusts §1.

tation of an intention to create it."[3] It is likely that the layman thinks of the trust in quite different terms, as some kind of basket or receptacle. How property gets into the basket and what role the trustee is supposed to play in the matter is never made entirely clear to most laymen.

This is a practical handbook that addresses the rights, duties, and obligations of the parties once the trustee takes title to the trust property, that is, once the property is in the basket. The focus is on "personal" trusts, that is to say trusts created by human beings for human beings. Some attention is paid as well to trusts created by corporations for their employees.

In this handbook, the term *settlor* encompasses any person who creates a trust, whether by lifetime transfer, by lifetime declaration, or by will. The reader should bear in mind, however, that the usual term for the creator of a testamentary trust is *testator*. A trust created by transfer pursuant to the terms of a will is referred to as a *testamentary* trust. A trust created by lifetime transfer or declaration is referred to as an *inter vivos trust*. The terms *inter vivos trust* and *living trust* are synonymous.

In this handbook, unless otherwise specified, the term *beneficiary* encompasses not only the person who during the life of the trust has some right to the income from — or use of — the trust property but also the remainderman. This interest of the beneficiary of an ongoing trust is known as an *equitable* or *beneficial* interest and is itself a property right.[4]

The trust is a complex legal organism that survives on private property. Its earlier forms predate even the Norman conquest.[5] The trust as we know it today is the product of centuries of evolution. It is "an 'institute' of great elasticity and generality; as elastic, as general as contract."[6] It provides enlightened property owners and their lawyers with a mechanism for seeing to the needs of the young, the disabled, and the elderly far more efficiently, far more cost-effectively, far more creatively, far more flexibly, far more

---

[3]Restatement (Second) of Trusts §2 (1959).

[4]Restatement of Property Introductory Note (1936).

[5]*See* W. F. Fratcher, Trusts *in* VI Intl. Encyclopedia of Comp. Law, ch. 11, pp.3, 8-20 (Frederick H. Lawson ed. 1973).

[6]Maitland, *supra* note 2.

Chapter 1   Introduction

expeditiously, and with far more dignity than the state could ever do. In this regard, even a charitable trust is no match for the private personal trust. Only one's imagination limits the purposes for which such trusts may be created. To be sure, the institution of the private personal trust can never accommodate the needs of everyone, but each person in need of assistance who is properly cared for pursuant to its terms is one less person who has to encounter — and be a burden to — the welfare bureaucracy.

For the institution of the trust to flourish, however, there must be a bench and bar that understand the concept of the trust and appreciate its myriad possibilities; and there must be a corps of incorruptible and conscientious trustees. Thus the law has demanded — and must continue to demand — that the trustee be absolutely loyal to the trust, that the trustee act solely in the interest of the beneficiary, and that any behavior on the trustee's part which compromises the trust be subject to judicial sanction.

The fountainhead of the trustee's powers is the trust instrument. The settlor has the right to include in the trust instrument any provision relating to management of property or to the duties and powers of the trustee, provided it is not contrary to public policy. These provisions, unless varied by the court, are binding upon the trustee and will supersede the general law applicable to trustees, the principles of which are threaded throughout this handbook. Thus, in the words of Mr. Loring, ". . . THE FIRST AND MOST IMPORTANT DUTY OF THE TRUSTEE IS TO STUDY AND BECOME THOROUGHLY FAMILIAR WITH THE PROVISIONS OF THE TRUST INSTRUMENT, AND THEREAFTER TO FOLLOW THEM OUT IMPLICITLY."

CHAPTER 2
The Property Requirement

§2.1 The Property Requirement

As a general rule, a trust cannot exist without property.[1] Any transferable property interest, legal or equitable, may be the subject of a trust. Usually, legal title to the property is in the trustee.[2]

---

§2.1 [1]*See generally* 1A Scott on Trusts §74. But see §2.2.1, noting that the Uniform Testamentary Additions to Trusts Act has been interpreted as allowing an inter vivos trust to arise without property.

[2]When a trustee holds the beneficial interest in another trust, however, title to the underlying property is in the trustee of the other trust.

§2.1.1   The Inter Vivos Trust

Under the common law, an inter vivos trust arises when title to some interest in property passes to the trustee during the lifetime of the settlor. Because a will is *ambulatory* (*i.e.*, it speaks only at death), the mere execution of a will that names a trustee as legatee or devisee under a so-called *pour-over provision* will not give rise to an inter vivos trust. This is because no property interest passes at the time of the will's execution. A will may be employed to add property postmortem to a trust established inter vivos[3] and, of course, to impress a testamentary trust upon probate property. The trustee should be aware, however, that some states have enacted statutes that have somewhat eroded this common law property requirement.[4]

In the context of postmortem additions to a trust in existence prior to the execution of the will, an *agency* is to be contrasted with a *will*. An agency terminates upon the death of the principal.[5] Thus an agent of the settlor acting under a Durable Power of Attorney may not make postmortem additions of the settlor's property to a trust. To effect such a transfer there must be compliance with the Statute of Wills.

Any transferable interest may be used to establish an inter

---

[3]As a general rule, under the common law the inter vivos trust must be in existence prior to the execution of the pour-over will. *See* Clark v. Citizens Natl. Bank of Collingswood, 38 N.J. Super. 69, 118 A.2d 108 (1955). *But see* Bogert, Trusts and Trustees §106 (suggesting that under the common law a pour-over provision may be effective even though the inter vivos trust comes into existence after the will is executed). *See also* Uniform Probate Code §2-511 comment, 8 U.L.A 125 (1993 Supp.).

[4]See §2.2.1.

[5]*But see* Uniform Probate Code §5-504 comment, 8 U.L.A. 516 (1969) which states:

> The death of a principal who has executed a written power of attorney, durable or otherwise, does not revoke or terminate the agency as to the attorney in fact or other person, who, without actual knowledge of the death of the principal, acts in good faith under the power. Any action so taken, unless otherwise invalid or unenforceable, binds successors in interest of the principal.

vivos trust.[6] All a settlor need do, for example, in order to make the settlor's 50 shares of stock the subject of a trust is to have the shares re-registered in the name of the trustee. A simple phone call to a broker should set the re-registration process in motion. Rights under an insurance contract may be transferred during the insured's lifetime to a trust by assigning the policy itself to the trustee or by merely filling out a form designating the trustee as recipient of the insurance proceeds.

A transferable interest in one trust (perhaps an interest in a realty trust) may be held in another trust (perhaps a revocable inter vivos trust), except if an effective spendthrift provision prevents a beneficiary from making such a transfer.[7]

The antialienation provisions of ERISA should not extend to preventing an employee from making a present revocable transfer of any employee's remainder interest in a qualified employee benefit plan to the trustee of an inter vivos personal trust.[8] Such a transfer could be accomplished merely by the employee's filling out a beneficiary designation form supplied by the employer's human resources office.

One's contractual rights to the personal services of another are probably nontransferable under the terms of the contract and therefore cannot be the subject of a trust.[9] As a matter of public policy, an unlitigated personal injury claim probably cannot be assigned to an inter vivos trustee,[10] although there would seem to be no public policy reason why such a claim should not be assignable for probate avoidance purposes to the trustee of a revocable inter vivos trust.

Transferable partial interests may be presently assigned to an inter vivos trustee. Thus one's interest in property as a tenant in

---

[6]*See generally* 1A Scott on Trusts §74.1.

[7]*See generally* 2A Scott on Trusts §152.4.

[8]Treas. Reg. §1.401-1(b)(4) (as amended in 1976).

[9]*See generally* S. Williston, Contracts §421 (W. Jaeger ed., 3d ed. 1960).

[10]A claim to unliquidated damages for tortious injury to person or reputation is generally nonassignable, but once such a claim is reduced to judgment it becomes a money debt which *is* assignable. *See generally* 4 A. Corbin, Contracts §857 (1951); 1A Scott on Trusts §79.

common may be so transferred.[11] Could an inter vivos trust be funded through a joint tenancy with right of survivorship, that is, could a nontrustee settlor hold property jointly with a trustee? Such an arrangement is probably not a viable way of effecting the funding of an inter vivos trust, not because there is no inter vivos transfer of a property interest associated with the creation of a joint interest — there is — but because there may not be a joint tenancy under such circumstances. The interests of the individual and the trustee, while perhaps concurrent, would not be *equal*,[12] for unlike the lifetime of an individual, that of the modern trust tends to be either fixed or perpetual, and not tied to the lifespan of the trustee.[13]

　　One cannot extinguish one's obligation as a debtor by transferring away the obligation to a trustee.[14] Presumably the right to extinguish the obligation (if any) is lodged with the creditor or his transferee — the one who has the property interest in the debt. Although some commentators disagree on the grounds that one cannot be indebted to oneself,[15] a debtor — at the direction of the creditor — ought to be able to hold the debt in trust for the benefit of another without causing the trust to fail as to that property. This is because in equity the debtor essentially is in-

　　[11]In a tenancy in common, each cotenant owns an interest, separate and distinct, that may be transferred at different times (independently of other cotenants). C. Moynihan, Introduction to the Law of Real Property 213-214 (2d ed. 1988).

　　[12]In a joint tenancy, cotenants have exactly the same rights in their individual proportional interests as the other cotenants have in theirs. Id. at 207.

　　[13]Under the common law, a corporation and an individual or two corporations could not hold property as joint tenants, but only as tenants in common. This is because a corporation might have a life of unlimited duration that would defeat the individual's right to survivorship. *See generally* 2 Scott on Trusts §103.1 n.1 and accompanying text. By analogy, this principle ought to apply to the trust as well as the corporation. But see 2 Scott on Trusts §103.1 on the related issue of whether an individual and a corporation may serve jointly as cotrustees.

　　[14]An individual must have an interest in property to make a present disposition. An obligor has no property interest in that obligation that is capable of being transferred. 1A Scott on Trusts §§74, 87.

　　[15]A "person cannot have a legal claim against himself, whether for his own benefit or for the benefit of another." 1A Scott on Trusts §87. Where a debtor is indebted to himself there is no longer an enforceable debt. Id. at §87.4 (1987). *See also* Bogert, Trusts and Trustees §115.

debted not to himself but to himself in a fiduciary capacity — to the office of trustee as it were. It should be noted that when a bank trust department invests trust assets in the bank's commercial deposit accounts, the bank is acting as a trustee of its own obligations.[16]

§2.1.2   The Testamentary Trust

The provisions of a testamentary trust are set forth in a will. A testamentary trust arises when title to a portion or all of the decedent's probate estate is transferred from the executor or personal representative to the testamentary trustee. Thus a testamentary trust cannot arise until after the testator dies. Only then does the probate property come into existence, because only then does the will speak. The term *pour-over* is generally not used in connection with a testamentary trust.[17] It refers to the transfer of probate assets to the trustee of an inter vivos trust.[18]

§2.2   Funding Issues

In recent years, the revocable trust, the life insurance contract, and the employee benefit plan (including the Individual Retirement Account) have been transferring postmortem as much property as the will, and perhaps more.[1] These flexible, ambulatory, will-like devices have come to be known as *will substitutes,* and their proliferation has raised some trust-related funding issues.

---

[16]*See generally* 2A Scott on Trusts §170.18; Bogert, Trusts and Trustees §598.

[17]*See generally* Polasky, "Pour-Over" Wills and the Statutory Blessing, 98 Trusts & Estates 949 (1959).

[18]*See generally* 1A Scott on Trusts §54.3.

§2.2   [1]*See generally* Langbein, The Nonprobate Revolution and the Future of the Law of Succession, 97 Harv. L. Rev. 1108 (1984).

§2.2.1   The Pour-over Statute

No property is passed at the time a will is executed. At common law, therefore, the execution of a will with a pour-over provision could not serve as the initial funding vehicle for an inter vivos trust. Something more was needed.

Thus the practice evolved of funding inter vivos trusts with nominal amounts of property (*token funding*). It can be argued that if there is no inter vivos transfer of property, there is no inter vivos trust; if there is no inter vivos trust, the will's pour-over provision will lapse or fail. Many states have adopted in one form or another the Uniform Testamentary Additions to Trusts Act,[2] which some courts have interpreted as essentially allowing an inter vivos trust to arise without property, provided the trustee is named a beneficiary of a portion of the settlor's probate estate pursuant to a pour-over provision in the settlor's will.[3] Presumably the inter vivos trust would come into existence at the time the will is executed.

---

[2] The Uniform Testamentary Additions to Trusts Act is a freestanding model statute, promulgated in 1960 and revised in 1991, to track §2-511 of the Uniform Probate Code, which was promulgated in 1969 and revised in 1990. Of course it is the prerogative of each state wishing to adopt such a statute to adopt either model, with or without modification. See 1A Scott on Trusts §54.3 for a list of states adopting the Uniform Testamentary Additions to Trusts Act. *See also* Uniform Probate Code §2-511, 8 U.L.A. 125 (1993 Supp.); 1991 Uniform Testamentary Additions to Trusts Act, 8A U.L.A. 426 (1993 Supp.).

[3] Earlier forms of the Uniform Testamentary Additions to Trusts Act and the Uniform Probate Code were somewhat ambiguous on the issue whether funding of an inter vivos trust was necessary during the lifetime of the settlor, provided there was a pour-over clause in the will. See Clymer v. Mayo, 393 Mass. 754, 473 N.E.2d 1084 (1985), involving a pour-over to an inter vivos trust that the court termed *unfunded*. The court suggested that the inter vivos trust was *unfunded* notwithstanding the fact that the trustee was a designated beneficiary of a life insurance policy. While it interpreted the Massachusetts Uniform Testamentary Additions to Trusts Act as not requiring that the inter vivos trust be funded at the time the will is executed, the court erred in characterizing the trust at issue as *unfunded*. The trust was in fact funded because the trustee had been designated the beneficiary of life insurance policies and beneficiary of the employee benefit plan and thus contained property in the form of contractual rights. *See* §2.2.2. In response to this confusion surrounding the term *unfunded*, the Uniform Probate Code and the Uniform Testamentary Additions to Trusts Act were revised to unequivocally provide that an inter vivos "trust" need not be funded during the lifetime of the settlor, provided there is an associated pour-over will. *See* Uniform Probate Code §2-511, 8 U.L.A. 125

§2.2.2 Life Insurance Beneficiary Designations

It is a popular misconception that the revocable inter vivos designation of a trustee as a beneficiary of future life insurance proceeds is, alone, not enough to fund an inter vivos trust.[4] It is believed that something more is required, such as the present transfer of title to the contract itself or token funding. Some incorrectly refer to such trusts as *unfunded*.[5] It is settled law, however, that even the revocable designation of a trustee as the recipient of life insurance proceeds upon the future death of the insured constitutes the present transfer of property to the trustee.[6] The inter vivos trustee is the third-party beneficiary of a contract under which there has been an inter vivos exchange of consideration between the insured and the insurance company, that is, the insured having transferred inter vivos a premium and the company having transferred inter vivos a promise to pay proceeds upon the death of the insured. The trustee has an enforceable claim against the insurance company in the event the designation remains unrevoked at the death of the insured. The revocable life insurance beneficiary designation differs from a pour-over provision in a will in that under the common law there has been no inter vivos transfer of a property interest to anyone pursuant to the terms of the will at the time the will is executed, whereas there *is* such a transfer at the time the insurance beneficiary designation is filled out.

§2.2.3 The Custodial IRA

A taxpayer's Individual Retirement Account may be administered pursuant to what amounts under state law to an invest-

---

comment (1993 Supp.). *See also* 1991 Uniform Testamentary Additions to Trusts Act, 8A U.L.A. 426 (1993 Supp.).

[4] *See generally* 1A Scott on Trusts §57.3.

[5] Id. *See also* U.P.C. §2-511, *supra* note 3.

[6] *See generally* 1A Scott on Trusts §57.3.

ment management agency agreement, known as a *custodial IRA*.[7] Because an agency terminates at the death of the principal, many jurisdictions have enacted statutes that provide that an IRA custodian may honor the postmortem dispositive provisions of the beneficiary designation form notwithstanding the requirements of the Statute of Wills.[8] In essence these statutes extend the life of these IRA agency arrangements beyond the death of the taxpayer-principal. Even if such a statute has been enacted in the trustee's jurisdiction, there remains the open question whether the designation of the trustee of an inter vivos trust as postmortem beneficiary of the taxpayer's custodial IRA constitutes an actual or constructive transfer of property that will cause the inter vivos trust to arise. It may well be that something more is needed, such as a token funding or the execution of a will with provisions that conform to the jurisdiction's pour-over statute.

§2.3 Wrongful Defunding

If trust property is wrongfully removed from a trust through the actions of a trustee or another, the trust ought not to be extinguished for want of trust property.[1] A reasonable argument can be made that the absent trust property has merely been transformed into another type of property, namely the personal equitable obligation of the wrongdoer.[2]

---

[7]I.R.C. §408(h) (1974) (effective for tax years beginning after December 31, 1974).

[8]*See, e.g.*, Mich. Comp. Laws Ann. §700.257 (West 1988); Mass. Gen. L. ch. 167D, §30 (1983); N.Y. Est. Powers & Trusts Law §13-3.2 (McKinney 1967); Conn. Gen. Stat. Ann. §45a-347 (West 1991); *see generally* Bogert, Trusts and Trustees §255 n.11 and accompanying text (second note 11).

§2.3 [1]*But see generally* 1A Scott on Trusts §74.2.

[2]Id.

CHAPTER *3*

The Trustee's Office

§3.1 Who Can Be a Trustee?

Legal capacity to receive, hold, and manage property in trust is one thing; fitness to serve as trustee is another. One with legal capacity to take title or hold property for oneself, may do so as trustee. A minor has the capacity to hold title to property either in his or her own right or as trustee,[1] but because a minor's contracts are voidable, a minor is unfit to administer a trust.[2] Likewise, a

---

§3.1 [1]*See generally* 2 Scott on Trusts §91.
[2]Id.

trust estate may vest in an insane person, but such an individual is unfit to administer a trust and will be removed.[3] A trust ordinarily does not fail because the individual or corporation named fails for whatever reason to serve or to continue to serve as trustee. The court will appoint another trustee to serve in his place, unless to do so would contravene the intentions of the settlor.[4] Thus the transfer of property in trust to a minor or an insane person ordinarily will not prevent the trust from coming into being.[5]

A nonresident individual generally may receive and administer trust property.[6] Many states require that nonresident testamentary trustees appoint resident agents for the purpose of accepting service of process.[7] The capacity of an alien to act as trustee may be limited in states where there are remnants of common law restrictions upon the capacity of an alien to hold property.[8]

The United States, a state of the United States, or a municipality may be a trustee, although principles of sovereign immunity may make the trust unenforceable absent a statute to the contrary.[9] A partnership can act as trustee if under state law it has the capacity to hold the legal title to property.[10]

At early common law, a corporation could not serve as trustee.[11] This is no longer the case.[12] A corporation may act as trustee in furtherance of and as an adjunct to its corporate purpose.[13] As a general rule, however, a corporation now needs statutory authority to have as its purpose the administration of trusts.[14]

---

[3]Id. at §92.

[4]*See* Restatement (Second) of Trusts §2 comment *i* (1959).

[5]Id.

[6]*See generally* 2 Scott on Trusts §§94 (nonresident individuals), 96.6 (nonresident corporations); Bogert, Trusts and Trustees §132.

[7]Bogert, Trust and Trustees §132.

[8]2 Scott on Trusts §93.

[9]*See generally* id. §§95, 96.4; Hughes, Can the Trustee Be Sued for Its Breach: The Sad Saga of United States v. Mitchell, 26 S.D. L. Rev. 447 (1981) (discussing the fate of a breach of trust claim against the United States).

[10]*See generally* 2 Scott on Trusts §98.

[11]*See* id. §96.

[12]Id.

[13]*See generally* id. §96.3; Restatement (Second) of Trusts §96 (1959).

[14]*See generally* 2 Scott on Trusts §96.3.

Thus, absent trust powers conferred by statute, an automobile manufacturing company, for example, may act as trustee of its own employee benefit plan but not as trustee of the plans of other companies.[15] Legislatures have traditionally conferred trust powers upon trust companies and banks, although the culture of the lender is to some extent incompatible with that of the trust fiduciary.[16] A few jurisdictions require that a corporation serving as trustee of a testamentary trust be domiciled in the state; those that do not will generally require the appointment of a local official as agent to accept service of process.[17]

A corporation acting as trustee without express statutory authority would be well advised to have in its file a legal opinion that it has the authority to so act. For example, a corporation in the business of transacting in real estate should have such a letter to the extent it utilizes trusts in the conduct of its business. The same also could be said for the charitable corporation administering a trust with a noncharitable component (perhaps a provision for the benefit of a benefactor's spouse).[18] A corporation acting as trustee under a statutory grant of authority — most often this will be a bank — should know the limits of its authority and the regulatory framework within which it must operate.[19] A national bank may be in danger that its commercial personnel may be operating without the oversight of its trust committee in violation of "Regulation 9," the collection of federal regulations governing the administration of national bank trust departments.[20] This could happen, for example, in the context of the marketing of trusteed IRAs, mini-trusts, and investment management agency services. This could

---

[15]Id.

[16]*See generally* id. §§96.5, 170.23A.

[17]Florida, for example, is a state that requires domicile. *See generally* 5A Scott on Trusts §558; Bogert, Trusts and Trustees §132.

[18]*See generally* 2 Scott on Trusts §96.3.

[19]National banks must operate within the guidelines set out in Comptroller of the Currency Regulations, 12 C.F.R. §9 (1963) (known as "Regulation 9") and are subject to the laws of the state in which they operate unless such laws conflict with federal laws or interfere with their purposes as defined by Congress. *See generally* 10 Am. Jur. 2d Banks §§15, 305 (1963); 2 Scott on Trusts §96.5.

[20]Comptroller of the Currency Regulations, 12 C.F.R. §§9.7-9.9. *See generally* 2A Scott on Trusts §172.1.

also happen when a bank enters into certain types of commercial relationships with a trust beneficiary or with the asset of one of its trusts. [21]

One's capacity to be a trustee is not affected by the fact that one is also a beneficiary of the trust. A person, however, may not be sole trustee and the sole beneficiary, because if there is a merger of the legal and equitable interests there is no trust. [22] A man may be trustee for himself and others, or with others be trustee for himself alone, and of course, may be trustee for himself for life with remainder for others or for others for life with remainder to himself. In each of these situations the trustee-beneficiary does not possess the *entire* legal and *entire* beneficial interest.

§3.2   Who Is Fit to Be a Trustee?

Trust administration is not for every personality and every ethic. It is not for the wheeler-dealer and the dabbler. A trust is a legally complicated relationship requiring sustained attention, often over a period of many years, to a myriad of details of which some are clerical in nature (*e.g.,* keeping track of dividends) and some are not (*e.g.,* making discretionary distributions). Stewardship of another's property in and of itself is serious business, and yet it is only one of the trustee's many nondelegable functions.

Above all the trustee must act solely in the interest of the beneficiaries. [1] The trustee may not transact with the trust property for personal benefit, absent authority from the settlor, the court, or from all the beneficiaries. One of the hallmarks of the trust relationship is the trustee's duty of absolute loyalty to the

---

[21] *See* §6.1.3.
[22] *See generally* Bogert, Trusts and Trustees §129; 2 Scott on Trusts §99. *See also* §8.7.
§3.2   [1] Restatement (Third) of Trusts §170(1) (1992).

16

trust. One should not accept the office of trustee if there are any doubts about one's ability to carry out the duty of loyalty.[2]

This does not mean that trust administration should be something other than a business. It *is* a business, and it should be. Compensation provides a trustee with the incentive to keep trust matters high on his list of priorities. But trusteeship should not degrade to a state where it is merely an adjunct to other businesses such as brokerage, law, accounting, banking, or financial planning. Trust administration is a worthy profession in and of itself; it is a profession that thrives on regular attention over the long term, stability of personnel, the tried and true, and slow incremental changes for the better.

The court may appoint a trustee, or the governing trust instrument may empower an individual to appoint one.[3] In appointing a trustee the court will have due regard for the wishes of the settlor but will decline to appoint an unfit person. Thus, if someone authorized by the governing trust instrument selects an unfit or incapable person as trustee, the court may review the appointment. Ordinarily, one should not appoint oneself as trustee. The responsible individual should, giving due regard to the intentions of the settlor, consult the beneficiaries and appoint someone agreeable to them; this is what a court is expected to do.

Courts are reluctant to appoint nonresidents but as a practical matter they often do, particularly where some or all of the beneficiaries or property are out of state, and especially if nominated by the testator.[4] In some states the court may appoint a cotrustee to serve with a nonresident trustee.[5]

A substance abuser[6] or person of dishonest or bad character will not be appointed since the property would not be in safe

---

[2]*See* §6.1.3.

[3]*See generally* 2 Scott on Trusts §108.2 (appointment by the court), §108.3 (noncourt appointments).

[4]*See generally* Bogert, Trusts and Trustees §132.

[5]*See, e.g.,* 20 Pa. Cons. Stat. Ann. §7103 (Purdon 1972).

[6]*See, e.g.,* Ohio Rev. Code Ann. §2109.24 (Anderson 1953) (intoxication grounds for removing a trustee). The Pennsylvania fiduciary removal statute, however, has been amended to eliminate a reference to intoxication. 20 Pa. Cons. Stat. Ann. §3182 (Purdon 1992).

hands.[7] The entire matter of appointment lies in the reasonable discretion of the court with due deference being given to reasonable provisions in the governing instrument.[8]

§3.2.1   The Professional Trustee and Single-Purpose Trust Company

In an ideal world, only single-purpose trust companies and individuals engaged full-time in the business of trust administration would serve as trustees. Experience in and knowledge of trust matters would be broad and deep. Attention to the welfare of the trust would be exclusive, focused, and sustained. Goods and services would be contracted for at arm's length on behalf of the trust.

Economic realities, however, are such that only a small percentage of the population has the wherewithal to purchase the services of trustees so single-mindedly committed. Moreover, there are those who feel that the professional trustee, no matter how competent, is unacceptable because of its inability to offer the personal attention that a family member ostensibly provides. In a less than ideal world, persons in other lines of work are called upon to serve as trustees. While their involvement is not per se undesirable, each category raises its own collection of red flags.

§3.2.2   The Lawyer

The advantage of having a lawyer serve as trustee is that lawyers understand the equitable rights and obligations of the parties. The disadvantage is that the lawyer who renders legal services to the trust for compensation over and above his or her reasonable trustees fees brushes with a conflict of interest.[9] The

---

[7]*See generally* 2 Scott on Trusts §107; Bogert, Trusts and Trustees §519 (the court's power to remove trustee).

[8]*See generally* 2 Scott on Trusts §108.2.

[9]*See, e.g.,* Kentucky Natl. Bank v. Stone, 93 Ky. 623, 20 S.W. 1040 (1893); Estate of Lankershim, 6 Cal. 2d 568, 58 P.2d 1282 (1936); Ontjes v. MacNider,

lawyer-trustee is after all transacting with the trust "for his own account." It is not always clear when one is acting as trustee and when one is acting as counsel, nor is it clear what portion of the compensation is attributable to actions as trustee and what portion is attributable to the rendering of legal services. But perhaps the fundamental problem is the loss to the trust of the independent perspective, of the checks and balances that operate when the functions are assumed by different entities.[10] It is a loss to the beneficiaries that cannot be mitigated or rationalized away by compensation adjustment. When functions are separated, the trustee to some extent monitors the lawyer and vice versa. When the functions coalesce in one person, there arises the danger that the lawyer as a practical matter is unaccountable as to performance and compensation.

§3.2.3   The Stockbroker

The trustee, under a duty to act solely in the interests of the beneficiaries, faces a built-in, structural incentive to violate that duty when he or she also serves as the trust's commissioned stockbroker. By selling when it is in the interest of the beneficiaries to hold and by buying when it is in the interests of the beneficiaries not to buy, the trustee-stockbroker personally benefits when the portfolio is "churned."[11]

One solution is for the trustee-stockbroker to place trades with another firm. This avoids the conflict inherent in placing trades with the trustee-stockbroker's firm, but it will not eliminate the indirect personal benefit — in good will and implied IOU's — that inevitably accrues to someone who parcels out business. Of course, this conflict is not confined to brokers of stock. It would also apply to brokers of insurance and real estate. If the trustee

---

234 Iowa 208, 12 N.W.2d 284 (1942); Florida Bar v. Della-Donna, 583 So. 2d 307 (Fla. 1989). *See generally* Kindregan, Conflicts of Interest and the Lawyer in Civil Practice, 10 Val. U.L. Rev. 423, 431 (1976); Krier, The Attorney as Personal Representative or Trustee, 65 Fla. B.J. 69 (1991).

[10]*Supra* note 9.

[11]*See, e.g.,* Armstrong v. McAlpin, 699 F.2d 79 (2d Cir. 1983).

intends to operate the trust out of a brokerage facility, at the very least the facility's infrastructure should be capable of accommodating the trust's specialized operational requirements.

§3.2.4   The Bank

A full-service bank is said to have two sides: the commercial side and the trust side. The trust side operates in the fiduciary's labor-intensive world, where beneficiaries are entitled to full disclosure, deference, and a degree of intimacy, while the commercial side operates in the world of the marketplace and by its rules. If a loan to a commercial customer goes bad, generally the lender is not bound by fiduciary ties and can take necessary steps to protect its interest. The bank in its role as creditor is different from the bank acting as trustee since as trustee the bank is the legal owner of the property and as trustee has a fiduciary duty to place the interest of the beneficiaries ahead of its own interests.

The cultures, too, are very different. If commercial officers run the full-service bank, they must strive to understand and adequately fund the trust function — a function that operates in a world that values, among other things, continuity of management and a smooth-running operational and administrative infrastructure.

§3.2.5   The Family Member

The seeds of family disharmony are too often sown when a beneficiary is appointed trustee. Particularly in the case where siblings and their issue are permissible beneficiaries of a discretionary trust, the appointment of one sibling can be a prescription for disaster. The sibling-trustee is tempted either to bend over backwards to the economic detriment of the sibling or the sibling's issue in order to avoid even the appearance of impropriety and conflict of interest (thus perhaps thwarting the settlor's wishes that all siblings and their issue be treated fairly) or the sibling is tempted to take unfair advantage of the office in furtherance of the sibling's economic interests to the exclusions of the interests of the other beneficiaries. On the other hand, it can be a prescription for gridlock and deadlock if all the siblings are serving as cotrustees. Moreover the matter of trustee compensation can become a sensitive issue when the trustee is also a beneficiary.

The appointment of a beneficiary's near relation brings with it its own set of problems, although in the United States relations are more often appointed than strangers. Laxness of management, the overweening influence of beneficiaries, and condonations of misconduct too often are the price of these family arrangements.

There is no rule against making the spouse of a beneficiary trustee. However, the risk does exist that the marriage will end in divorce before the trust terminates. In addition, it would be a tragedy if the spouse's appointment itself were to have a destabilizing effect on a marriage which till then had been solid.

§3.2.6   Considerations in the Selection of a Trustee

The expected duration of the trust, the complexity of its assets, the needs of the beneficiaries, the level of administrative and investment expertise required and the fees a professional trustee will charge must be considered in the selection of a trustee. The settlor should take the long view. A trust for a retarded child or an orphaned grandchild, for example, could extend 50, 60, or 70 years beyond the settlor's lifetime, long after the settlor's close friends and relatives have died. In other words, the trust needs a spine. This could take the form of an institution in the first instance, an institution as a cotrustee, or an institution as a fallback in default of named individuals.

The settlor should not confuse the function of a *guardian* of the person with the function of a *trustee*. The loving grandfather may be the perfect guardian of the orphaned grandchild's person, but he may be totally unsuited because of his age to act as trustee. Moreover, if both positions are held by different people, the guardian benefits from the trustee's independent perspective and the child benefits from the checks and balances inherent in a separation of these responsibilities. A separation of responsibilities is also preferable if the settlor intends that the guardian of the person receive generous discretionary distributions of income and principal for domestic help, the construction of an addition on the guardian's house, or such other purposes as will lessen the financial burden of the guardianship. It is always awkward for trustees, even though duly authorized, to make discretionary distributions to themselves.

The settlor ought not to measure one's suitability to be a trustee solely by his or her investment successes. There is much more to a trusteeship than merely investing.

If the settlor intends to name himself as trustee in the first instance, he should make sure that matters of trustee succession are adequately addressed in the governing instrument. It is very important that the matter of the settlor's incapacity be addressed.

Finally, the settlor should be reminded that the selection is not an either/or choice between the bank or the lawyer or the family member. Many permutations and combinations of cotrusteeships and orders of succession can exploit strengths and mitigate weaknesses. For the settlor wishing to build in a measure of nonjudicial oversight, there are provisions for trustee removal and appointment that need not create tax problems if properly drafted.[12]

§3.3   Involuntary Trustees

With the following exceptions, one cannot be forced to serve as a trustee:

[12]*See generally* Wall Estate v. Commissioner, No. 15311-91, 101 T.C. No. 21 (Oct. 12, 1993); Priv. Ltr. Rul. 93-03-018 (Oct. 23, 1992).

(1) Once a trusteeship is voluntarily accepted, the law may require the trustee to remain in office until a qualified successor is in place.[1] Thus a trustee who at some point wants to resign may end up serving a portion of the trusteeship involuntarily. This is yet one more reason why the decision to serve as a trustee is not to be taken lightly.

(2) If the trustee dies and there is no provision for a successor, the trustee's personal representatives or those having an interest in the trustee's personal estate may find themselves de facto successor trustees until such time as qualified successors are in place.[2]

(3) *The constructive trust.* This is an equitable remedy employed by the courts to avoid unjust enrichment. It is a device more often employed to remedy breaches of contract than breaches of trust, and works as follows: If a person comes into possession of property as a result of fraud, undue influence, or some other such intentional wrong (with a few minor exceptions), he will hold the property not for himself or the perpetrator of the wrong but as a constructive trustee for the person who, but for the wrong, would have received the property. The constructive trustee's primary responsibility is to get title and possession safely into the hands of the rightful owner.[3]

(4) *The purchase money resulting trust.*[4] A purchase money re-

---

§3.3   [1]*See generally* Bogert, Trusts and Trustees §§511-512; 2 Scott on Trusts §106.1.

[2]*See generally* Bogert, Trusts and Trustees §529.

[3]A constructive trust, unlike an express trust, is not a fiduciary relation. Restatement of Restitution §160 comment *a* (1937). *See also* 5 Scott on Trusts §462.1. Although the constructive trust is technically a legal mechanism for transferring title, the prudent constructive trustee will act as a short-term fiduciary with respect to the property until title is transferred.

[4]*See generally* 5 Scott on Trusts §440.

sulting trust[5] may arise where property is purchased and
the purchase price is paid by one person and at his direction the seller transfers the property to another person.[6] If
there is no intent that the transferee take the beneficial
interest, the titleholder (*i.e.*, the resulting trustee) must
turn the property over to the person who paid the consideration. A purchase money resulting trust does not arise
automatically. For example, when there is an intent on the
part of the person who paid the consideration to make a
gift to the transferee, no purchase money resulting trust
will arise.

(5) It has long been the practice of federal, state, and local
governments, in lieu of taking property for just compensation, to place restrictions on how certain types of properties may be used by their owners.[7] These restrictions are
intended to further certain state interests, such as land
and wildlife conservation, historic preservation, and resi-
dential zoning. In times when public treasuries are
strapped for funds, trusteeships by restriction have a

---

[5]*See generally* id. §440.1. If *A* purchases land and puts the legal title in
B's name, or *A* gives *B* money to purchase land on *A*'s behalf, and if there is no
intention by *A* to make a gift to *B*, a *purchase money resulting trust* will arise.

[6]Id.

[7]*See, e.g.,* Penn Central Transp. Co. v. City of New York, 438 U.S. 104
(1978); Nollan v. California Coastal Commn., 483 U.S. 825 (1987). A point is
reached, however, when a body of restrictions so circumscribes how an
owner may use his property that he becomes a de facto trustee of the property for the benefit of the public. While the matter of restraints on coastal
development has received considerable publicity because of the de facto
takings cases, and while the spotted owl and the snail darter have brought
public attention to matters of wildlife conservation, efforts to regulate the
use of Native-American burial sites discovered on private property or the
interiors of historic homes in private hands perhaps show the trusteeship by
restriction at its most intrusive. *See also* Rounds, Protections Afforded to
Massachusetts' Ancient Burial Grounds, 73 Mass. L. Rev. 176 (1988). The
better approach, both for the property owner and the public, is for the state
to take a particular asset by eminent domain for just compensation and then
irrevocably transfer it into a common law charitable trust, together with
sufficient funds for its perpetual maintenance and for the adequate compensation of willing competent trustees.

certain superficial appeal: They appear to be effective, cost-free mechanisms for limiting the use of property on behalf of the public. But one has to question the long-term effectiveness of such involuntary arrangements that require de facto trustees to serve without compensation and without reimbursement for expenses.

In the case of state-imposed restrictions on archaeological sites and the interiors of homes, there can be no credible enforcement of such trusts over the long-term without massive state expenditure and intrusion. Another problem is that the trusteeship by restriction is essentially a passive arrangement that neither makes provision for the perpetual maintenance of assets nor protects an asset in the event it is constructively abandoned (*e.g.,* due to the property owner's impoverishment).

§3.4   Avoiding, Assuming, and Vacating the Office

A trust arises as a result of the settlor's general intention to create it. The transfer of title to the trustee is a legal consequence of that intention. A trust, however, will not fail for want of a trustee. Thus, if property is transferred to one who cannot act, or if the one nominated disclaims, or if the trustee has died or is unable to act, the property will be held by the person in possession until a proper trustee can be appointed. The power to appoint a trustee will arise whenever the circumstances make it necessary, either (1) in the nature of things (as in the case of the death of the trustee), (2) whenever the provisions of the trust instrument prescribe it, (3) when the number of trustees sinks below the prescribed number, or (4) when the safety of the property or the proper administration of the trust requires an additional trustee.

§3.4.1 Appointment

The appointment of the trustee under a declaration of trust requires no action by the court and no act of property transfer.[1] The declarant becomes trustee simply by intending to impress a trust upon his property. However, the segregation of the property and the re-registration of securities and other such items of intangible personal property are advisable in order to generate factual evidence of the intent to impress a trust upon the property.

A trust created by inter vivos transfer from *A* to *B* also requires no judicial act of appointment.[2] A completed transfer of the trust property must occur before the appointment is effective.[3] When the property is land, delivery of a deed completes the transfer; when the property is intangible personal property (*e.g.,* stocks and bonds), re-registration in the name of the trustee completes the transfer. But what if the securities remain in the name of the original owner who, in lieu of re-registration, places them in the hands of the trustee with the intention that they be held in trust? Has the appointment of a trustee been consummated? The better view is that it has. It is settled law, for example, that notice to an insurance company is not a requirement for impressing a trust in equity upon rights under an insurance contract.[4] Nor is notice to a bank required to impress a trust upon a bank account.[5] Likewise no notice to a transfer agent is required to impress a trust in equity upon a block of securities.[6] Thus it logically follows that the trustee's appointment can be effected in equity by the transfer of physical possession in lieu of re-registration, provided the act is coupled with the appropriate intent.

Of course no rational person would purposely forgo re-registration, settling only for a transfer of physical possession. The absence of a paper trail would hamper efforts to defend the trust

---

§3.4   [1]*See* 1 Scott on Trusts §17.1.
[2]5A Scott on Trusts §557.
[3]*See* 1 Scott on Trusts §§32.1-32.2.
[4]*See generally* 1A Scott on Trusts §57.3.
[5]*See generally* id. §§58-58.6.
[6]*See generally* 2A Scott on Trusts §179.3.

against those who would attack the transfer. But what if the securities are physically inaccessible and their precise descriptions not readily ascertainable? Could an appointment be effected if the settlor executes and delivers a general unspecific assignment of all the securities he owns to the trustee? In this case there is no re-registration *and* no physical transfer of the underlying paper. It is suggested that in cases of emergency (*e.g.,* the imminent death of the settlor), the transfer is sufficiently complete in equity to effect an appointment, because the owner has done all that can be done under the circumstances to place the property in the hands of a trustee.

Whether an agent acting under a durable power of attorney can effect the appointment of a trustee for the principal's property remains to be seen.[7] The proliferation of Durable Powers of Attorney makes it likely that such appointments will be attempted — they certainly will be challenged.[8] However, if a particular appointment is in the interest of the principal and within the scope of the agent's authority, it ought to be upheld in equity.

In the case of testamentary trusts the common requirement is that the trustee nominated must obtain appointment by the court.[9] Some authorities describe this procedure as a mere confirmation of the appointment made by the will inasmuch as it is conceded that the trustee's powers, after appointment, mainly flow from the trust instrument and not from the court. However, the trustee's powers also arise partly from the general body of the law, and it is at least certain that no valid exercise of any testamentary trust power may be made by the trustee prior to his court appointment and qualification.[10]

Trustees who are appointed by decree of court may be required to give bond to the court for the faithful performance of their trust.[11] In testamentary trusts the trustee's bond ordinarily is

---

[7]*See generally* 11 Institute on Estate Planning §305.2 (P. E. Heckering, ed. 1977).

[8]*See generally* McGovern, Trusts, Custodianships, and Durable Powers of Attorney, 27 Real Prop. Prob. & Tr. J. 1 (Spring 1992).

[9]*See generally* 5A Scott on Trusts §557.

[10]Id.

[11]*See generally* Bogert, Trusts and Trustees §151.

required to be with sureties unless the testator expressly has excused the trustee from furnishing them or unless all persons beneficially interested join in requesting the exemption.[12] In many jurisdictions corporate fiduciaries are exempt from providing sureties on their bonds.[13]

Probate courts (usually by virtue of statute) and courts acting under statute or under their general equity jurisdiction have broad powers with regard to the appointment of trustees.[14] The court's power to appoint a trustee is exercised wherever circumstances make it necessary.[15] In case of need, such as the death of a sole trustee, the court will appoint a temporary trustee or receiver. In New York, apparently the court will undertake to administer the trust itself.[16] The cardinal principle is that a trust will not be allowed to fail for lack of a trustee.[17]

The trust instrument, testamentary or inter vivos, may specify a manner of appointment of a successor trustee. If so, the prescribed method should be followed strictly whether or not the matter is before the court. If the instrument does not provide for a successor trustee, when a vacancy occurs the court will appoint a successor.[18]

The carefully drawn trust instrument provides for the contingency of vacancy and succession in the office of trustee and commonly states that upon appointment the new trustee shall have title to the trust property. This sort of provision, if accurately followed, has been held sufficient to pass title.[19] Similarly, in cases where the new or successor trustee was appointed by the

---

[12]Id.

[13]Id.

[14]*See generally* 2 Scott on Trusts §§108.2, 556; Bogert, Trusts and Trustees §151.

[15]2 Scott on Trusts §108; Bogert, Trusts and Trustees §151.

[16]*See generally* Bogert, Trusts and Trustees §529 n.13 and accompanying text.

[17]*See* Restatement (Second) of Trusts §101 (1959). *But see* 2 Scott on Trusts §101.1 (discussing failure of the trust when the named trustee was deemed essential to the creation, purpose, and maintenance of the trust).

[18]*See generally* 2 Scott on Trusts §108.

[19]*See* id. §110.

court, the decree has operated to vest title in him.[20] In many states today, doubt as to the vesting of title in the successor trustee pursuant to court appointment has been removed by statute.[21] In any case, where the court appoints a new trustee it is good practice to incorporate an order for conveyance in the decree.

§3.4.2   Acceptance and Disclaimer

Acceptance of the duties of the trustee may be shown by words or by conduct.[22] In the case of testamentary trusts, the intent to accept is ordinarily demonstrated by the filing of a petition of appointment, usually in the probate court.[23] In the case of declarations of trust, the existence of intent to accept is obvious, since the owner declares himself trustee. In the case of inter vivos transfers in trust, receipt of the property coupled with the transferee's failure to disclaim within a reasonable time will amount to an acceptance of the office.[24] In order to avoid a period of uncertainty it is good practice to require a nontestamentary trustee to immediately and formally accept either by signing the trust instrument or an instrument of acceptance.[25] An instrument of acceptance need not be in any particular form; a letter will be sufficient.

[20]*See* id. §109.

[21]*See* id. §109 nn.2-3 and accompanying text.

[22]*See* Restatement (Second) of Trusts §102 (1959); *see generally* 2 Scott on Trusts §102.1.

[23]*See, e.g.,* Uniform Probate Code §3-601 (1990) (a personal representative shall qualify by filing with the appointing court any required bond and a statement of acceptance of the duties of the office).

[24]*See generally* Bogert, Trusts and Trustees §150.

[25]Many instruments will specify procedures for acceptance, and it is good practice to follow these procedures to the letter. However, acceptance may be construed even in the absence of compliance with procedures set forth in the governing instrument. Thus, the nominee should not assume that mere noncompliance will suffice as a disclaimer. If a nominee wishes not to assume fiduciary responsibilities, he should take positive steps to disclaim. Id.

As a general rule, no one need be a trustee involuntarily.[26] Usually the trustee nominated has the alternative of acceptance or disclaimer. No particular form of disclaimer is necessary; it may be by words or by conduct.[27] A trustee who wishes to disclaim obviously will desire to be certain of complete lack of responsibility from the outset. It is good practice to make certain that the disclaimer is in writing and is affirmative and unequivocal in nature. It can be recorded in the place where the trust instrument is recorded, or delivered to the person having custody of the instrument. It is also good practice to serve notice on cotrustees, if any, current beneficiaries, if any are known to the nominee, as well as to other parties having an equitable interest in the trust property, if known. If the trust instrument is a will, a disclaimer filed in the probate court is appropriate and a printed form generally is used. As many states have enacted statutes establishing procedures and timeframes for the filing of disclaimers, a person contemplating the disclaimer of a trusteeship would be well advised to search the annotated laws for any statutes that may apply.[28]

Disclaimer is not allowable after acceptance of the office has taken place; resignation then becomes the only available option if a trustee no longer wishes to serve as such.[29] Thus, since acceptance may be shown by actions as well as by words, it will be important for the nominee to make up his mind one way or the other speedily and unequivocally.

If the nominee decides upon disclaimer, meticulous care should be taken to avoid any assumption of authority or voluntary interference with or control of the trust property, as such action may be construed as an acceptance. Of course, one's actions are

---

[26]*See generally* Restatement (Second) of Trusts §102 (1959); 2 Scott on Trusts §102. *See* §3.3 for a few exceptions.

[27]*See generally* 2 Scott on Trusts §102.1; Restatement (Second) of Trusts §102, comment *b* (1959).

[28] For a list of statutes expressly providing that a person named as trustee may disclaim, see 2 Scott on Trusts §102 n.4.

[29]*See* §3.4.3.

always open to reasonable explanation,[30] but it is easier to avoid the burden of such explanation.[31]

The effect of a disclaimer of one of several trustees is to vest the entire title in those who accept,[32] and it is said that in the case of a sole trustee who disclaims, the title is temporarily revested in the settlor or the settlor's successors as of the time of the transfer.[33] It is certain that the disclaiming trustee is relieved ab initio of any liability.[34] This does not mean destruction of the trust, however, since equity will not allow the trust to fail because of the failure of the individual trustee, except in the rare case where a particular trustee is deemed essential to the whole trust purpose.[35] If for some reason the settlor has expressed an intent that the person nominated is to be the only trustee qualified, it can be said that the nominee's acceptance is necessary to the creation of the trust.[36] Once one has disclaimed, one cannot thereafter withdraw it except with the permission of the court.[37]

[30]If a person proceeds to administer the trust property as would a trustee, such action may be construed as an acceptance. *See* Carter v. Carter, 184 A. 78, 321 Pa. 391 (1936) (acceptance indicated by collecting insurance proceeds due the trust); Lentz v. Lentz, 5 N.C. App. 309, 168 S.E.2d 437 (1969) (acceptance indicated by executing assignment of option to purchase real estate). However, if the nominee is merely protecting the property temporarily until a trustee is appointed, such action ought not to be construed as acceptance. *See generally* Bogert, Trusts and Trustees §150.

[31]Disclaimer has been implied under the following circumstances: lack of interest and inconsistent conduct; lack of acceptance; failure to give bond and to qualify as trustee; failure to act for a prolonged period. *See* 2 Scott on Trusts §102.2.

[32]*See* Bogert, Trusts and Trustees §150.

[33]*See* Restatement (Second) of Trusts §102 comment *g* (1959); 2 Scott on Trusts §102.3.

[34]*See generally* 2 Scott on Trusts §102.3.

[35]*See generally* id. §101.1.

[36]*See generally* Bogert, Trusts and Trustees §150 n.22 and accompanying text.

[37]*See* 2 Scott on Trusts §102.3.

§3.4.3   Death and Resignation

Trustees (where there is more than one) take a joint estate that is not subject to partition.[38] A conveyance out of the trust from one cotrustee acting alone is void.[39] This means that a contract that relates to the trust property between one of the cotrustees and a third party with notice of the trust is ineffective absent a statute to the contrary.[40] Of course, the trust instrument may permit action by fewer than all of the trustees.

When one trustee dies the whole estate vests in the survivors.[41] Even in states in which there is a statutory presumption that multiple parties take title to property as tenants in common, cotrustees generally take as joint tenants.[42] If the trust instrument specifies a definite number of trustees and the death of one or more of them reduces the number below the required amount, the whole estate will still vest in the surviving trustees and will remain there until a successor or successors assumes responsibility for the trust property whether pursuant to court order or the terms of the governing instrument.[43] In certain situations where the trustees and the beneficiaries are one and the same, the fact that the trustees hold the legal title jointly with right of survivorship and the beneficiaries hold the equitable interest as tenants in common may prevent the destruction of the trust through merger.[44]

At common law, if a sole trustee died without leaving a will, the title to the trust property passed to the trustee's heirs, in the case of real estate, or to the trustee's personal representative in

---

[38]The joint tenancy of trustees does not share all of the characteristics of the classic joint tenancy. The parties to a classic joint tenancy are entitled to convert the interest into a tenancy in common (a *petition to partition*). Cotrustees, however, have no power to partition the trust or extinguish the trust by a conveyance or other action. Their powers are confined to joining with their cotrustees in conveying the whole estate or a part of it. *See generally* Bogert, Trusts and Trustees §145.

[39]Id. *See also* 3 Scott on Trusts §194.

[40]*See generally* 3 Scott on Trusts §194.

[41]*See* Restatement (Second) of Trusts §103 (1959).

[42]*See* id. §103 comment *a.*

[43]*See* §3.4.4.3.

[44]*See generally* 2 Scott on Trusts §99.5; First Alabama Bank of Tuscaloosa v. Webb, 373 So. 2d 631 (Ala. 1979). *See* §8.7.

the case of personal property. The heirs or personal representatives were not permitted to administer the trust unless authorized to do so by the terms of the trust.[45] If a sole trustee died leaving a will, title to the trust property passed at common law to the general takers under the trustee's will unless it happened that the testator-trustee expressed an intention to confine the testamentary disposition to that in which the testator-trustee had a beneficial interest.[46] Fortunately, in many jurisdictions statutes have been enacted to address the issue.[47]

Some statutes provide that both title and the office of trusteeship pass to the takers under the will; others provide that the title and right to possession vest in a court and that the court is to appoint a successor trustee; still others provide that the title and right to possession vest in the successor trustee.[48] In general a clear distinction is made between the deceased trustee's own property and the property that is held in trust. Thus the surviving spouse of the deceased trustee does not take an interest in the trust property as statutory heir or by dower or curtesy.[49]

One may not be relieved of one's obligations as trustee by mere transfer and abandonment.[50] Essentially the trustee will be held to have improperly delegated to the transferee — or the world at large in case of abandonment — responsibility for administering the trust.[51] The trustee may resign either upon permission of the court or in accordance with the terms of the trust instrument or with the consent of all of the beneficiaries, including the remaindermen, be their interests vested or contingent.[52] The consent of the beneficiaries will not be a complete protection to the trustee, of course, unless every one of them is of full capacity and has joined in the consent.[53] More often than not, consent will not be a viable option as there are likely to be unborn and unascer-

---

[45]See generally Bogert, Trusts and Trustees §529; 2 Scott on Trusts §104.
[46]Id.
[47]See generally Bogert, Trusts and Trustees §529.
[48]Id.
[49]See generally 2 Scott on Trusts §104 n.6 and accompanying text.
[50]See generally Bogert, Trusts and Trustees §§511, 512.
[51]See generally Bogert, Trusts and Trustees §512.
[52]See 2 Scott on Trusts §106.
[53]Id. See also §5.5.

tained individuals with beneficial interests under the trust. Statutes in most states govern the resignation of trustees.[54]

The mere resignation and acceptance thereof may not, in the absence of statute or appropriate language in the governing instrument, operate to transfer the title to a successor trustee. Thus the resigning trustee may need to execute suitable conveyances of the trust property to the successor in office.[55] The outgoing trustee will want to in any case so as to put others on notice of the succession.

The resignation of a testamentary trustee will likely require court involvement. In inter vivos trust instruments, a nonjudicial method of resignation always should be provided. If the trust expressly provides a method for the trustee's resignation, then the trustee must follow these requirements.[56] Many trusts provide that upon written notice to the beneficiary or beneficiaries then entitled to receive income, the trustee may resign.[57] Often the instrument specifies that the resignation becomes effective after a period of time from the date notice is mailed. In the interim, the resigning trustee remains responsible for the administration of the trust. Written notice should be sent by certified mail to ensure receipt by the beneficiary, and regardless of what the instrument may say, the prudent trustee should assume that he is not discharged until the trust property has been transferred to a qualified successor.[58]

§3.4.4   Exercise and Devolution of Powers

Upon acceptance of the trusteeship, the trustee acquires the panoply of express and implied powers needed to carry out the

[54]*See* id. §106 n.4 (a list of statutes governing the resignation of trustees).

[55]Restatement (Second) of Trusts §106 comment *b* (1959).

[56]*See* 2 Scott on Trusts §106.2; *see also* Croslow v. Croslow, 38 Ill. App. 3d 373, 347 N.E.2d 800 (1976) (holding ineffective a resignation not in accordance with the terms of the trust).

[57]*See* Bogert, Trusts and Trustees §1293, for examples of trustee resignation provisions.

[58]*See* §3.3 note 1.

terms of the trust.[59] If a power is not confined to the doing of a single act or restricted in point of time, it remains available throughout the trust and may be executed in part or in whole at any time.

§3.4.4.1   Multiple Trustees

Where there are several trustees, the powers, like the title, vest jointly.[60] Thus, with possible exception of the charitable trust, trust powers can only be executed by the joint action of all trustees; an action by fewer than all, even though a majority, is void unless permitted by the instrument or by statute.[61] A theoretical result of this principle would be that refusal to concur on the part of one of several trustees would block all action. It has long been settled, however, that if a trustee unreasonably refuses to concur in the joint exercise of a power, the court may remove the trustee.[62] It has also been held that, in an emergency, one trustee may exercise joint powers without the concurrence of the others.[63]

All of several trustees must join or be joined in any suit, or to the settlement or compromise thereof, because trustees are joint tenants. For the same reason it is always safer to insist that receipts and other papers be signed by all of the trustees, for, although payment received by one of them may amount to a good discharge at law, the validity of the receipt may well remain open to question in equity.

§3.4.4.2   Surviving Trustees

When for any reason one of several trustees ceases to hold his office, the trust powers ordinarily remain in the surviving trust-

---

[59]See §3.5.3, which discusses the nature and scope of these powers.

[60]See Restatement (Second) of Trusts §194 (1959).

[61]Id. See also 3 Scott on Trusts §194.

[62]See generally 3 Scott on Trusts §194. See also Restatement (Second) of Trusts §107(a) comment b (1959).

[63]See 3 Scott on Trusts §194.

ees.[64] This may be the case even when a delay in filling vacancies occurs.[65] Only in cases where there are special reasons for believing that the settlor intended to limit discretion to all the trustees originally named, or to those times when all vacancies are filled, will the court conclude that the powers do not vest in the survivors.[66] This is in contrast to what was once the rule, namely that transfers in trust to two or more individuals specified by name implied an intention that neither could exercise discretionary powers alone.[67]

§3.4.4.3 Successor Trustees

It is an equitable maxim that a trust shall not fail for want of a trustee. Furthermore the settlor is presumed to intend that the trust shall continue until its purposes are accomplished. This leads to the general rule that all express and implied powers vested in the original trustee shall pass to the successor trustees, unless the settlor expresses a contrary intention.[68]

The cardinal principle, however, is that *the intention of the settlor as expressed in the trust instrument is controlling.*[69] A well-drawn trust will specify that successor trustees shall have all powers granted the original trustees. In the absence of such specific language, however, the settlor's intentions on the matter must be inferred from the general terms of the instrument.[70] It has been said that the settlor who names a corporate trustee intends that discretionary powers will pass to the successor trustees.[71] On the other hand, the fact that discretionary powers are conferred on a named individual may be a slight indication that the powers were

[64]*See* Restatement (Second) of Trusts §195 (1959); *see generally* 3 Scott on Trusts §195.

[65]*See* 3 Scott on Trusts §195 n.6 and accompanying text.

[66]*See generally* 3 Scott on Trusts §195.

[67]*See, e.g.,* Weeks v. Frankel, 128 A.D. 223, 112 N.Y. Supp. 562 (N.Y. App. Div. 1908).

[68]*See* Restatement (Second) of Trusts §196 (1959).

[69]*See* id.

[70]*See generally* 3 Scott on Trusts §196.

[71]*See* Restatement (Second) of Trusts §196, comment *f* (1959).

not intended to be exercised by anyone except the individual named. [72] The modern trend however is to disregard this distinction. In the great bulk of cases all powers, express and implied, have been found to be transmitted. [73]

§3.5   Trustee's Relationship to the Trust Estate

Professor Fratcher notes that the trust — in contrast to the corporation — is not a legal entity; rather it is "an aggregation of property," where the rights and duties associated with its ownership "are divided between the trustee and the beneficiary." Thus "the trust, as such, is incapable of owning property, acquiring claims or incurring liabilities." [1] Because the trust is not an entity, it is more legally accurate to say that "a trust has been impressed on Blackacre" or "Blackacre has been transferred to a trustee" than it is to say that "Blackacre has been put into a trust."

§3.5.1   Nature and Extent of the Trustee's Estate

In every trust there are two estates: the trustee's *legal* estate and the beneficiary's *equitable* estate. [2] Though these two estates are separate, they are bound together and tend to travel on parallel lines. [3] Legal title to the trust property is held by the trustee,

---

[72]Id. comment *a*.

[73]Id. comment *a*.

§3.5 [1]W. F. Fratcher, Trust §95 at 77, *in* VI Intl. Encyclopedia of Comp. Law ch. 11 (F. H. Lawson, ed., 1973) (hereinafter "Fratcher").

[2]The *legal estate* is the whole estate, and the holder of the legal title is the sole owner. When the title is held for the benefit of another, as in a trust, the beneficial interest thus created is called an *equitable estate. See generally* C. Moynihan, Introduction to the Law of Real Property §173 (2d ed. 1988).

[3]*See generally* 2 Scott on Trusts §130.1; Bogert, Trusts and Trustees §181.

unless one of the following exceptions applies: it is a nondiscretionary trust involving real estate;[4] the subject of the trust is an equitable interest; or the settlor expresses a contrary intent.[5] Thus it is said that the trustee owns the property.

To the nonlawyer this splitting of interests is as mysterious as the Trinity. How can it be that the trustee and the beneficiaries both own the property? Perhaps it would be helpful to look at it this way: The trustee has all rights to the trust property except the right to its benefit. That right is given to the beneficiary. Of course it is the prerogative of the settlor to withhold from the trustee other rights, such as the right to sell the trust property.[6] In England in earlier times the beneficiary would look to the ecclesiastical courts for help in protecting his beneficial interest. Today the beneficiary looks to the secular courts in the exercise of their equitable powers.[7]

What then is the practical difference between a trust and a contract, or between a trust and an agency such as a power of attorney, when it comes to the property that is the subject of these arrangements? By way of illustrating how the trust fits into the framework of fundamental common law legal relationships, let us take the village inn. Assume that one evening the building inspector is about in the village, and he notices that the fire escapes have fallen off the building. Whom then does he cite for an infraction of the building code? Certainly not the guests. The innkeeper is cited because he owns the inn. Now the guests may well find themselves out in the cold that evening. Their recourse however is a *legal* one against the innkeeper with whom they have a contractual relationship.[8] In earlier times this would have been a legal matter for the secular courts. That is still the case today.

Let us now assume that the innkeeper is trustee of the inn and that the guests are beneficiaries, not parties to a contract with the

---

[4]*See generally* 1A Scott on Trusts §88.

[5]*See generally* id. §88.1.

[6]*See generally* 3 Scott on Trusts §190. *See also* §3.5.3.1(a).

[7]*See generally* id. §197.

[8]A breach of contract gives the injured party a right to damages (usually a sum of money based on an expectation interest) against the party in breach. Restatement (Second) of Contracts §§346-347 (1979).

innkeeper. Whom does the building inspector now cite? Again the innkeeper is cited because, as far as the inspector is concerned, the innkeeper legally owns the inn. Any complaint the guests may have with the innkeeper is not the inspector's problem. In earlier times, the beneficiary, not being in a contractual relationship with his trustee, would have had recourse against the innkeeper only to the ecclesiastical courts for any breach of trust; today the beneficiary must invoke the *equitable* powers of the secular courts. It always should be kept in mind that even though the innkeeper receives the citation as legal owner of the trust property, the equitable or beneficial interests of the guests are very much interests in property as well.[9] A beneficiary's equitable right of enjoyment, for example, may not be seized by the trustee's personal creditors.[10]

It is out of more than mere historical interest that we ponder the nature of the trustee's estate. As one can see, rights are affected. For example, what about the ironmonger who improperly installed the fire escapes? Who pursues him, the trustee or the beneficiaries? Under the common law, the trustee is the plaintiff because, as owner of the property, the trustee is in a contractual relationship with the ironmonger.[11] What if the fire escape fell on a passerby? Is the trustee personally liable above and beyond the value of the trust property for any negligent harm caused? Under the common law the trustee's liability probably would not be limited to the value of the trust estate.[12] What if the trustee sells the inn in violation of the terms of the trust to someone who has no notice of the trust? Under the common law the sale is probably good with the result that the beneficiaries have no recourse against the purchaser.[13] When the trust terminates, must the trustee convey the property to the remaindermen or do the remaindermen take automatically? Under the common law a conveyance would be required, with the possible exception of certain trusts involving real estate.[14]

---

[9]*See* 1 Restatement of Property at 3 (1936) (introductory note to chapter 1).
[10]*See generally* Bogert, Trusts and Trustees §146.
[11]*See generally* 4 Scott on Trusts §280.2.
[12]*See generally* id. §264.
[13]*See generally* id. §284.
[14]*See generally* 1A Scott on Trusts §88.

The trustee's ownership interest in the trust estate is subtle and complex and thus the rights, duties, and obligations of those who come in contact with the trust estate are entangled. As the trustee may be exposed to potential personal liability to third parties as an incident of the "ownership" interest in the trust estate, the potential trustee should seek the advice of counsel before venturing into this strange world of bifurcated interests. With respect to a given situation, the trustee should also understand the extent to which these common law duties and obligations may be altered by statute, by decision, and by the terms of a particular governing instrument.

Finally, what about the agency? What if the guests own the inn and the innkeeper is operating the inn under a power of attorney? In that case the innkeeper is their agent and he receives the citation on their behalf, as they possess both the legal estate and the equitable estate.

§3.5.2   Rights of the Trustee

In the tangle of legal relationships that is the trust, the trustee as well as the beneficiary has certain rights. The trustee's rights are incident to holding the *title* (*e.g.*, the right of possession and alienation) and the *office* (*e.g.*, the right of reasonable compensation and reimbursement).

§3.5.2.1   Right at Law to Possession

In the absence of statute, decision, or the settlor's contrary intention, the trustee, as holder of the legal title, is entitled to the possession of the real property; thus the trustee may eject the beneficiary.[15] With the same qualifications the trustee is entitled also to the possession of the personal property.

---

[15]*See generally* 2A Scott on Trusts §175.

§3.5.2.2   Right at Law to Transfer Title

The trustee, being the legal owner, may make conveyance, and the transferee will stand at law entitled in place of the trustee.[16] But if the settlor bestowed on the trustee no power to convey, any transferee with notice of the restriction takes the property subject to the trust, receiving no larger title than the trustee is authorized to convey.[17] Under these circumstances, the sale is voidable at the option of the beneficiary.[18]

Because of the trustee's right to transfer title, it is said that the trust is not a restraint on the alienability of property.[19] This is because "if the trustee makes a transfer under powers conferred by law or the terms of the trust, the transferee acquires the whole title, free of trust; if he makes a transfer in breach of trust to a bona fide purchaser, the transferee also acquires the whole title, free of trust; [e]ven a transfer in breach of trust to a donee, or to a purchaser with notice of the breach, carries the title, subject to the trust, which is all the trustee ever owned."[20]

§3.5.2.3   Right in Equity to Exoneration and Reimbursement

Inasmuch as there is a rigid restriction against personal participation by the trustee in any of the profits and gains resulting from the administration of the trust estate, equity takes pains to hold the trustee harmless from personal liability for obligations properly incurred.[21]

Inherent in the right of exoneration is the trustee's right to pay directly from the estate all of the expenses properly incurred as owner, including taxes, repairs, insurance, and other legitimate

---

[16]See generally 4 Scott on Trusts §283.
[17]See generally id. §284.
[18]See generally id. §291.
[19]See generally Broadway Natl. Bank v. Adams, 133 Mass. 170 (1882).
[20]Fratcher, supra note 1, §108 at 89.
[21]See generally Bogert, Trusts and Trustees §718.

expenses of management, traveling expenses, the cost of justifiable litigation, and expenses of consulting counsel when there is reasonable cause.[22] This right of exoneration is coupled with a right of reimbursement for sums paid from the trustee's own pocket for expenses properly incurred.[23]

§3.5.2.4   Right in Equity to Compensation

The English rule is that the trustee is not entitled to compensation unless the instrument expressly provides for it.[24] In the United States and some parts of the British Commonwealth, however, the trustee is entitled in equity to reasonable compensation, even when the instrument is silent upon the subject.[25] In some jurisdictions, a trustee's compensation is set by statute.[26]

§3.5.3   The Powers of the Trustee in Equity to Manage the Trust Estate

A trustee, being the absolute legal owner of the property, has all the rights of an absolute owner, subject however to the paramount equitable rights of the beneficiary.[27] Thus, the courts of equity will restrain the trustee from exercising any power inconsistent with the beneficiary's rights.[28] As a rule of thumb the trustee has only the powers — and all the powers — needed to carry out the terms of the trust and to protect the trust corpus.[29] When the two goals are in conflict or when the terms of the trust or the law is ambiguous, the trustee is entitled to petition the court for guidance.

[22]Id.; *see generally* 3 Scott on Trusts §188.
[23]*See generally* Bogert, Trusts and Trustees §718.
[24]*See generally* 3A Scott on Trusts §242.
[25]Id.
[26]*See generally* Bogert, Trusts and Trustees §975.
[27]*See generally* id. §146.
[28]*See* 3 Scott on Trusts §199.
[29]*See* id. §186.

Ascertaining the limits of the trustee's equitable authority (in other words, the limits of the trustee's powers) is more an art than a science. The panoply of powers with respect to a given trust are drawn from long-established customs and practice, the common law, statute, the express language of the governing instrument, and by implication from the general purposes of the trust. The trustee's general powers incidental to the office are numerous; to name just a few, they include: the power to sell,[30] lease,[31] sue and defend,[32] contract and incur expense,[33] and to vote stock proxies.[34] In short, the trustee has all the powers needed to carry out the duties of a trustee.

When it comes to trust powers, however, things are not always as they seem. Trustees should be cautious in exercising an express power that expands the common law authority of a trustee. For example, one would be ill advised to rely on an expansive general power in the governing instrument "to do all things which the settlor could have done with his own property." Courts are unlikely to interpret such language as a license to speculate or self-deal or otherwise engage in acts that are inconsistent with the concept of a trust.[35] On the other hand, a tightly drafted specific power to retain a particular investment remains outstanding only so long as the investment furthers the general purposes and economic well-being of the trust.[36] If, for example, the investment is in an industry whose products are becoming obsolete and thus unmarketable, the trustee may have a duty to sell the investment notwithstanding the express retention authority.[37] The trustee who mechanically relies on powers expressly bestowed in the governing instrument does so at his peril. (On the other hand, when the law is ambiguous as to whether the trustee has an implied

---

[30]See §3.5.3.1(a).
[31]See §3.5.3.1(b).
[32]See §3.5.3.1(c).
[33]See §3.5.3.1(d).
[34]See §3.5.3.1(e).
[35]See Restatement (Second) of Trusts §186 comment f (1959).
[36]See id. §167 comments g & h.
[37]See, e.g., Mueller v. Mueller, 28 Wis. 2d 26, 135 N.W.2d 854 (1965).

power in a given situation, the trustee is entitled and advised to seek judicial guidance.)

§3.5.3.1 Implied General Powers

Implied powers are granted to the trustee by operation of law, because without them it would be impossible to carry out the trustee's fiduciary responsibilities. They are not expressly granted in the governing instrument. The power to sell intangible personal property, lease, sue and defend, bind the trust in contract, and vote proxies are some of the more important powers that the trustee possesses incidental to his office. Thus they are powers that the trustee possesses unless the settlor expressly or by implication denies them to the trustee.

(a) **The power to sell.** Absent statutory authority or authority in the governing instrument, does the trustee have an implied power on behalf of the trust to sell the trust property to a third party for reasonable consideration? At early common law the answer was "no" when it came to land.[38] This was appropriate for a time when a family would derive its very identity from a specific parcel of land.[39] In the United States today courts will generally find a power of sale unless it appears from the language of the trust instrument, interpreted in light of the circumstances, that the settlor intended that the land should be retained by the trust.[40] Such a presumption is appropriate for a society that has come to look upon real estate as just one form of investment. Moreover, unless there is an indication of a contrary intention on the part of the settlor, the trustee has had the implied or inherent authority to sell intangible personal property (*e.g.,* stocks and bonds) since the concept of the *Prudent Man Rule* took root.[41]

---

[38]*See generally* 3 Scott on Trusts §186.
[39]*See generally* id. §190.
[40]Id.
[41]*See generally* Restatement (Third) of Trusts at 3 (1992) (introduction to Topic 5).

With the express or implied duty to invest comes the power to buy and sell.[42] In many jurisdictions the trustee is given by statute the power to sell personal property, unless the terms of the trust indicate a contrary intention.[43] The Restatement of Trusts provides that a trustee has an implied power of sale unless the terms of the trust indicate a contrary intent.[44]

A power of sale does not necessarily include the power to sell the trust property on credit.[45] Whether a sale on credit is allowed depends in large part on whether the receipt of notes in lieu of cash would put the trust at unnecessary risk.[46] If the buyer has a good credit rating, the sale may be proper, particularly if the sale is desirable and cannot otherwise be made.[47] A trustee would have the implied power to sell on credit, that is, in exchange for an unsecured promissory note, provided the promissory note is an appropriate trust investment. Likewise, a power of sale does not automatically bring with it a power in the trustee to grant an option.[48] It depends upon whether to do so is in the best interests of the trust, taking into account all the facts and circumstances.[49]

A general power of sale or investment would allow the trustee to exchange trust property for property other than cash, provided the property received is a proper trust investment.[50]

It appears to be the current state of the law that a power of sale, in and of itself, will not bring with it the power to incorpo-

---

[42]See Restatement (Third) of Trusts §190 comments *b* & *d* (1992).

[43]See 3 Scott on Trusts §190 n.10 & §190.4 n.10 for statutes governing the sale of trust property. *See also* Uniform Trustee's Powers Act, §§3(c)(7), 12 (a trustee has power "to acquire or dispose of an asset, for cash or on credit, at public or private sale").

[44]Restatement (Third) of Trusts §190 (1992).

[45]*See generally* 3 Scott on Trusts §190.7.

[46]Id.

[47]*See* Restatement (Third) of Trusts §190 comment *j* (1992).

[48]*See* 3 Scott on Trusts §190.8.

[49]*See* id. §190.8 n.3 and accompanying text.

[50]*See* Restatement (Third) of Trusts §190 comment *m* (1992). *See also* 3 Scott on Trusts §190.9 n.2 and accompanying text. The trustee should be aware that, under certain circumstances, like-kind exchanges may offer income tax advantages for the trust. See I.R.C. §1031.

rate the trust property.[51] Let us assume, for example, that a portion of the trust estate comprises an unincorporated business enterprise. The trustee may wish to exchange the assets of the enterprise for shares in an incorporated entity in order to insulate the other trust assets from the risks of the business.[52] Some commentators have suggested that court approval may be needed to effect such an incorporation, absent express authority in the governing instrument.[53] It would seem, however, that any concerns regarding incorporating the trust property have more to do with issues of improper delegation than issues of the abuse of the power of sale.

It should be emphasized that a general express or implied power of sale does not contemplate sales to third parties for less than reasonable consideration.[54] Nor does it contemplate sales to the trustee himself.

(b) The power to lease. Associated with the trustee's duty to make the trust property productive is the power in the trustee to lease the real estate, unless to do so would violate the express or implied intentions of the settlor.[55] However, because the remaindermen are entitled to the entire interest upon termination, the lease may not extend beyond the period of the trust.[56] A lease that extends beyond the reasonably anticipated duration of the trust may not be binding on the remaindermen, but such a lease will be valid for the duration of the trust.[57] Thus, the trustee should take care to limit his lease to a reasonable or customary term.

What *is* a "reasonable and customary duration" may depend upon facts peculiar to each case. Thus, long-term leases have been approved when necessary to preserve the trust property.[58] If the trustee enters into a lease where the lessee undertakes to make

---

[51]*See generally* 3 Scott on Trusts §190.9A.
[52]Id.
[53]Id.
[54]*See* Restatement (Third) of Trusts §190 comment *i* (1992).
[55]*See generally* Restatement (Second) of Trusts §189 (1959).
[56]Id. comment *c* (1959).
[57]Id.
[58]*See generally* 3 Scott on Trusts §189.2.

improvements to the property in partial or total satisfaction of the lessee's rental obligation, the trustee should understand that such an arrangement could have the effect of shifting beneficial interests from the income beneficiary to the remaindermen.[59] Therefore, absent express or implied authority in the governing instrument, the trustee should refrain from entering into such a lease unless a way can be found to compensate the income account for the portion of the lessee's rental obligation that has taken the form of capital improvements.

(c) **The power to sue and defend.** The trustee has the duty of gathering in and protecting the trust property,[60] hence the implied power to sue for it or for any damage to it; to defend suits against the trust; and to employ counsel and incur all necessary costs at the expense of the trust fund, whether successful or not in the litigation, unless the trustee has been imprudent.[61] These expenses are allowed, not only in cases directly affecting the property, but also where the trustee has acted reasonably and in good faith in attempting to protect the beneficiary (*e.g.,* where the trustee has attempted, though unsuccessfully, to have a guardian appointed for the beneficiary).

(d) **The power to bind the trust in contract.** If there is a fiduciary duty, the trustee has the power to enter into contracts, binding on the trust, for goods and services that are reasonably needed by him to carry out that duty.[62] This would include the costs of judicial proceedings and the expenses of managing, repairing, and improving the trust property.[63] The trustee has the inherent power to hire at trust expense agents such as attor-

---

[59]*See generally* id. §189.5.

[60]*See* §6.2.1.

[61]*See* Restatement (Second) of Trusts §188 comment *b* (1959); *see generally* 3 Scott on Trusts §188.4.

[62]*See generally* 3 Scott on Trusts §188; Restatement (Second) of Trusts §271 (1959).

[63]*See generally* 3 Scott on Trusts §188.4 (judicial proceedings), §188.2 (repairs and improvements).

neys and brokers, provided their services are needed for the proper administration of the trust.[64] The trustee, however, has no implied power to hire an agent for the purpose of performing services that the trustee ought personally to perform.[65] The trustee, for example, could not hire at trust expense an agent to decide who among a class of beneficiaries is entitled to discretionary distributions of principal.[66]

(e) **The power to vote proxies.** One of the duties of the trustee is to actively manage and protect the trust estate.[67] Thus with respect to shares of stock the trustee has the power to exercise all of the ordinary rights of a stockholder, including the right to vote on corporate matters.[68] It is the duty of the trustee in voting shares of stock to act solely in the economic interest of the beneficiary in light of the manifested intentions of the settlor.[69] One has no power as trustee to indulge one's own social and political predilections with the stockholder franchise.[70] The lodestars must always be the economic well-being of the trust and the intentions of the settlor.

If a minority interest in a corporation comprises a portion of the trust estate, the trustee probably has the implied power to vote the shares by proxy, provided the trustee is acquainted with the questions to be voted upon, has used due care in selecting the proxy, and has given suitable instructions with regard to the vote.[71] If the trust's interest in the corporation is a controlling one, the trustee has no power to give a general proxy.[72]

---

[64]*See* id. §188.3.
[65]*See* §6.1.4.
[66]*See* §6.1.4.
[67]*See* §6.2.1.
[68]*See generally* 3 Scott on Trusts §193.
[69]*See* id. §193.1.
[70]*See* §6.1.3.
[71]*See* 3 Scott on Trusts §193.3. For a list of statutes providing that fiduciaries may vote by proxy, see id., §193.3 nn.2-3.
[72]*See* id. §193.3.

§3.5.3.2   Powers to Engage in Acts That Might Otherwise Be Breaches of Trust

Sometimes it is in the interest of the trust — and the proper execution of its purposes — for the trustee to engage in acts that, at least technically, are breaches of trust. Thus most trust instruments bestow powers that the trustee might not otherwise possess under the common law. Courts will construe such provisions narrowly. The following is a catalog of some standard powers that fall into this category.

(a) **The power to make discretionary applications of income and principal.** Most trust instruments give the trustee the power to pay income to or for the benefit of the beneficiary. However, if the instrument simply requires the trustee to pay the trust's income to the beneficiary, the common law would require that payment be made directly to the beneficiary at reasonable intervals less expenses allocable to income. [73] The trustee would not have the power to choose the alternative of expenditure for the benefit of the beneficiary. [74] Thus, if the beneficiary is incapacitated a guardian would have to be appointed by the court to receive the income payments on behalf of the beneficiary — an expensive, time-consuming, and inconvenient process. [75] Statutes have now been enacted in some jurisdictions allowing trustees to make payments to or for the benefit of the beneficiary absent express authority in the governing instrument. [76]

Under a simple trust — A to B for C for life, then to D — C receives all income accrued to the date of death, and upon C's death, D receives the principal outright and free of trust. Because of the duty of impartiality, the trustee has no power to withhold

---

[73] *See generally* 2A Scott on Trusts §182.
[74] Id.
[75] Id. §182.1.
[76] Id.

income from C or take principal from D and give it to C.[77] To do so would be a breach of trust.[78] Moreover if there are multiple C's, the trustee has a common law duty to be impartial as among them.[79] Thus each C would receive an equal portion of the income stream.

It is now common practice for settlors to bestow on trustees, in derogation of the common law duty of impartiality, the authority to favor the income beneficiary over the remainderman and vice versa, and to discriminate between and among members of a class of income beneficiaries. These discretionary powers to sprinkle, spray, accumulate income, and to invade principal are governed by standards set forth in the governing instrument.[80] A standard can be broadly drafted (*e.g.*, the power to invade principal for C's "benefit") or narrowly drafted, (*e.g.*, the power to invade principal to pay C's "medical bills"). A typical standard found in many trusts permits payment for the "maintenance and support" of the beneficiary. This standard falls somewhere between the underwriting of utility bills and the underwriting of a world cruise. Precisely *where* is not always easy to determine. Much may depend on the beneficiary's station in life at the time the inter vivos trust was established, or in the case of a testamentary trust, during the testator's lifetime.[81] The menu of standards available to the settlor is limited only by one's imagination.

The permissible income beneficiaries and the presumptive remaindermen have standing to bring an action against the trustee for abuse of discretion. As a general rule, however, courts will not second guess the trustee's exercise of discretionary powers unless there has been clear abuse.[82] The trustee must be aware that the exercise of a discretionary power to pay income or distribute

[77]*See* §6.2.5.
[78]Id.
[79]Id.
[80]*See generally* 2 Scott on Trusts §§128.3, 128.7. For an example of a discretionary provision see Bogert, Trusts and Trustees §1707 art. 3(e).
[81]*See generally* Halbach, Problems of Discretion in Discretionary Trusts, 61 Colum. L. Rev. 1425 (1961); *see also* IRC §2041(b)(1)(A) (providing that a power holder's right to invade principal for his own "maintenance or support" is *not* treated as a general power for federal estate tax purposes).
[82]*See generally* 3 Scott on Trusts §187.

principal affects the property rights of the beneficiaries. Thus, discretionary decisions should be well documented: A trustee is well advised to keep accurate records of all requests, granted and denied.

The common law offers little useful guidance when it comes to whether the trustee shall take into account assets available to the beneficiary outside of the trust (*e.g.*, a portfolio of securities) or take into account the beneficiary's collateral sources of support (*e.g.*, welfare entitlements or a wealthy spouse). The issue most often arises when the standard is "maintenance" or "support." The Restatement of Trusts takes the position that in trusts for support the inference is that the trustee does not need to take into account other resources available to the beneficiary.[83] This position is followed by many, though not all jurisdictions.[84]

In any case, a court asked to rule on the issue will ground its ruling in the presumed intentions of the settlor as extracted from the particular language at issue.[85] The prudent prospective trustee will thus attempt to avoid the problem by insisting that the governing instrument reflect clearly whether the trustee shall take into account the beneficiary's other resources.

If the trust instrument grants the trustee the discretionary power to pay income or distribute principal to the beneficiary for the beneficiary's maintenance and support, the trustee may well be under an affirmative duty to determine if the beneficiary needs funds. Some recent cases seem to suggest this.[86]

If authorized to pay income and principal to or for the benefit of a beneficiary, may the trustee pay the beneficiary's funeral bills? Absent express authority to do so, probably not. This is because the equitable property interest is now in someone other than the beneficiary's estate.[87]

---

[83]*See* Restatement (Second) of Trusts §128(e) (1959).
[84]*See generally* 2 Scott on Trusts §128.4.
[85]Id.
[86]*See, e.g.,* Marsman v. Nasca, 30 Mass. App. 789, 573 N.E.2d 1025 (1991); Old Colony Trust Co. v. Rodd, 356 Mass. 584, 254 N.E.2d 886 (1970). *See generally* Hayes & Wall, Fiduciary Discretion — Where Is the Better Part of Valor, 132 Trusts & Estates 8 (1993) (discussing the practical considerations of making and documenting discretionary distributions).
[87]*But see* 2 Scott on Trusts §128.4.

Inherent in a trustee's right to make discretionary distributions is the lesser right, in lieu thereof, to make loans. As a practical matter, however, the trustee may not wish get into the business of administering loans to beneficiaries. Moreover, what if the beneficiary defaults? Should the trustee seek to collect on behalf of the trust or should discretion be exercised and the original transaction treated as an outright distribution? Absent special circumstances, the trustee should keep things as clean and simple as possible.

If there are competing requests for discretionary distributions it is up to the trustee, not counsel to the trust, to determine the proper allocation. In making discretionary payments among a group of several beneficiaries, the trustee has reasonable latitude in favoring one beneficiary over the other, since in the absence of abuse the trustee's discretion is final.[88] Under no circumstances, however, should the trustee make any discretionary distribution without a full understanding of the generation-skipping tax consequences.

(b) The power to lease beyond the term of the trust. Under certain circumstances, it may be in the economic interest of the trust for the trustee to enter into a lease that extends beyond the term of the trust.[89] It is good practice, therefore, to provide express language in the governing instrument authorizing such leases. Otherwise the trustee might be held liable for failing to turn over to the remainderman the entire interest in the trust property.

(c) The power to borrow on behalf of the trust or to pledge or mortgage the trust property. Whether the trustee has the power to borrow money on behalf of the trust and whether he or she has the right to pledge or mortgage the trust property as security for the loan are separate questions.[90] The trustee, for

---

[88]*See* 2A Scott on Trusts §183.
[89]*See generally* 3 Scott on Trusts §189.2.
[90]*See* 2A Scott on Trusts §191.3.

example, may have a power to borrow money on the general credit of the trust for a particular trust purpose without any authority to pledge or mortgage a specific part of the trust property.[91]

Because the trustee has a common law duty to exercise direct continuing control over the trust property, there is no inherent power to borrow on behalf of the trust absent express statutory authority or express authority in the governing instrument.[92] It follows from this that the trustee would have no implied general power to pledge or mortgage the trust property. However, under limited circumstances (*e.g.,* an emergency threatening the economic well-being of the trust), the powers to borrow and to encumber the trust property may be implied.[93]

Some courts have construed certain expressed powers of management as including the power to borrow.[94] What about the power to borrow for investment purposes? Is that implied in the direction "to invest and reinvest?" Probably not, because such a power is tantamount to a power to speculate.[95] The mere power of sale would not carry with it a power to pledge or mortgage.[96]

If the trust expressly permits the trustee to borrow on behalf of the trust, may the trustee become the lender? This question usually arises in the context of a corporate fiduciary that has general banking powers. While there is no absolute prohibition against the trustee lending funds to the trust, if at all possible the practice should be avoided. Any loans that *are* made must be at competitive rates and terms. The issue of conflict of interest is always present whenever the trustee enters into transactions involving the trust estate for the trustee's own account.

It should be noted that the recently revised Restatement of Trusts now grants the trustee an implied power to borrow, pledge,

---

[91]*See* id.

[92]*See* Restatement (Second) of Trusts §175 (1959). For a list of statutes enlarging the power of trustees to mortgage or pledge trust property, see 2A Scott on Trusts §191 n.17.

[93]Id. §167.

[94]*See generally* 3 Scott on Trusts §191.3.

[95]*See* id. §227.6.

[96]*See generally* 2A Scott on Trusts §191.

or otherwise encumber trust property for trust purposes, unless prohibited from doing so by statute or the terms of the trust.[97]

(d) The power to invest in mutual funds, common trust funds, and common funds. In a jurisdiction where the investment of trust property in a mutual fund is considered a breach of the common law duty not to delegate investment discretion, the trustee will need express authority in the governing instrument.[98] To invest in a common trust fund, the trustee will need statutory authority or express authority in the trust instrument;[99] otherwise the trustee runs afoul of the common law duty not to commingle the assets of the trust with the assets of other trusts.[100]

Nowadays many trusts fracture into separate trust shares upon the happening of a contingency. It may be in the economic interest of all concerned, however, to keep the assets of the separate trusts together in a common fund for investment purposes. Because of the common law prohibition against commingling, the trustee will need express authority in the governing instrument to do so.[101]

(e) The power to hold the trust property in the name of a third party or in the trustee's own name without disclosing the fiduciary relationship. The trustee has a common law duty to earmark the trust property as the property of the trust.[102] On the other hand, the trustee may, for legitimate reasons, prefer not to disclose the fiduciary relationship. The process of security transfer, for example, is less complicated when securities are registered in the name of someone other than the trustee (there being no need to prove authority to brokers and transfer agents). Any

[97]See Restatement (Third) of Trusts §191 (1992).
[98]See §6.1.4.
[99]See Restatement (Third) of Trusts §227 comment *m* (1992). *See generally* Bogert, Trusts and Trustees §677.
[100]See §6.2.1.
[101]See generally 2A Scott on Trusts §179.2.
[102]See id. §179.3. See §6.2.1.

power in the trustee not to disclose the fiduciary relationship must be set forth expressly in the governing instrument or in a statute.[103]

It should be noted that some methods of nondisclosure are riskier than others. If, for example, trust securities are registered in the name of a partnership established under the auspices of a bank trust department (*a nominee*),[104] the securities are segregated from the general assets of the bank. If the securities are registered in the name of a brokerage house (*street name*),[105] they may not be segregated from the general assets of the brokerage house.[106] Thus if the brokerage house goes bankrupt, the trustee may have no greater rights than all the other customers similarly situated.[107] The settlor and the trustee will want to give careful consideration to whether investor protection insurance adequately mitigates the risk of registering securities in street name.

(f) The power to compromise, arbitrate, and abandon claims. A trustee has the duty to collect that which is owed the trust.[108] On the other hand there is a duty not to squander trust assets in litigating claims that should be dealt with in some other way.[109] Thus the trustee has the inherent common law power to compromise, arbitrate, and abandon claims to the extent it is in the economic interest of the trust to do so.[110] Because of the tension between the two duties, the cautious trustee will seek judicial approval before compromising, arbitrating, or abandoning substantial claims, unless there is clear statutory authority to do so or the matter is expressly addressed in the governing instrument.

[103]*See generally* Bogert, Trusts and Trustees §596.
[104]Id.
[105]*See generally* 5 Scott on Trusts §521.6 n.9 and accompanying text.
[106]Id.
[107]Id.
[108]*See* Restatement (Second) of Trusts §177 (1959).
[109]Id. comment *c*; 3 Scott on Trusts §192.
[110]Id.

(g) The power to resolve questions as to what is income and what is principal. Absent authority in the governing instrument, the trustee has no inherent power to deviate from generally accepted practices of fiduciary accounting when determining what is income and what is principal for purposes of crediting receipts or charging disbursements.[111] Nor would most settlors want to bestow on the trustee such a power, for to do so would permit the trustee to shift beneficial interests arbitrarily between the income beneficiary and the remaindermen.[112] On the other hand, when the law provides no clear guidance on how to characterize a particular item, the trustee ought to have the power to decide such questions without resort to the courts. Thus the settlor should give the trustee the power in doubtful cases to determine which receipts are income and which are principal, and which expenses should be paid out of the income account and which out of the principal account.

(h) The power to exclude the remainderman from the accounting process. The trustee has a duty to render accounts at reasonable intervals not only to the income beneficiaries but also to the remaindermen.[113] The process of accounting to remaindermen can be expensive and time-consuming, particularly when interests are contingent or diffused.[114] Moreover, when remaindermen are unborn or unascertainable during a given accounting period, the involvement of a guardian ad litem may be required.[115] A trustee therefore welcomes an express power to exclude the remaindermen from the accounting process. A word of caution: In some jurisdictions, the assent of the income benefi-

---

[111]*See* Restatement (Second) of Trusts §233 comment *p* (1959).

[112]In Old Colony Trust Co. v. Silliman, 352 Mass. 6, 223 N.E.2d 504 (1967), the court held that broad discretion in the trustee to decide whether accretions are to be treated as income or principal did not empower trustee to shift the beneficial interests. It noted that "[a] fair reading of the whole of most trust instruments will reveal a 'judicially enforceable, external, and ascertainable standard' for the exercise of even broadly expressed fiduciary powers." Id. at 9.

[113]*See* §6.1.5.

[114]*See generally* Westfall, Nonjudicial Settlement of Trustees' Accounts, 71 Harv. L. Rev. 40, 49 n.34 and accompanying text (1957).

[115]Id.; *see also* Restatement (Second) of Trusts §214 comment *a* (1959).

ciary cannot bind the remaindermen no matter what the governing instrument may say, particularly when the assent relates to a shifting of beneficial interests.[116]

(i) Special investment powers. The trustee has a duty to invest the trust property prudently, balancing the obligation to preserve the principal for the remaindermen against the obligation to produce a reasonable rate of return for the income beneficiary.[117] Over the years, courts and legislatures have set down guidelines for trustees to follow in the carrying out of this duty.[118] A trustee who keeps within them will be protected regardless of how the portfolio actually performs.[119]

Many instruments, however, provide the trustee with powers to deviate from established guidelines, such as a power to speculate, or to hold wasting assets or assets that present a high degree of risk. As a practical matter, the more general the fiduciary's power to veer from established investment practice the more likely the power is illusory.[120] If a settlor, for example, wants the family business retained in trust even though such an investment may amount to a speculation under the common law, the trustee will want an express power of retention that makes reference to the business itself[121] as well as appropriate express powers to enable the trustee to run the business efficiently and cost-effectively. Absent express authority to hold the settlor's business in trust, the trustee is under a duty to liquidate the business.[122] Certainly a general authority to speculate is insufficient, because the trustee is at risk that some court would dismiss such language as "boiler-

---

[116]*See, e.g.,* In re Crane, 34 N.Y.S.2d 9 (1942); *see generally* Westfall, supra note 114.

[117]*See* §6.2.2.1.

[118]Id.

[119]Id.

[120]"A trust provision that authorizes investments to be made 'in the trustee's discretion,' or that confers on the trustee 'all of the powers of an owner' is not ordinarily to be construed as granting the trustee wider latitude than conferred by the prudent investor rule." Restatement (Third) of Trusts §228 comment *g* (1992).

[121]Id. §229 comment *e*.

[122]Id.

plate" and then rule that the trustee's reliance upon it was unreasonable.[123]

(j) The power to loan money to the trust and charge a reasonable rate of interest. As the trustee has no inherent power under the common law to transact with the trust property for his own account, it would seem he has no inherent power to loan his own money to the trust at interest. The cases suggest otherwise, however.[124] All things being equal, however, it is preferable that the trustee refrain from such activity in the absence of statutory or regulatory authority or authority in the governing instrument.[125]

(k) The power to terminate the trust. The trustee has no inherent power to terminate the trust before its purposes have been fulfilled.[126] The settlor may wish to provide such a power should the trust become impractical or uneconomical to administer. Absent an express power of termination, for example, the trustee might feel obliged to seek judicial approval before terminating a trust that had become too small to cost-effectively manage.[127] Many jurisdictions now have statutes authorizing the nonjudicial termination of small trusts.[128] It is important to keep in mind, however, that for an express termination provision to have any utility, it must direct where the property is to go once the power of termination has been exercised.[129]

[123]Id. §228 comment *g*.
[124]*See generally* Bogert, Trusts and Trustees §543(L).
[125]Id.
[126]*See generally* 4 Scott on Trusts §337.
[127]*See* Procedures for Terminating Small Trusts: Report of the Committee on Formation, Administration and Distribution of Trusts, 19 Real Prop. Prob. & Tr. J. 988 (1984).
[128]Id.
[129]Id.

§3.5.4   Nature of Trustee's Liability

At common law, the trustee's liability was personal. This is still the law when it comes to the trustee's internal dealings with the beneficiary.

§3.5.4.1   Personal Liability

The trustee can take no benefit from ownership of the trust estate, nor deal with it for personal profit or for any purpose unconnected with the trust.[130] The trustee is nevertheless the "owner" of the property.[131] Thus, subject to certain exceptions (statutory and otherwise),[132] the general rule is that the trustee is personally liable as owner to nonbeneficiaries such as contract creditors, tort creditors, and the federal, state, and local governments in the same way and to the same extent as if the property were owned by the trustee individually.[133] Moreover, the trustee is personally liable in equity to the beneficiaries for any breach of fiduciary duty,[134] subject however to a right of indemnity or exoneration from the trust estate for certain liabilities.[135]

§3.5.4.2   Insuring Against Personal Liability

As owner of the legal interest, the trustee is vulnerable on two fronts when it comes to personal liability. As the *owner* of the trust estate, the trustee is personally liable to nonbeneficiaries for negligent and intentional torts committed by him and his servants against nonbeneficiaries in the course of the administration of the trust estate. As the *fiduciary*, the trustee is also personally liable to

---

[130]*See* §6.1.3.
[131]*See* §3.5.1.
[132]*See* §§3.5.2.3., 7.3.
[133]*See* §7.3.
[134]*See* §7.2.
[135]*See* §3.5.2.3.

the beneficiaries for any negligent or intentional breaches of trust that cause injury to the trust itself.

As a practical matter, the individual trustee cannot obtain insurance that would cover the trustee's personal liability for intentional torts committed against nonbeneficiaries and for intentional breaches of trust.[136] Even if such insurance could be obtained, the premiums would have to be absorbed by the trustee personally as a cost of doing business — they may not be charged by the trustee to the trust estate.[137] The insurance company that underwrites the trustee's coverage for negligent acts against nonbeneficiaries essentially underwrites as well the costs of the trustee's defense against allegations that the acts were intentional.

The individual trustee who is not also an attorney will have a hard time finding inexpensive fiduciary liability insurance that will cover the trustee's personal liability for negligent breaches of trust, particularly in the carrying out of investment and property disbursement responsibilities.[138] Such insurance falls outside the scope of coverage of most homeowner and umbrella policies. It is generally underwritten on a per trust basis, with the insurance company requiring the trustee, as part of the application process, to submit a copy of the governing instrument. If the terms of the trust are amendable in any manner that would change the potential liability of the trustee, a substantive amendment will terminate coverage unless approved in advance by the insurance company.

Many insurance companies have a substantial minimum premium for such fiduciary liability insurance. The individual trustee of a personal trust who seeks customized fiduciary liability insurance that would cover the trustee's negligent breaches of trust probably should start with those companies that write policies for

---

[136]*See generally* R. Keeton & A. Widiss, Insurance Law, Guide to Fundamental Principles, Legal Doctrines, and Commercial Practices, Practitioner's Edition §5.4 (1988) (suggesting that it would be against public policy to be able to obtain insurance against one's intentional tortious acts).

[137]*See generally* Bogert, Trusts and Trustees §599.

[138]Phone interviews with insurers offering professional liability products yielded no insurer with a standard policy for the private trustee. Those insurers willing to consider underwriting policies would negotiate the price and the coverage.

fiduciaries of pension plans or directors and officers of corporations.[139] Remember that premiums for that type of coverage may not be charged against the trust estate.

The attorney acting as trustee has an advantage over the layman when it comes to coverage for negligent breaches of trust. Standardized legal malpractice policies are available to the lawyer who acts as trustee of trusts in the ordinary course of his or her practice. Most of these policies, however, exclude discrimination and environmental injury claims.

The trust officer who is employed by a corporate trustee seems particularly exposed when it comes to liability for breaches of trust. While the doctrine of respondeat superior will inevitably draw in the corporate trustee as a codefendant, it is the employment contract itself that determines whether the employer must defend and indemnify the trust officer or obtain insurance that will achieve the same result. If the terms are nonexistent or ambiguous in this regard, the trust officer would be well advised to consult with his or her insurance carrier. Again, little comfort will be found in the terms of personal homeowner and umbrella policies.

The trustee's liability for injury to nonbeneficiaries occasioned by negligent acts (committed personally and by servants) is readily insurable, and in most cases its costs are chargeable to the trust estate. For example, the cost of insuring an automobile that comprises a part of the trust estate is properly a trust expense.

[139]A list of such companies is published by the International Risk Management Institute, 12222 Merit Drive, Suite 1660, Dallas, Texas 75251, which can be reached at (214) 960-7693.

CHAPTER *4*

Interests Remaining with the Settlor

§4.1   Interests and Powers Remaining with the Settlor by Operation of Law

Whether the law reserves for the settlor some interest in the trust property is a question of more than academic interest, particularly in the charitable context where property worth billions of dollars is currently held in trust.[1] If some property rights remain back with the settlor at the time property is transferred in

---

§4.1   [1]The value of the combined endowments of Harvard, University of Texas, Princeton, Yale, Stanford, Columbia, Emory, M.I.T., Washington (St. Louis), and Texas A&M alone is $25.33 billion. Frank, Endowment Officials' Pay Is Mixed Bag, Wall St. J., July 26, 1993, at C1, col. 3.

trust, then the settlor may have standing to compel the trustee to carry out the terms of the trust. Thus, for example, the trustee of a college endowment fund could be accountable not only to the attorney general but also to benefactors. Presently there is much authority to the effect that the settlor of an irrevocable trust has no interest that would allow him to bring an action against the trustee for breach of trust.[2] However, some case law and commentary suggest that the settlor may not be entirely out of the picture (*e.g.*, a spendthrift trust may not be terminated without the settlor's consent).[3] Of course, the settlor with expressly retained interests or powers may bring an enforcement action against the trustee.[4]

§4.1.1   The Reversionary Interest

If the settlor or the settlor's estate is entitled by operation of law to a return of the trust property should the trust fail, it is said that the settlor possesses a *reversionary interest*. Moreover this right is vested in the settlor from the trust's inception whether or not the trust ever does fail.

§4.1.1.1   The Noncharitable Trust

The governing instrument of a noncharitable trust — if properly drawn — designates those who take title to the property

[2]*See, e.g.*, 3 Scott on Trusts §200.1; Bogert, Trusts and Trustees §42.

[3]*See, e.g.*, Carr v. Carr, 171 N.W. 785 (Iowa 1919) (holding that the donor of a trust has such interest therein as to entitle him to maintain a suit in equity to compel the carrying out of the terms thereof); 2A Scott on Trusts §151 ("It is held that even though the trust is a spendthrift trust, it can be terminated by the beneficiaries and the settlor if they all consent and are under no disability); Bogert, Trusts and Trustees §1006 n.13 and accompanying text; *see generally* Gaubatz, Grantor Enforcement of Trusts: Standing in One Private Law Setting, 62 N.C. L. Rev. 905, 941 (1984); Note, Right of a Settlor to Enforce a Private Trust, 62 Harv. L. Rev. 1370 (1949); Rounds, Social Investing, IOLTA and the Law of Trusts: The Settlor's Case Against the Political Use of Charitable and Client Funds, 22 Loy. U. Chi. L.J. 163 (1990).

[4]*See* Bogert, Trusts and Trustees §§42, 415.

once the trust terminates. In the absence of such express or implied designation, or if the anticipated takers are not then in existence, the beneficial interest does not accrue to the trustee. Or to put it another way, the trustee may not walk away with the trust property. The property returns to the settlor or the settlor's estate upon a resulting trust.[5]

A *resulting trust* is the equitable mechanism that gets the title from the trustee back into the hands of the settlor or the settlor's estate when a trust fails. From the trust's inception, the settlor possesses the possibility of reverter, which is a vested reversionary interest in the property.[6] This is nothing more than a beneficial interest in the property superior to that of the trustee and which may become possessory by operation of law through the mechanism of the resulting trust should the trust fail.

The resulting trust represents the law's commitment to protecting the settlor's property rights. The concept of the trust begins with the settlor, exists to fulfill the settlor's wishes, and ultimately ends with the settlor or the settlor's estate to the extent that the settlor's wishes cannot be fulfilled or are unknown. The trustee is the steward of someone else's property — in part the steward of the reversionary interest. The scrupulous trustee understands this.

§4.1.1.2   The Charitable Trust

Occasionally, the charitable purpose for which the settlor establishes a charitable trust will become impossible of fulfillment. This most often arises where the charity ceases to exist. In those cases a cy pres petition may be brought to determine if the settlor had a general charitable intent.[7]

A settlor possesses no reversionary interest under a trust with a general charitable purpose. Should such a trust become impossible of fulfillment, the court, instead of enforcing a result-

---

[5] 5 Scott on Trusts §411. *See also* National Shawmut Bank v. Joy, 315 Mass. 457, 463, 53 N.E.2d 113, 119 (1944).

[6] J. Gray, Rule Against Perpetuities §§113, 603.9 (4th ed. 1942).

[7] *See* §9.1.3.

ing trust, will apply the doctrine of *cy pres*.[8] This involves the judicial modification of the terms of the trust so that a charitable purpose as near as possible to the one generally specified by the settlor can be carried out. The development of the concept of cy pres as an alternative to the resulting trust has had the effect of making general charitable intent and the reversionary interest mutually exclusive.[9] The settlor of a trust with a limited charitable purpose, however, does have a vested reversionary interest that becomes possessory if the purpose becomes impossible of fulfillment.[10]

§4.1.2   The Expectation Interest

Let us assume for the sake of argument that a certain settlor reserves no power and no beneficial interest. Would that settlor nonetheless have any standing to seek judicial redress for a breach of trust? It is generally assumed that neither the settlor nor the settlor's representatives can compel performance of the trust or redress a breach.[11] This assumption appears to take support from the Restatement of Trusts:

> Neither the settlor nor his heirs or personal representatives, as such, can maintain a suit against the trustee to enforce a trust or enjoin or obtain redress for a breach of trust. Where, however, the settlor retains an interest in the trust property, he can of course maintain a suit against the trustee to protect that interest. Thus, if the settlor is also a beneficiary of the trust, or if he has an interest by way of a resulting trust, or if he has reserved power to revoke the trust, he can maintain a suit against the trustee to protect his interest.[12]

Upon reflection, however, one realizes that while under this

---

[8]Id.

[9]Id.

[10]J. Gray, The Rule Against Perpetuities §603.9 (4th ed. 1942); 4A Scott on Trusts §§399.3, 401.2-401.3.

[11]*See generally* 3 Scott on Trusts §200.1; Bogert, Trusts and Trustees §42.

[12]Restatement (Second) of Trusts §200 comment *b* (1959).

section the settlor of a trust with a general charitable purpose would lack standing to enforce the trust, perhaps the settlor of either a personal trust or a charitable trust with a limited purpose would not.

The settlor of a personal trust or a limited-charitable purpose trust retains a vested reversionary interest in the trust property that exists because of the possibility that the trust may fail at some future date for want of a purpose or beneficiary. Upon the trust's failure, a resulting trust arises in favor of the settlor or the settlor's estate. Thus the Restatement may support the proposition that the reversionary interest — an interest that becomes possessory should the trust fail — provides a settlor with sufficient standing to compel the trustee to carry out the provisions of his trust. On the other hand, the authors of the Restatement may have intended that the settlor acquire standing only in the event the trust actually fails.

Taking a different tack, in 1949, a Note in the Harvard Law Review questioned the now widely-held assumption that the settlor lacks standing to seek enforcement of the trust and suggested that Professor Scott's positions were unsupported by judicial decision.[13] Thirty-five years later Professor Gaubatz put forth in an article the thesis that in some situations a settlor has standing to enforce a trust based on the settlor's "expectation interest" in having the terms of the trust carried out.[14]

To be sure, enforceability and accountability are two features

---

[13]*See* Note, Right of a Settlor to Enforce a Private Trust, 62 Harv. L. Rev. 1370 (1949).

[14]Gaubatz, Grantor Enforcement of Trusts: Standing in One Private Law Setting, 62 N.C. L. Rev. 905 (1984). Professor Gaubatz suggests that "the grantor's standing is analyzed better on the basis of whether he has an interest, economic or otherwise, in the performance of the trustee's duties. If he possesses such an interest, and that interest is within the zone of interests sought to be protected by those duties, then the grantor can bring an action to enforce the trust. In a broad sense, if the grantor has an economic, *expectation* (emphasis added), or representational interest in the trust, such that he can be trusted to fully and fairly litigate the validity of the transactions that he challenges, and his interest was foreseeable at the time the trust was created, he can maintain an action." Id. at 940-941. *But see* Sanders v. Citizens Natl. Bank of Leesburg, 585 So. 2d 1064 (Fla. 1991) (court, having denied a settlor standing to enforce a trust that he had impressed upon his property, made an oblique reference to Professor Gaubatz's article).

that distinguish the trust from the *gift*.[15] If a settlor has an expectation interest in having the terms of the trust carried out — and thus standing to seek judicial redress — this may add an extra measure of accountability to the trust relationship consistent with the imposition of fiduciary duties. It is that imposition, after all, which distinguishes a trust from a gift. Without some right of enforcement remaining back with the settlor, there is no practical way to prevent the trustee from colluding with beneficiaries to effect a breach of trust. In the context of charitable trusts, an element of "privatization" is called for as attorneys general no longer have the resources to systematically police the administration of the nation's inventory of charitable trusts.[16] Moreover, in construing the terms of a trust, a court will attempt to divine the intent of the settlor as manifested at the time the interest was created.[17] Is there not then some irony when that settlor, himself, is denied standing to bring before the court issues relating to that intent?

One cannot deny the practical downside for the trustee if the settlor is to remain in the picture, particularly in situations where the trustee and settlor disagree as to how certain trust provisions should be interpreted and administered. And there will always be the situation where the settlor and beneficiaries are at loggerheads and the trustee is caught in the middle.

§4.1.3 Creditor Accessibility as a General Inter Vivos Power of Appointment

It is becoming a general rule that a settlor's creditors may reach the trust property to the extent the settlor reserves a benefi-

---

[15]*See generally* Restatement (Second) of Trusts §§25 comment *c*, comment *a* (1959). The settlor's standing, if any, to enforce a trust may have its roots in Anglo-Norman law. In the fourteenth century, if the *feoffee to uses* failed to perform his duties, the *feoffor* could seek enforcement in the Court of Common Pleas. Later, the *cestui que use* also gained a right to seek enforcement, but in the Court of Chancery. *See generally* W. F. Fratcher, 6 Intl. Encyclopedia of Comp. Law, at 14 (F. H. Lawson, ed. 1973).

[16]*See generally* 4A Scott on Trusts §391.

[17]*See generally* Restatement (Second) of Trusts §164 comment *b* (1959).

cial interest.[18] For example, a trust for the benefit of the settlor —
fully discretionary as to income and principal — will expose the
entire property to creditor attack.[19] The law thus bestows on the
settlor the ability to indirectly extract value from the trust by
incurring debts and leaving it to the creditors to collect.[20] This
right to direct trust property to creditors conforms to the Restatement of Property's definition of a general inter vivos power of
appointment.[21] The possession of such a right may have estate and
gift tax consequences,[22] and may also bear on the settlor's eligibility for Medicaid and on the rights of the settlor's spouse to reach
the trust property.[23]

§4.2   Expressly Reserved Beneficial Interests and Powers

A settlor may expressly reserve a beneficial interest in the
income or the principal, or both, of the trust.[1] The settlor may
reserve special and general powers of appointment.[2] If a power
is exercisable by will it is known as a *testamentary power*. A power
exercisable by deed is known as an *inter vivos power*. The settlor
may reserve a power to amend the trust.[3] This right is tantamount to a general inter vivos power of appointment because
such a power can be inserted into the instrument through the
amendment process. At the outset, the settlor may appoint himself trustee or cotrustee or reserve the right to do so thereafter.[4]

[18]*See* §5.3.3.1.
[19]Id.
[20]Id.
[21]Restatement (Second) of Property §11.4 (Donative Transfers).
[22]*See* §5.3.3.1.
[23]*See* §5.3.5 (Medicaid eligibility); §5.3.4 (spousal rights).
  §4.2   [1]*See generally* Restatement (Second) of Trusts §114 (1959).
  [2]*See generally* National Shawmut Bank v. Joy, 315 Mass. 457, 53 N.E.2d 113
(1944).
  [3]*See generally* 4 Scott on Trusts §§331, 331.1, 331.2.
  [4]*See generally* 2 Scott on Trusts §100.

These are the traditional ways the settlor may remain in the picture.

Nowadays settlors are resorting to more limited, more subtle means of maintaining involvement, such as by reserving rights to control investments, to remove trustees, or to receive accountings. These reservations are less burdensome for the settlor than the assumption of a cotrusteeship, but not necessarily less burdensome for the trustee. The practice of reserving the right to direct investments is a particularly worrisome development from the trustee's perspective because the law is not entirely clear whether the trustee has some fiduciary responsibility to monitor and react to the settlor's investment activities.[5] Any ambiguity in the arrangement will pose a trap for the unwary trustee and an extraordinary burden for the cautious trustee. The trustee should not accept directed trust business unless these ambiguities can be resolved by express language in the governing instrument. There is some authority to the effect that, in the case of an irrevocable trust, a nontrustee in whom investment discretion has been allocated will be held to a fiduciary standard in the exercise of that discretion.[6] It should be emphasized, however, that this will in no way diminish the general fiduciary duties of the trustee.

As to devices aimed at riding herd on the trustee — reserved rights of removal, consultation, and disclosure — the law has not settled on what constraints, if any, are placed on the holders of these rights. If they are fiduciaries, they are like cotrustees and presumably assume the burdens commensurate with that office, such as the risk of surcharge for unreasonable behavior. If they are *not* fiduciaries, then what are they? How does the law protect the trustee from assertions of these rights that are arbitrary, unreasonable, or imprudent — in short, in ways that are not in the interest of the beneficiaries?

---

[5]*See generally* 2A Scott on Trusts §185; Restatement (Third) of Trusts §185 comments *b-h* (1992). See also Cal. Prob. Code Ann. §16462 (1990).
[6]*See supra* note 5.

CHAPTER **5**
The Beneficiary

§5.1 Who Can Be a Beneficiary?

A trust beneficiary's interest is an equitable interest.[1] This interest, be it vested or contingent, is property.[2] Thus entities

§5.1 [1]*See* Restatement of Property §6 comment *a* (1936); Restatement (Second) of Trusts §2 comment *f* (1959); *see generally* §3.5.1.

[2]*See generally* 2 Scott on Trusts §130 (the property subject to the trust); 1 Restatement of Property at 3 (1936) (introduction to chapter 1) (the equitable interest).

capable of owning property are eligible to be trust beneficiaries; these are entities to whom enforceable personal rights with respect to tangible and intangible things may attach.[3] Such entities would include minors,[4] the insane,[5] certain corporations,[6] unincorporated associations, trustees, persons who are unborn or unascertained,[7] the United States or a state of the United States. In the noncharitable context, the equitable interests of the unborn and unascertained are represented by the guardian ad litem.[8] In the charitable context, future unascertained recipients of charity are entitled to beneficiary status because the attorney general is charged with enforcing trusts established on their behalf.[9]

The dead, who are without any status whatsoever under the common law, are entitled to beneficiary status provided the legislature authorizes trusts for the perpetual care of gravesites and legal mechanisms for their enforcement.[10] In the absence of such statutory authority, the relatives of the dead have common law standing to enforce gravesite protection trusts during the period permitted by the Rule Against Perpetuities.[11] It could be argued that for all intents and purposes such trusts would exist for the benefit of the relatives who themselves possess the common law right to visit, honor, and protect gravesites of their deceased relatives.[12]

Under the definition of property adopted by the Restate-

---

[3]*See generally* W. N. Hohfeld, Fundamental Legal Conceptions 23-124 (1923) (suggesting that property is a collection of rights, privileges, powers and immunities with respect to a thing rather than the thing itself); *see also* I Restatement of Property at 3 (1936) (introduction to chapter 1).

[4]*See* 2 Scott on Trusts §116.

[5]Id.

[6]*See* 2 Scott on Trusts §117.1.

[7]*See* 2 Scott on Trusts §112.1.

[8]*See* Restatement (Second) of Trusts §214 comment *a* (1959). *See generally* Begleiter, The Guardian Ad Litem in Estate Proceedings, 20 Willamette L. Rev. 643, 651-653 (1984).

[9]*See* 4A Scott on Trusts §§364, 391.

[10]*See generally* P. Jackson, The Law of Cadavers and of Burial and Burial Places (2d ed. 1950); G. Newhall, Settlement of Estates and Fiduciary Law in Massachusetts §10 (4th ed. 1958); 4A Scott on Trusts §374.9.

[11]*But see* 2 Scott on Trusts §124.2.

[12]*See generally* Rounds, Protections Afforded to Massachusetts' Ancient Burial Grounds, 73 Mass. L. Rev. 176 (1988).

ment, the holder of a general inter vivos power of appointment would be a beneficiary because the holder would possess an enforceable equitable personal right relating to a tangible or intangible thing.[13] In the pre-Restatement world, when personal rights and property rights were considered mutually exclusive, a power holder had only a personal right.[14]

Where there is no beneficiary, there is no trust.[15] In the case of private trusts (as opposed to charitable or public trusts), the beneficiary must be definite.[16] This does not mean that the beneficiary specifically must be named — a designation by description is sufficient.[17] The beneficiary is sufficiently definite only if it is certain at the time when the trust takes effect that the beneficiary will be identified before the expiration of the period allowed by the Rule Against Perpetuities.[18]

Despite the usual rule that a beneficiary must be a definite ascertainable individual, it commonly is held that a trust for the benefit of the members of a class of persons is valid.[19] However, a trust created for the benefit of a class of persons which is not sufficiently definite to be capable of ascertainment within the period of the Rule Against Perpetuities will fail, and a resulting trust will be imposed.[20] Trusts for the benefit of animals or of inanimate objects have been sustained, even when not charitable.[21] These trusts, however, depend upon the honor of the trustee since there is no person who as beneficiary can apply to the court for enforcement.[22] If the named trustee does not carry out the trust, the property will be held upon a resulting trust.[23] In the case of

---

[13]*Supra* note 3. *See generally* 1 Restatement of Property at 43 (1936) (introduction to chapter 1).

[14]*See generally* National Shawmut Bank v. Joy, 315 Mass. 457, 472, 53 N.E.2d 113, 123 (1944) (suggesting that power of appointment is not property).

[15]Restatement (Second) of Trusts §66 (1959).

[16]Id. §112 (1959).

[17]Id. comment *b*.

[18]Id. comment *a*.

[19]*See* id. §120.

[20]*See* id. §123; *see generally* 2 Scott on Trusts §123; *Joy*, 315 Mass. at 463, 53 N.E.2d at 118.

[21]*See generally* 2 Scott on Trusts §124.

[22]*See generally* Restatement (Second) of Trusts §124 comment *d* (1959).

[23]*See generally* id. §404.

charitable trusts, where the beneficiaries are indefinite, the attorney general is charged with the duty of informing the court of any breach of duty by the trustee.[24]

§5.2   Class Designation: "Issue" and "Heirs"

When the settlor properly designates by name related beneficiaries such as children, there is little room for ambiguity as to who qualifies as a beneficiary. What is lost however is the flexibility, adaptability, and economy of language that comes when the beneficiaries are designated not by name but by group membership. Suppose a trust provides that the trustee, upon the death of the settlor's spouse, shall distribute the corpus outright and free of trust to "the children then living of the settlor." It would accommodate children born after the trust was executed and exclude children predeceasing the spouse. Were the children specifically named, considerable additional language would be required to address such contingencies.

But class designations must be drafted properly or they will only cause problems for the trustee. Take for example the term *issue*, perhaps the most commonly used and most useful of the class designations:

1. *Issue* includes not just children but the descendants of all generations of the designated ancestor, that is, grandchildren, great-grandchildren and the like.[1] Thus, the term *issue* can lead to unfortunate misunderstandings and misconceptions on the part of beneficiaries and amateur trustees who are inclined to understand the term as meaning only someone's "children."

[24]*See* §9.1.2.
§5.2 [1]Uniform Probate Code §1-201(25), 8 U.L.A. 32 (1993 Supp.).

2. *Issue* ought not to stand alone. It should be accompanied by language explaining the proportions in which the issue take, be it *equally* or *by right of representation* or *equally within a generation* (the new *equally near, equally dear* concept of the Uniform Probate Code).[2] The inherently contradictory phrase *issue in equal shares, by right of representation* should be avoided at all costs.[3] Trustees unable to avoid administering such a provision will be faced with rationalizing this patently ambiguous phrase. It may well be that the phrase *in equal shares* refers to equality among the stocks with the term *by right of representation* referring to the proportions that the issue within each stock take.

3. Legislatures and courts are redefining the term *issue* and

---

[2]To illustrate the difference between *per stirpes* (by right of representation) and *per capita at each generation* (equally near, equally dear), let us assume that a settlor provided that his trust shall terminate at his death and that the property shall then pass to his then living issue, per stirpes. Let us also assume that the settlor had three children (X, Y, and Z) during his lifetime: X predeceased the trust's termination, leaving one child who survived the termination; Y predeceased the trust's termination, leaving two children who survived the termination; Z survived the termination as did her three children. Under the traditional per stirpital approach, X's child would take one third, Y's children would share one third, and Z would take one third. *See generally* M. Reutlinger, Wills, Trusts, and Estates 18-23 (1993). On the other hand, if the settlor had provided that his then living issue were to take *per capita* (equally), then Z and all the then-living grandchildren would have taken equal shares.

A hybrid concept, known as *per capita at each generation* or *equally near, equally dear*, has recently been approved by the National Conference of Commissioners on Uniform State Laws. Uniform Act on Intestacy, Wills, and Donative Transfers, 8A U.L.A. 154 (1993 Supp.). It is derived from the intestacy sections of the Uniform Probate Code, §2-106. It has been suggested that "[t]he per-capita-at-each-generation system is more responsive to the underlying premise of the original UPC system, in that it always provides equal shares to those equally related; the pre-1990 UPC achieved this objective in most but not all cases." 8A U.L.A. at 167. To continue with our example, if the classic pre-1990 per stirpital approach is applied, the child of X receives one third; under the new "equally near, equally dear" approach, the child of X receives $2/9$, because the children of deceased X and the children of deceased Y would share equally. Id.

[3]*See generally* U.S. Trust, 1992 New York Trusts and Estates Legislation: Meanings of "Per Stirpes" and "In Equal Shares per Stirpes," Practical Drafting 2939-2972 (1992).

other such group designations to include persons adopted and born out of wedlock.[4] Such alterations in meaning should not apply retroactively to trusts already in existence — no matter how appealing on a personal level retroactivity may be. Such alterations in meaning should apply only prospectively, unless the settlor has expressed a contrary intention. Otherwise, this shifting of property interests from one group to another amounts to the state's "taking by redefinition" of property.

To illustrate the last point, let us assume that in 1900 an irrevocable trust was created that provided that, upon its termination at the death of the last survivor of the settlor's children, the property passes outright and free of trust to the "then living issue" of the settlor. Let us assume further that the term *issue* as understood in 1900 did *not* include persons who were adopted or who were born out of wedlock. At the time the trust was created, members of the class of the settlor's grandchildren and more remote descendants, whether born or unborn, acquired property rights in the form of equitable contingent remainders. It is a popular misconception that contingent interests under trusts are not property interests — nothing could be further from the truth. The office of the guardian ad litem itself has evolved to represent just such property interests on behalf of minors, the unborn, and the unascertained.[5] Thus when the state retroactively redefines a term such as *issue* to bring in persons not intended by the settlor, the state dilutes the property interests, contingent or otherwise, of the persons whom the settlor did contemplate, whether those persons are born or unborn.[6]

---

[4]*See generally* Restatement (Second) of Property §§25.2-25.5 (1988) (Donative Transfers). *See also* In re Trusts of Harrington, 311 Minn. 403, 250 N.W.2d 163 (1977) (adoptees deemed issue of the body); In Will of Hoffman, 53 A.D.2d 55, 385 N.Y.S.2d 49 (1976) (redefining the term *issue* to include illegitimates).

[5]*See* §3.5.3.2(h); Restatement (Second) of Trusts §214 comment *a* (1959).

[6]Wachovia Bank & Trust Co. v. Andrews, 264 N.C. 531, 142 S.E.2d 182 (1965) (holding that the state may not retroactively redefine a class to include adopteds and thus dilute the property interests of nonadopted members).

Heirs is another term that often appears in trust instruments.[7] That term, accompanied by appropriate qualifying language, can serve as a convenient formula for coming up with takers in default of named beneficiaries, but it can also carry with it all kinds of problems if it is used alone. To illustrate, let us assume that upon the death of a settlor's spouse the trustee shall distribute the trust property outright and free of trust to the settlor's "heirs." Most courts will construe *heir* as someone who takes, or would take, under some statute dealing with intestate succession.[8] But the statute of which jurisdiction? And is it the statute in effect at the creation of the trust, the death of the settlor, or the death of the spouse? What if the statute treats real property differently from personal property? And what is intended by the term if the settlor died testate? Perhaps it imports the subjunctive, that is, those persons who would take the property of the settlor if he or she had died intestate.[9]

A prospective trustee should insist that the term *heirs* be accompanied with appropriate assumptions, exclusions, and qualifications to wring out such gaps and ambiguities.[10] In 1939, Professor Casner offered the following "basic form" which was intended to do just that in the context of devises under wills. Over the years since then it has been revised and adapted to accommodate equitable interests under trusts:

[7]The Uniform Probate Code narrowly defines *heirs* as "those persons, including the surviving spouse, who are entitled under the statutes of intestate succession to the property of a decedent." Uniform Probate Code §1-201(21), 8 U.L.A. 32 (1993 Supp.).

[8]*See* Casner, Construction of Gifts to "Heirs" and the Like, 53 Harv. L. Rev. 207, 208-209 (1939): "When the devisees in a will are described as the 'heirs' . . . of a designated person, almost all courts agree that some statute dealing with the intestate succession of property is to be employed to ascertain the persons described, in the absence of additional language or circumstances which indicate a contrary intent on the part of the testator."

[9]*See* National Shawmut Bank of Boston v. Joy, 315 Mass. 457, 462-467, 53 N.E.2d 113, 117-120 (1944) (construing a default clause to be in the subjunctive); *see generally* Casner, Construction of Gifts to "Heirs" and the Like, 53 Harv. L. Rev. 207 (1939).

[10]*See generally* Casner, Construction of Gifts to "Heirs" and the Like, 53 Harv. L. Rev. 207 (1939).

. . . then to those persons, and in such shares, as would have taken real property owned by me and situated in State *X* if I had died immediately after the termination of all prior interests in the land which is the subject of this devise, intestate and domiciled in State *X*, unless all prior interests expire by their terms before the will has taken effect, in which case, to those persons and in such shares as would have taken real property owned by me and situated in State *X* if I had died intestate and domiciled in State *X*; my intention is to include all persons who would take on such assumed intestacy whether they are related to me by blood or not, whether legitimate or illegitimate, and whether or not they have received any interest under this will.[11]

If the trust instrument uses the term *heirs* without any language that qualifies the term, then prior to distribution the trustee should seek the advice of counsel. This will reduce the risk of misdelivery.

§5.3   The Beneficiary's Property Interest

The beneficiary's equitable interest is an interest in property. However, it is a type of interest that may, under certain circumstances, be inalienable or immune from attachment, or both.

§5.3.1   Nature and Extent of Property Interest

"When uses were first enforced in England by the chancellors of the fifteenth century, it is clear that they looked at the use primarily as a personal relationship between the feoffee and the cestui que use."[1] Today, a beneficiary has more than mere rights

[11]Id. at 249-250.
§5.3 [1]2 Scott on Trusts §130. The phrase *cestui que trust* has evolved into a synonym for *beneficiary*. It is not known when this Norman-French phrase was

against the trustee.[2] The beneficiary possesses an interest in the trust property itself that is either vested or contingent.[3] The outcome of a tax or other dispute may hinge on the beneficiary's legal relationship with the underlying trust property.[4]

The extent of the beneficiary's equitable interest is usually governed by the terms of the instrument. The settlor of the trust may create equitable interests that correspond to the comparable legal estates (*e.g.*, the beneficiary may be given an equitable life estate or an equitable estate for years). With respect to vested equitable interests, if the trust principal is personal property the beneficiary's interest is personal property, too, and follows personal property rules; if it is real estate, the beneficiary's interest is also regarded as realty.

The interest of the beneficiary may be a future interest, vested or contingent; may rest solely in the discretion of the trustee; it may be limited to the occupation of the trust property.

Co-owners of a beneficial interest ordinarily hold the interest jointly unless there is a statute to the contrary.[5] Of course, the terms of a governing instrument may specify how the beneficial interest is to be held (jointly or as tenants in common) notwithstanding any common law or statutory presumption.[6]

The issue of the beneficiary's relationship to the underlying property is separate from the issue of whether a particular equitable interest is vested or contingent. A beneficiary's equitable inter-

---

introduced into our language, but it is believed to have been in the seventeenth century. For a discussion of such borrowings from the Norman French see Sweet, 'Cestui Que Use': 'Cestui Que Trust,' 26 L.Q. Rev. 196 (1910).

[2]*See generally* 2 Scott on Trusts §130.

[3]*See generally* Bogert, Trusts and Trustees §182.

[4]*See, e.g.*, Cohen, Massachusetts Estate Tax Planning For Non-Massachusetts Residents Owning Real Estate in Massachusetts, 70 Mass. L. Rev. 124, 126 (Sept. 1985) (tax); In re Grand Jury Subpoena, 973 F.2d 45 (1st Cir. 1992) (Fifth Amendment privilege not available to trustees of nominee trust).

[5]In many states such statutes have been enacted. *See generally* 2A Scott on Trusts §143. Many states' statutes impose a presumption of tenancy in common. *See, e.g.*, N.Y. Est. Powers & Trusts Law §6-2.2 (Consol. 1979); Ill. Ann. Stat. ch. 76, §§1-1a, 2 (Smith-Hurd 1987); Cal. Civ. Code §683 (West 1982); Mass. Gen. Laws. Ann. ch. 184, §7 (West 1987).

[6]*See, e.g.*, Anderson v. Bean, 220 Mass. 360, 107 N.E. 964 (1915).

est, for example, may be so contingent as to be for all intents and purposes little more than a right of action against the trustee.

"Interests of beneficiaries of private express trusts run the gamut from valuable substantialities to evanescent hopes. Such a beneficiary may have any one of an almost infinite variety of the possible aggregates of rights, privileges, powers and immunities."[7] Equitable interests in trusteed IRAs and realty trusts tend to crowd the substantial end of the rights spectrum.[8] They are often distinguishable only in form from vested legal interests in the underlying property.[9] At the opposite extreme are the contingent interests in charitable trusts.[10] Such interests tend to be little more than evanescent hopes. A beneficiary's interest in a trust associated with a qualified employee benefit plan tends to move over time from the contingent end to the vested end of the rights spectrum.[11]

§5.3.2 Voluntary Transfers

In the absence of restraint imposed by the trust instrument or by statute, the beneficiary's equitable estate may be transferred by the beneficiary as freely as might be done if it were a legal estate (beneficial interests after all being property interests).[12] (This is a matter separate from whether the beneficiary holds a power of appointment.[13]) The beneficiary may not transfer the equitable interest if it is subject to the discretion of the trustee or if it is inseparable from that of others.[14] These are restraints imposed by the instrument. Although not literally a restraint of the trust in-

---

[7]Farkas v. Williams, 5 Ill. 2d 417, 422-423, 125 N.E.2d 600, 603 (1955) (*citing* 4 Powell, The Law of Real Property, at 87).

[8]*See* §§9.2.2, 9.3.

[9]Id.

[10]*See* §9.1.

[11]I.R.C. §§401(a)(7), 411; ERISA §203 (ERISA vesting standards).

[12]*See generally* Restatement of Property §5 (1936); id. at 3 (introduction to chapter 1); 2A Scott on Trusts §132; Restatement (Second) of Trusts §133 (1959); Brown v. Fletcher, 235 U.S. 589, 599 (1915).

[13]*See* §8.1.

[14]*See generally* 2A Scott on Trusts §§132, 155, 161; E. Griswold, Spendthrift Trusts §§435-445 (2d ed. 1947) (discussing the separability of the beneficial interests).

strument, a beneficial interest may be so personal in nature as to be unassignable.[15]

Unless it terminates with the beneficiary's death, the beneficial interest may pass by will or by intestacy, or be transferred by deed. The transfer may be in whole or in part, outright or by way of security, or in trust.[16] Requirements of capacity and intention are identical at law and in equity.[17] The transferee of a legal or equitable interest need not know of the transfer or assent to it, but both interests are of course disclaimable.[18] Testamentary transfers of beneficial interests as well as legal interests require compliance with the Statute of Wills.[19]

The Statute of Frauds may apply to the transfer of an equitable interest, particularly if the underlying property is realty.[20] Such a transfer may also require attention to the rules and regulations of the Securities and Exchange Commission.[21] On the other hand, some of the formalities required for the transfer of a legal interest may be dispensed with in the case of the transfer of the equitable interest. Thus, as a general rule, the transfer of a beneficial interest in a trust containing real estate need not be recorded in a registry of deeds.[22] This then raises the question whether assignments of beneficial interests take priority in the order made or in the order in which notice is given to the trustee. There is a division of authority on the issue.[23]

What if a trustee honors the beneficiary's assignment of an equitable interest in a spendthrift trust? Courts tend to absolve the

[15]*See generally* 2A Scott on Trusts §160.

[16]*See generally* id. §132; *see also* Blair v. Commissioner, 300 U.S. 5, 13 (1937) (holding valid life beneficiary's assignment of portions of trust income).

[17]*See generally* Restatement (Second) of Trusts §133 (1959); 2A Scott on Trusts §§133-134 (capacity, intention); Chase Natl. Bank of N.Y. v. Sayles, 11 F.2d 948, 955 (1st Cir. 1926) (a valid unrestricted assignment is irrevocable); Restatement (Second) of Trusts §134 (1959).

[18]*See generally* Restatement (Second) of Trusts §137 (1959); 2A Scott on Trusts §137.

[19]*See generally* Bogert, Trusts and Trustees §188; 2A Scott on Trusts §132.1.

[20]*See generally* Bogert, Trusts and Trustees §190; Restatement (Second) of Trusts §138.

[21]*See* §§7.3.3.3, 7.3.4.2(a).

[22]*See generally* Bogert, Trusts and Trustees §249.

[23]*See generally* 2A Scott on Trusts §163; Bogert, Trusts and Trustees §195.

trustee by treating the assignment as a revocable order to transfer accrued income or principal once it becomes possessory.[24] The trustee is essentially deemed an agent of the beneficiary. The relationship being an agency, it is revocable by the principal (in this case the beneficiary) up until the time accrued income or principal is transferred by the trustee outright and free of trust to the assignee.[25]

§5.3.3 Rights of Beneficiary's Creditors and Others to Trust Property

In the case of involuntary transfers of the beneficiary's interest, the equitable estate is treated in many respects as if it were a legal estate.[26] Thus, as a general rule a beneficiary's creditors and spouse may reach that portion of the equitable interest over which the beneficiary possesses an affirmative right of consumption.[27] There are three important exceptions to this rule.

1. *Powers of appointment.* As a general rule, a nonsettlor holder of a general power of appointment cannot be compelled to exercise it.[28] This is a remnant of the pre-Restatement of Property distinction between personal rights and property rights.[29] However, if the power is exercised, the property subject to the power may be fair game for the holder's creditors.[30] It should be noted that in a few states, statutes permit the creditors of the holder of a general power of appointment to reach the property even if the power is unexercised.[31] Property subject to a

---

[24]*See* Restatement (Second) of Trusts §152 comment *i* (1959).
[25]Id.
[26]Bogert, Trusts and Trustees §193.
[27]*See generally* 2A Scott on Trusts §§147, 157.
[28]*See* State Street Trust Co. v. Kissel, 302 Mass. 328, 333, 119 N.E.2d 25 (1939); Ritchie et al., Decedent's Estates and Trusts 961-964 (8th ed. 1993).
[29]Id.; *see also* National Shawmut Bank v. Joy, 315 Mass. 457, 472, 53 N.E.2d 113, 124 (1944).
[30]Id.
[31]Bogert, Trusts and Trustees §233.

nongeneral power to appoint, of course, can never be reached by the holder's creditors, whether or not the power is exercised.

2. *Employee benefit plans.* Even though employees have un-trammeled access to their interests in trusts associated with qualified employee benefit plans, it does not necessar-ily mean that their creditors do as well. This is due to federal pension law.[32]

3. *Indivisible equitable interests.* If the debtor-beneficiary holds the equitable interest jointly with another or as a tenant by the entirety, the creditors may not reach the trust property during the life of the cotenant.[33]

An example of an equitable interest that is vulnerable to involuntary transfer would be an irrevocable, nondiscretionary, income-only trust created by *A* for the benefit of *C*: where, after the expiration of ten years, the property passes outright and free of trust to *D*; where *B* is the trustee; where *D* is ascertained at the time the property is transferred to *B*; and where there is no spendthrift provision. Under such a trust, the income stream itself would be reachable and attachable by *C*'s spouse and credi-tors during the ten-year period. If *C* were to die intestate during the ten-year period, the income stream would inure to the bene-fit of *C*'s heirs at law for the balance of the period, subject to any rights of the creditors and the spouse to the equitable interest. In addition, the present vested right to the future unrestricted en-joyment of the property would be reachable by *D*'s spouse and creditors during the ten-year period.[34] If *D* were to die intestate before ten years, the vested equitable remainder interest — that right of future enjoyment — would pass in accordance with the laws of distribution to *D*'s heirs at law, unless the underlying

---

[32]*See* I.R.C. §401(a)(13) (1954) (trusts that are part of qualified plans must prohibit assignment or alienation of benefits); Patterson v. Shumate, 112 S. Ct. 2242 (1992) (holding that assets held in a trust associated with a qualified plan may not be reached by the bankruptcy trustee though the trust would not qualify for spendthrift protection under state trust law).

[33]*See generally* Bogert, Trusts and Trustees §230.

[34]*See generally* Bogert, Trusts and Trustees §193.

trust property were realty, in which case the equitable interest would pass to them by descent.[35] D could also designate by will who is to succeed to D's interest if death occurred during the ten-year period.

While a vested equitable interest may be vulnerable to creditor attack, it may also be entitled to the same statutory protections as legal interests.[36] Homestead exemptions, for example, apply to equitable as well as legal interests.[37]

An example of an equitable interest that probably would not be subject to involuntary transfer is a fully discretionary trust established by A for the benefit of C during C's lifetime. Here C possesses no affirmative right to consume the income and principal: C gets whatever B chooses to release and no more, as do C's spouse and creditors. Moreover, should C die intestate nothing would pass to C's heirs at law, the interest having extinguished at C's death. All bets are off, however, with respect to reserved equitable interests, even under discretionary trusts. Where the settlor is also a beneficiary, that is to say, where A and C or A and D are the same, the equitable interest is vulnerable to attack by A's spouse and creditors. This is a manifestation of an evolving public policy that if you are a settlor-debtor you may not eat your cake and have it too.[38]

§5.3.3.1 Reaching Settlor's Reserved Beneficial Interest

As a matter of public policy, the settlor cannot place property in trust for the settlor's own benefit and keep it beyond the reach of creditors. This is true even though the trust may contain a spendthrift provision, even though the remaindermen may be

---

[35] 2A Scott on Trusts §142.
[36] Bogert, Trusts and Trustees §187.
[37] Id.
[38] *See generally* 2A Scott on Trusts §156; Restatement (Second) of Trusts §156 (1959); Ware v. Gulda, 331 Mass. 68, 117 N.E.2d 137 (1954) (holding the property of a fully discretionary trust to be reachable by the settlor-beneficiary's creditors).

harmed, and even if the settlor has not retained the right to revoke or amend the trust.[39] The policy is reflected in §156(2) of the Restatement (Second) of Trusts,[40] which has been adopted in whole or in part by an ever-increasing number of jurisdictions: "[W]here a person creates for his own benefit a trust for support or a discretionary trust, his transferee or creditors can reach the maximum amount which the trustee under the terms of the trust could pay to him or apply for his benefit."[41] While unanimity across the jurisdictions on the rights of creditors to reach reserved beneficial interests has not been achieved, the law seems to be settling rapidly on the spirit, and in some cases even the language, of §156(2).[42]

In jurisdictions that are following the letter or spirit of §156(2), a transfer to an irrevocable trust by the settlor for the settlor's own benefit will not be a completed inter vivos transfer for federal gift tax or estate tax purposes.[43] This is true even if the settlor is only a discretionary beneficiary.[44]

(a) The vulnerability of principal. It is important to understand how radically §156(2) alters the common law of property and trusts. Let us assume that a settlor creates a trust for his own benefit giving the trustee discretion over income and principal. Under §156(2) the principal is vulnerable to attack by the settlor's creditors even if: (1) the trustee never chooses to exercise this discretion; (2) the trustee is independent; (3) the remaindermen are unrelated third parties. Suppose the settlor reserves no beneficial interest, only a naked right of revocation. The current state of the common law seems to be that an unexercised, naked reserved right of revocation will not expose the principal to attack by the

[39]*See* Restatement (Second) of Trusts §156 (1959).
[40]*See also Ware, supra* note 38.
[41]*See* Restatement (Second) of Trusts §156 appendix (1959).
[42]*See* 2A Scott on Trusts §156 n.1.
[43]Paolozzi v. Commissioner, 23 T.C. 182, 186 (1954); Outwin v. Commissioner, 76 T.C. 153 n.5 (1981).
[44]Id.

settlor's creditors.[45] The trustee however, should expect form to give way to substance sooner rather than later. Courts will be hard pressed to justify why, as a matter of public policy, the settlor's creditors should be thwarted by naked reserved rights of revocation under which settlors retain rights of consumption over the subject properties, but should not be thwarted by reserved beneficial interests in discretionary trusts where control is transferred to independent trustees.

Is principal safe from attack when the settlor creates an income-only trust for the settlor's own benefit? Probably so — at least for the foreseeable future. There is a counter argument, however: The principal — the engine that generates the income — is employed for the benefit of the settlor. Thus, because the entire principal is dedicated to the benefit of the settlor, the spirit and letter of §156(2) dictate that the principal itself should be vulnerable to creditor attack.[46] While the engine argument is essentially the rationale in the estate tax context for the reserved life estate sections of the Internal Revenue Code,[47] it has so far proven of little utility to the settlor's creditors.

(b) The postmortem creditor. The current trend of the law favors allowing the settlor's postmortem creditors, and the surviving spouse as well, access to the principal of an inter vivos trust if the settlor reserved a power to consume the property at the time of the settlor's death.[48] This should be contrasted with the lot of the inter vivos creditor where the focus is on the retention of a

[45]*See* Restatement (Second) of Trusts §330 comment *o* (1959); for statutes providing otherwise, see 4 Scott on Trusts §330.12.

[46]*See generally* Rounds, The Vulnerability of Trust Assets to Attack by the Deceased Settlors Creditors, by the Commonwealth Should It Seek Reimbursement for Medicaid Payments, and by the Spouse, 73 Mass L. Rev. 67, 70 (1988).

[47]I.R.C. §2036 (a)(1) (1978) (*reversing* May v. Heiner, 281 U.S. 238 (1930)); *see also* Omnibus Budget Reconciliation Act of 1993 §13611 (1993) (making the principle of self-settled income-only trusts countable for Medicaid eligibility purposes).

[48]*See, e.g.*, State Street Bank v. Reiser, 7 Mass. App. Ct. 633, 389 N.E.2d 768 (1979) (power of consumption at time of debtor's death); Sullivan v. Burkin, 390 Mass. 864, 460 N.E.2d 572 (1984) (power of consumption during marriage).

beneficial interest rather than a power to consume. [49] Thus we have such anomalies as the naked reserved right of revocation exposing a trust to the reach of the settlor's postmortem creditor but not the inter vivos one. [50] In the future the law will evolve to the point where the settlor-beneficiary's inter vivos and postmortem creditors will have coextensive access to the property of an inter vivos trust, but until that time such subtle divergences in the law will continue to complicate the already complicated life of the trustee.

Life insurance proceeds paid to the insured's inter vivos trust upon the death of the insured may, by statute, be beyond the reach of the settlor's postmortem creditors. [51] Prior to paying the settlor's postmortem creditors from life insurance proceeds payable to the trustee by reason of the settlor's death, the trustee should consult counsel.

§5.3.3.2   Reaching the Equitable Interest of Beneficiary Who Is Not the Settlor

The trustee should understand that because the equitable interests of nonsettlor trust beneficiaries and remaindermen are property interests, these interests may be subject to the claims of the beneficiaries' creditors. [52] If, however, the settlor has reserved beneficial interests or if the settlor has qualified the beneficiaries' equitable interests, [53] then the trust property may well

---

[49]*See* 4 Scott on Trusts §330.12; Restatement (Second) of Trusts §330 comment *o* (1959).

[50]*See Reiser*, 7 Mass. App. Ct. at 638, 389 N.E.2d at 771 (in the postmortem context, a reserved general inter vivos power may be enough to expose trust property to creditor attack); Restatement (Second) of Trusts §330 comment *o* (1959) (in inter vivos context a naked reserved general inter vivos power may *not* be enough to expose property to creditor attack).

[51]*See generally* 5 Scott on Trusts §508.4; Bogert, Trusts and Trustees §243.

[52]*See* 2A Scott on Trusts §147.

[53]*See* §§5.3.3.1, 5.3.3.3.

not be available to the creditors of the nonsettlor beneficiaries.[54] Let us look at a classic creditor-vulnerable trust that contains no such reservations or qualifications: *A* establishes an income-only trust for the benefit of *C* for *C*'s life. The principal passes outright and free of trust to *D* at the death of *C*, *D* being a person ascertained at the time of the trust's creation. *C* has a vested property interest in the stream of net income.[55] *C*'s creditors can seize the stream itself.[56] *D* has a vested nonpossessory property interest in the remainder. That interest is reachable by *D*'s creditors even before *C* dies, although it would not be possessory until *C* dies.[57]

The trustee should understand that *all* equitable interests — contingent or otherwise — are *property* interests.[58] As such they may not be taken by the state without just compensation.[59] Some equitable interests, however, such as those under the just-described trust, may be reached by the beneficiaries' creditors. While an equitable interest in trust property may be vulnerable to the reach of creditors, property subject only to a power of appointment — even a general inter vivos power — may well not be vulnerable.[60] The trustee should be aware of this subtle but substantive difference in vulnerability, a difference that has its origins in a vestigial distinction between property rights (*e.g.*, the equitable interest) and personal rights (*e.g.*, the power of appointment).[61]

---

[54]*See* Restatement (Second) of Trusts §§152, 155 (1959). *But see* id. §157.

[55]*See generally* Bogert, Trusts and Trustees §182 (section entitled "Vested and Contingent Interests").

[56]*See generally* id. §193.

[57]*See* 2A Scott on Trusts §147.2.

[58]*See* id. §130.

[59]*See* Webb's Fabulous Pharmacies, Inc. v. Beckwith, 449 U.S. 155 (1980); Sinibaldi, The Taking Issue in California's Legal Services Trust Account Program, 12 Hastings Const. L.Q. 463 (1985). *But see* Washington Legal Found. v. Massachusetts Bar Found., 993 F.2d 962 (1st Cir. 1993) (holding that the interest earned on certain funds entrusted by a client to his attorney is not the client's property; rather, it "belongs to no one").

[60]State Street Trust Co., Trustee v. Kissel, 302 Mass. 328, 19 N.E.2d 25 (1939).

[61]National Shawmut Bank v. Joy, 315 Mass. 457, 53 N.E.2d 113 (1944).

§5.3.3.3   Discretionary Provisions and Other Restraints Upon Voluntary and Involuntary Transfers Including the Spendthrift Trust

The settlor may limit the circumstances under which income and principal shall benefit the holder of an equitable interest.[62] Some limitations can so qualify the equitable interest that the beneficiary, as a practical matter, has no transferable and attachable property right.[63] The trustee should keep in mind — and this bears frequent repeating — that these limitations are not likely to thwart the settlor-beneficiary's creditors,[64] and that, even in the face of such limitations, once income or principal is distributed from the trust to the beneficiary (*i.e.*, once title passes from the trustee to the beneficiary), the distributed property becomes alienable by the beneficiary and is reachable by the beneficiary's creditors.

(a) The discretionary trust. The *discretionary trust* is perhaps the most effective means of keeping the beneficiary's creditors away from the equitable interest.[65] This is because the beneficiary has no enforceable right to an identifiable portion of the income stream or to the principal. The classic discretionary trust grants the trustee broad discretion to pay income and distribute principal to the beneficiary.[66] A cousin of the discretionary trust is the *support trust*, in which the trustee's discretion is limited by a standard such as health, maintenance, and support. No matter what the type of noncharitable discretionary trust, a member of the

---

[62]Farkas v. Williams, 5 Ill. 2d 417, 422-423, 125 N.E.2d 600, 603 (1955) (*citing* 4 Powell, The Law of Real Property, at 87).

[63]*See, e.g.*, Brownell v. Leutz, 149 F. Supp 98 (1957) (the interest of permissible beneficiary of a discretionary trust who was German alien was held not to be property interest susceptible of seizure during wartime by Alien Property Custodian).

[64]*See* §5.3.3.1.

[65]*See* Restatement (Second) of Trusts §155 comment *b* (1959); Pemberton v. Pemberton, 9 Mass. App. Ct. 9, 20, 411 N.E.2d 1305, 1308 (1980).

[66]*See* Bogert, Trusts and Trustees §228.

class of eligible beneficiaries would have standing to sue the trustee for abuse of discretion.[67] As a general rule a creditor, not being a beneficiary, would lack such standing and thus could not force the trustee to make discretionary distributions.[68] Limited exceptions to this general rule may include support trusts where the claimant is the beneficiary's spouse or child, or a governmental entity.[69] When the beneficiary is not the settlor, the creditor will find it difficult if not impossible to reach property held in a fully discretionary trust because the trustee's fiduciary duty runs to the debtor-beneficiary, not to the creditor.[70]

(b) Forfeiture provisions. Another mechanism for thwarting a trust beneficiary's creditors is a provision that terminates altogether the beneficiary's equitable interest upon the happening of some event such as the beneficiary's entering a nursing home, assuming debtor status, or attempting the alienation of the income stream.[71] If the beneficiary has no property interest then there is nothing to alienate and nothing for the creditors to attach.

(c) The spendthrift trust. Unlike the settlor of a discretionary trust, the settlor of a *spendthrift trust* directly confronts the creditor by withholding from the trustee the right to honor assignments and attachments of the equitable interests.[72] What the beneficiary

---

[67]*See* Restatement (Second) of Trusts §187 comment *k* (1959).

[68]*See* id. §155 comment *d*.

[69]*See* id. §157 (1959); Miller v. Department of Mental Health, 432 Mich. 426, 442 N.W.2d 617 (1989) (suggesting that Michigan may not seek reimbursement from discretionary trusts for public assistance rendered to nonsettlor beneficiaries but that support trusts may be vulnerable). *See also* Silber, The Effect of a Trust on the Eligibility or Liability of the Trust Beneficiary for Public Assistance, 26 Real Prop. Prob. & Tr. J. 133 (1991).

[70]*See* 2A Scott on Trusts §154; Restatement (Second) of Trusts §170 (1959).

[71]*See generally* 2A Scott on Trusts §150.

[72]*See* 2A Scott on Trusts §151, §152 (restraint on alienation of income), §153 (restraint on alienation of principal); Bogert, Trusts and Trustees §222 n.59 (for the current status of spendthrift trusts in all states).

cannot alienate, the creditor cannot attach.[73] The rationale for upholding the spendthrift trust is that it is the prerogative of the settlor — the owner of the property — to determine what restrictions (if any) shall be placed on the use of his property.[74] It is a privilege that comes with ownership.[75] After all, the settlor need not have created the trust in the first place, but could have instead consumed the property or given it away outright and free of trust.

The express reference in many spendthrift clauses to creditors over the years has invited assaults on the very institution of the spendthrift trust.[76] Some assaults have been partially or wholly successful, leading to noteworthy divergences across the jurisdictions.[77] A few states, such as North Carolina, will not enforce a spendthrift provision.[78] On the other hand, Massachusetts will, with one possible divorce-related exception.[79] Some states allow spendthrift provisions to protect the income stream only,[80] while others allow principal to be protected as well.[81] Some spendthrift jurisdictions draw a line when it comes to the beneficiary's spouse and children or to a creditor who has supplied "necessaries"[82] which has been held in some cases to include a government agency that has provided institutional care to the beneficiary.[83] A spendthrift provision will not prohibit the United States or a state from attaching the beneficial interest for taxes owed by the beneficiary.[84]

---

[73]Ritchie et al., Decedent's Estates and Trusts 630 (8th ed. 1993); 2A Scott on Trusts §152.3. *But see* Bank of New England v. Strandland, 402 Mass. 707, 529 N.E.2d 394 (1988) (honoring restraint on involuntary alienation only).

[74]Broadway Natl. Bank v. Adams, 133 Mass. 170 (1882).

[75]Id.

[76]*See* Bogert, Trusts and Trustees §222 (arguments for and against spendthrift trusts).

[77]Bogert, Trusts and Trustees §222 n.59.

[78]Id.

[79]*See* Lauricella v. Lauricella, 409 Mass. 211, 565 N.E.2d 436 (1991) (nonsettlor beneficiary's interest in realty trust subject to equitable division in divorce proceeding notwithstanding spendthrift clause).

[80]2A Scott on Trusts §152.

[81]Id. §153.

[82]*See* id. §§157.1, 157.2.

[83]Id.

[84]Id. §157.4.

At this point a comment on *alienation restraints* is in order. It is a cardinal principle of the law that a restraint upon alienation of a legal fee simple, or of an absolute interest in personal property, is invalid.[85] Courts that enforce spendthrift provisions circumvent this rule by drawing a distinction between legal interests and equitable interests.[86] Because the spendthrift restraint goes to the equitable interest and not to the trustee's legal interest, the power of alienation under a spendthrift provision continues unimpaired.[87]

(d) Trusteed employee benefit plans and IRAs. An employee benefit plan may well include an associated trust that serves as a receptacle for employer and employee contributions. Under federal law, contributions and the income generated by their investment are entitled to favorable tax treatment, provided the plan meets certain requirements (is *tax-qualified*). One such requirement is that the associated trust contain a spendthrift provision.[88] An ERISA-mandated antialienation provision prevents a trustee in bankruptcy from reaching the employees' interest in a tax-qualified plan, even though the associated trust would not have enjoyed spendthrift protection under state trust law.[89] The trustee should be aware that no federal spendthrift requirement applies to trusts associated with IRAs.[90] Thus state statutes and the common law of trusts will determine whether property held by an IRA trustee is reachable by the taxpayer's creditors.[91]

The administration of employee benefit and IRA arrangements is a topic beyond the scope of this handbook. Trustees of property associated with tax-qualified employee benefit arrangements, however, should at least understand the federal and state laws governing the rights of creditors to reach such property. And

---

[85]*See* 2A Scott on Trusts §152.
[86]*See* Broadway Natl. Bank v. Adams, 133 Mass. 170 (1882).
[87]Id.
[88]*See* I.R.C. §401(a)(13) (1986).
[89]*See* Patterson v. Shumate, 112 S. Ct. 2242 (1992).
[90]*See* I.R.C. §408 (1986).
[91]*See, e.g.*, Dicken, Is an IRA-Exempt Property Under the Kentucky Exemption Statute KRS §427.150(1)(b)?, 73 Ky. L.J. 1127 (1984).

all trustees should be aware of how beneficiaries and their creditors may be affected by the movement of property from the shelter of tax-qualified employee benefit trusts to other types of trusts.[92]

§5.3.4 Rights of Beneficiary's Spouse to Trust Property

If a trust is accessible to a beneficiary's creditors, it will be accessible to the beneficiary's spouse for the spouse's support.[93] Under certain circumstances the spouse will have access while the creditors will not.[94] He or she, for example, may be entitled to pierce a spendthrift trust for alimony and child support, even when the beneficiary is not the settlor,[95] although as a general rule a trust created by someone other than the beneficiary under which the trustee has uncontrolled discretion is immune from spousal attack.[96] Whatever the degree of the trust's vulnerability, always keep in mind that the trustee's primary allegiance is to the beneficiary, not to the nonbeneficiary spouse. Thus, when there is domestic conflict, the trustee must suppress any personal feelings as to who may be "at fault" and vigorously defend — within reason and to the extent the law allows — the beneficiary's equitable property interest.

Upon the death of the nonsettlor beneficiary, the surviving spouse will not have access to the trust unless the terms of the governing instrument provide that the beneficial interest shall pass outright and free of trust to the spouse or to the deceased beneficiary's estate.[97] In an ever-increasing number of jurisdictions, however, the spouse may be afforded postmortem access to

---

[92]I.R.C. §401(a)(13); *Patterson, supra* note 89.

[93]*Lauricella, supra* note 79.

[94]*See* Restatement (Second) of Trusts §157 (1959); *Lauricella, supra* note 79.

[95]Id.

[96]*See* id. §155. *See also* Pemberton v. Pemberton, 9 Mass. App. 9, 411 N.E.2d 1305 (1980).

[97]*See* 2A Scott on Trusts §§144, 145, 146A.

the trust if it was created by the deceased spouse *and* if the deceased spouse had reserved the power to revoke or amend the trust or a general inter vivos power of appointment.[98] The law in this area is unsettled.[99]

§5.3.5 Medicaid Eligibility and Recoupment

Medicaid (not to be confused with Medicare) is a medical assistance welfare program established under the federal Social Security Act, administered by the states, and supported by federal and state tax revenues.[100] To be eligible for Medicaid benefits (*e.g.*, reimbursement for nursing home costs), an applicant in theory must be "needy."[101] Over the years, attorneys have resorted to the trust device as a means of having their clients render themselves "needy" and thus "eligible" for Medicaid; legislatures and welfare bureaucracies have responded with statutes and regulations designed to thwart these efforts.[102]

Often trustees have been left to administer poorly drawn instruments long after the settlors have died and memories faded as to why such arrangements were made in the first place. The prospective trustee of a trust designed to render the settlor eligible for Medicaid should pay particular attention to the provisions that kick in *after* the settlor has died. In addition, whether the trust is long- or short-term, the prospective trustee should be particularly wary of taking on a trust that contains a single illiquid asset

[98]Bogert, Trusts and Trustees §233 (surviving spouse's marital rights). *See also* Sullivan v. Burkin, 390 Mass. 864, 460 N.E.2d 572 (1984).

[99]*See Sullivan*, 390 Mass. at 864 n.4, 460 N.E.2d at 572 n.4.

[100]*See* Dobris, Medical Asset Planning by the Elderly: A Policy View of Expectations, Entitlement and Inheritance, 24 Real Prop. Prob. & Tr. J. 1, 10 (1989).

[101]Id.

[102]*See* Rounds, The Vulnerability of Trust Assets to Attack by the Deceased Settlor's Creditors, by the Commonwealth Should It Seek Reimbursement for Medicaid Payments, and by the Spouse, 73 Mass. L. Rev. 67, 79 n.94 and accompanying text (1988); *see, e.g.*, 42 U.S.C. §1396a(k)(i) (deeming property in certain self-settled trusts to be countable for Medicaid eligibility); *see also* K. M. Coughlin, Here Come the Trustbusters: States Move to Restrict Medicaid Planning, The ElderLaw Report, Nov. 1992, at 1.

such as a residence. How are the expenses and commissions to be paid?

While Medicaid planning issues are well beyond the scope of this handbook, several points are worth making here:

First, the trustee should understand that Medicaid planning has two parts: *eligibility* and *recoupment*. A trust, for example, that contains the settlor's residence may not jeopardize the settlor's eligibility for Medicaid assistance,[103] but the residence may be subject to postmortem recoupment by the state.[104] The two should not be confused.

The second point concerns whether the beneficiary is also the settlor. If so then even the settlor-beneficiary's contingent interest in a discretionary trust is likely to cause the trust property to be considered to be "owned" by the beneficiary for Medicaid eligibility purposes.[105] Moreover, there is no value discount for the contingency of the trustee exercising its discretion.[106] On the other hand, when the beneficiary is not the settlor, the rule of thumb is that the trust property will be countable for Medicaid eligibility purposes to the extent the property is accessible to the beneficiary's creditors.[107] Thus a true discretionary trust (*i.e.*, one that gives the trustee uncontrolled discretion over payment of income or distribution of principal) created by someone other than the beneficiary may not render a beneficiary ineligible for Medicaid. If the trust grants the trustee the discretion to pay income or distribute principal to the beneficiary for the beneficiary's support, then it is a matter of interpretation as to whether the assets of the trust will prevent the beneficiary from obtaining Medicaid. In matters of Medicaid, the trustee should understand that the treatment of trusts created by the beneficiary is likely to be different from trusts created by a third party.[108]

Finally, when it comes to postmortem recoupment for life-

---

[103]*See* 24 Real Prop. Prob. & Tr. J. 1, 15 (1989).
[104]Id. at 17.
[105]*See* U.S. Trust, Practical Drafting 1746-1747 (April 1989).
[106]Id.
[107]*See* Dobris, *supra* note 100.
[108]Id.

time Medicaid payments, the welfare department essentially has the status of a creditor.[109] The trustee thus should keep in mind the duty to the successor beneficiaries to allow the state only such access to the trust as the law requires. The trustee wishing to keep abreast of trust-related developments in the Medicaid area would do well to subscribe to the ElderLaw Report.[110]

§5.4   Rights of the Beneficiary

The beneficiary has, by virtue of the equitable interest in the trust property, rights against the trustee. The trustee must perform certain duties or be held accountable to the wronged beneficiary. The beneficiary may protect the equitable interest against all attacks.

§5.4.1   Certain Incidental Rights of the Beneficiary Against the Trustee

The beneficiary's equitable interest is an interest in property, a property right being a bundle of personal rights associated with something of value.[1] It could be said that the various rights of the beneficiary are subsumed in the general right that fiduciary duties be carried out. However, to the trustee operating on the front lines, such a general description does not offer much practical guidance. Accordingly, this section addresses some of the more important specific rights incidental to that general right.

---

[109]*See generally* Rounds, *supra* note 102.
[110]Published 11 times a year, the ElderLaw Report is edited by Harry S. Margolis and published by Little, Brown.
§5.4   [1]*See* Restatement of Property §§1-5, 6 comment *a* (1936); 2 Scott on Trusts §130.

§5.4.1.1   Right to Information and Confidentiality

A trustee has a duty to account to the beneficiary.[2] As a practical matter this duty translates into a right in the beneficiary to all information needed to protect the beneficiary's equitable interest.[3] The beneficiary has a right to full information about the concerns of the trust at all reasonable times[4] and may examine the deeds or opinions of counsel consulted by the trustee in respect to trust affairs.[5]

The most important thing that the trustee must keep in mind is that the income beneficiary does not possess this right to information alone: The remaindermen, including in some cases those with contingent interests,[6] also share this right. Unless limited by the terms of the trust, a trustee must not succumb to the pressure of a beneficiary to withold information about the trust from other beneficiaries. This situation usually occurs when the current beneficiary is a member of a generation older than the remainder interests and does not want the existence of the trust disclosed. Typically the current beneficiary is a parent of the beneficiaries who will take the remainder. To be sure, the settlor by express language may limit the rights of the remaindermen to information, but there is a limit to what a court will tolerate when it comes to limiting a beneficiary's right to protect the equitable interest. A trustee who may operate in secret is essentially unaccountable — a condition that is inimical to the concept of the trust.

On the other hand the beneficiary's right to information, under certain circumstances, may conflict with another beneficiary's right to confidentiality, the latter right being an incident of the trustee's duty of loyalty.[7] The conflict arises not in the context of the trustee's duty to refrain from making unnecessary

---

[2]*See* §6.1.5.
[3]*See* §6.1.5.1.
[4]Bogert, Trusts and Trustees §961, 861.
[5]*But see* 2A Scott on Trusts §173 n.5 and accompanying text.
[6]*See* id. §172; *but see* Bogert, Trusts and Trustees §961 n.23 and accompanying text.
[7]*See* §6.2.3.

disclosures of the affairs of the trust to third parties, which is virtually absolute; it arises in the context of balancing the interests of multiple classes of beneficiaries. Is someone with a remote contingent remainder interest, for example, entitled to all the information that the trustee was privy to when a discretionary distribution to a permissible life beneficiary was made? That information might include medical information or intimate details of the beneficiary's marital situation. The answer is "of course not." On the other hand, an abuse of the trustee's discretion could improperly eliminate the remainderman's property interest altogether.[8]

There are no easy answers. The trustee must exercise good judgment in distinguishing the fishing expedition from legitimate efforts to protect one's property. While the contingent remaindermen ought not to be furnished with all the details of the discretionary distribution, they at least are entitled to know that discretion has been exercised; they certainly are entitled to a copy of the governing instrument. The practice of furnishing certain classes of beneficiaries with excerpts only of a governing instrument is a questionable one, absent express, unambiguous authority in the governing instrument.

§5.4.1.2   Right to Prompt and Efficient Administration

The beneficiary's equitable interest is an interest in property. Thus to the extent the trustee is dilatory or inefficient in the administration of his trust, he interferes with that property interest and is in breach of trust.[9] The beneficiary has a right to expect that his checks will arrive on time, that tax returns will be filled out properly and filed when due, that investment decisions will be

[8]*See* Bogert, Trusts and Trustees §961 n.4 and accompanying text; 2A Scott on Trusts §173 n.3.

[9]*See* Bogert, Trusts and Trustees §541 n.60 and accompanying text (the requirement of diligence applies to the uncompensated as well as the compensated trustee).

made and executed in a timely fashion, and that accountings will be submitted at regular intervals.

§5.4.1.3   Right to Income or Possession

A trust is *income only* unless the governing instrument clearly indicates that the settlor intended to bestow on the trustee a right to invade principal in furtherance of the trust's purposes.[10] The beneficiary has no right to the possession of the trust property unless there is clear indication that the settlor intended otherwise.[11] If the trust requires a mandatory distribution of income to the beneficiary, the trustee must remit the income at regular intervals.

Ordinarily the right to possession of real estate and chattels belongs to the trustee,[12] but if the settlor intended that the beneficiary have the use of the property in specie, the beneficiary will be entitled to possession.[13]

§5.4.1.4   Right to Enjoin Abuse of Discretion

By express language in the governing instrument, the settlor may provide — in lieu of the common law right to the income from or the use of the trust property — that the beneficiary shall have a right to income or principal or both, in the discretion of the trustee.[14] Usually the settlor provides some standard to guide the trustee in the exercise of discretion ("support" and "education" being some common examples).[15] While the general rule is that a court will not second-guess the trustee's exercise of discretion, a

[10]Id. §812 n.72 and accompanying text.
[11]Id. §181 n.14 and accompanying text.
[12]Id.
[13]Id.
[14]*See* §3.5.3.2(a).
[15]Bogert, Trusts and Trustees §182 (support or education), §229 (support).

beneficiary does have the right to seek judicial relief should the trustee abuse that discretion.[16]

§5.4.1.5 Right to Remedies for Breaches of Trust

The beneficiary has standing to seek judicial enforcement of the terms of the trust and to have the trust made whole for any loss occasioned by the trustee's breach of trust.[17] This is true whether the beneficiary's interest is vested or contingent, or whether the beneficiary is a life beneficiary or a remainderman. The judicial remedies available to the beneficiary are covered elsewhere in this handbook.[18]

§5.4.1.6 Express Rights to Appoint, Remove, Direct, and Advise in the Absence of Fault

The trustee is not an agent of the beneficiary. Thus the beneficiary has no inherent common law right to appoint or remove the trustee, nor to direct the trustee or even have the beneficiary's advice considered by the trustee.[19] The beneficiary can bring an action to remove the trustee, but there must be grounds for removal, and the ultimate decision rests with the court. The settlor, however, may bestow on the beneficiary by express language in the governing instrument any one or more of these rights as against the trustee. These rights may be exercised even when the trustee is not at fault, if such is the wish of the settlor. The prospective trustee should be aware of all such common law derogations that may lurk in a governing instrument. The existence of certain ones — such as the right to give

---

[16]2 Scott on Trusts §128.3.
[17]Bogert, Trusts and Trustees §871.
[18]*See* §7.2.3; *see also* Bogert, Trusts and Trustees §§861-871.
[19]*See* 2 Scott on Trusts §§107.3, 185.

investment directions — may bear on how the trustee's services should be priced or on the advisability of even taking on the trusteeship at all,[20] because the law has not yet settled on what monitoring obligations the trustee has in the face of such a right of direction in the beneficiary.[21]

§5.4.1.7   Right to Conveyance

The remainderman has a right to conveyance of the trust property within a reasonable time after the trust has terminated, assuming title has not already vested in the remainderman by operation of law.[22]

Are there any circumstances under which a remainderman is entitled to a conveyance before the end of a trust's natural life? Assume the following transfer in trust: A to B for C for ten years, remainder to C; the trust is inter vivos; no other person has a beneficial interest; and C is of full age and legal capacity. Does C have a right to the property outright and free of trust before the expiration of the ten-year period? The American Rule is that if the trust has a purpose (e.g., if it is a spendthrift or discretionary trust), C would have no such right.[23] (The English Rule is to the contrary.[24]) If the trust has no purpose, or its purpose had been accomplished, C would have a right to conveyance before the period's expiration.[25]

As a practical matter, C may be able to persuade the trustee to convey in the face of an unfulfilled trust purpose. However, some have suggested that the settlor ought to have a cause of action against the trustee for interfering with the settlor's expectation

---

[20]Bogert, Trusts and Trustees §122.

[21]*See* §6.1.4.

[22]Restatement (Second) of Trusts §345 comment *e* (1959).

[23]*See* Claflin v. Claflin, 149 Mass. 19, 20 N.E. 454 (1889); Restatement (Second) of Trusts §337 (1959).

[24]Restatement of Trusts §337, reporter's notes (1959).

[25]*See* Bogert, Trusts and Trustees §1006, 1007.

interest in having the terms of the trust carried out.[26] In any case, while C may succeed in obtaining the property, there is no enforceable right to a premature conveyance in the face of an unfulfilled purpose as would be the case under the more liberal English Rule.[27] Thus, if the aid of the court is sought in accelerating C's remainder interest, it will not be given.[28]

In any event, nothing less than the whole of an absolute estate will entitle the beneficiary to a conveyance, even under the English Rule.[29] Therefore, if there are contingent or unascertained interests there can be no agreement to convey, and a beneficiary who has a life estate, with power of disposition by will, has not such an absolute estate as entitles him to a conveyance. Thus the settlor can prevent the beneficiary's call for a conveyance even under the English Rule by the simple expedient of making a small provision for some person unascertained.[30]

§5.4.2 Rights of the Beneficiary Against Those Other Than the Trustee

The trustee holds the legal title for the benefit of the beneficiary; each person who receives the legal title from the trustee in breach of trust also holds the property in trust, unless the transferee has a special and valid equitable claim of his own.[31] The law has concluded that the transferee has such an equitable claim when title is acquired in a wholly innocent manner in exchange for value.[32] Whenever a person acquires the title under these circum-

---

[26]See §4.1.2. But see Bogert, Trusts and Trustees §1006 n.13 and accompanying text (premature terminations upheld when the trustee and beneficiary joined in a transfer of trust property outright and free of trust back to the settlor). See also §1008 (implying that settlor has standing to litigate issues of premature termination).

[27]Id. §1008.

[28]See id.

[29]See id. §1007 n.7 and accompanying text.

[30]See id. §1007 n.9 and accompanying text.

[31]See 4 Scott on Trusts §288.

[32]See id. §284.

stances, the equity court declines to interfere.[33] This is the doctrine of *bona fide purchase*; it is substantially a rule of inaction.[34] Thus, if the trustee transfers trust property to a bona fide purchaser (that is, one who has no actual or constructive knowledge of the trust), the purchaser acquires the title free of trust.[35] In many jurisdictions the rule has been codified. For the transferee to be protected each of the rule's three conditions must be satisfied: actual acquisition of title, the payment of value, and a lack of notice.[36]

Thus, even when the trustee wrongfully contracts to sell the trust property to an innocent purchaser, the beneficiary's right remains unclouded if the purchaser then learns of the trust relationship before the transfer.[37] To enforce the contract under these circumstances would be to order a breach of trust.

One who receives the trust property by *gift* must disgorge it, even when the donee is ignorant of the trust's existence.[38] The innocent donee who has restored the property to the trust is under no further duty.[39] The donee who sold it need only restore the proceeds. Should the donee, while still ignorant of the trust, in turn give it away to someone else, he or she is not liable.[40] If on the other hand the innocent donee sells or gives away the property after acquiring knowledge of the trust, liability attaches.[41]

The innocent donee who has consumed the trust property may be liable if these expenditures qualify as "ordinary";[42] if they are "extraordinary," and if the donee has changed position det-

---

[33]Id.
[34]Id.
[35]Id.
[36]Bogert, Trusts and Trustees §885 (title), §887 (value), §891 (notice), §894 (facts putting on inquiry).
[37]*See* Restatement (Second) of Trusts §311 (1959).
[38]Id. §289.
[39]*See* 4 Scott on Trusts §292.
[40]*See* id. §292.1.
[41]*See* id. §292.3.
[42]Restatement (Second) of Trusts §292 comment *j* (1959).

rimentally in reasonable reliance upon the transfer, then the donee may not be liable.[43]

A person who actually pays for and receives title and possession knowing that the transfer is in violation of the beneficiary's
prior rights holds the property in constructive trust for the beneficiary.[44] This holds true if the person ought to have known of the
outstanding beneficial interest.[45]

§5.5   Loss of the Beneficiary's Rights

The trustee has an affirmative equitable duty to act solely in
the interest of the beneficiaries. Thus a former or present trustee
may not acquire the property of the trust by adverse possession.[1]
In theory, however, the trustee may acquire the property with the
informed consent of all beneficiaries.[2] Likewise, their informed
consent, ratification, or release may be sufficient to discharge the
trustee from breaches of trust.[3]

It is clear, however, that such discharge is not binding if
given in reliance upon fraudulent representations or under circumstances of concealment of material facts.[4] It equally is well
settled that the beneficiary must be of full age and legal capacity
else the beneficiary's consent is not binding.[5] In acts involving
the shifting of beneficial interests, the assent of one beneficiary
will not bind the others,[6] nor is the assent of the income benefi-

---

[43]Id.
[44]5 Scott on Trusts §462.4.
[45]Bogert, Trusts and Trustees §894.
§5.5 [1]5 Scott on Trusts §495.
[2]Id. §496.
[3]Id. §216.
[4]Id.
[5]Id. §216.3.
[6]Id. §216.2; *see also* In Re Crane, 34 N.Y.S.2d 9 (1942).

ciaries binding on the remaindermen.[7] Thus it is impossible for a trustee to obtain release by private agreement when there are beneficiaries who are unborn, unascertained, or under some legal disability.[8] (Such would certainly be the case for most cemetery trustees and trustees of charitable trusts.[9]) On the other hand the assent of the beneficiary who holds a general inter vivos power of appointment or reserved right of revocation may well be binding on all other beneficiaries, including the unborn and unascertained.[10]

Delay on the part of the beneficiary in compelling a trustee to redress negligent breaches of trust apparent from a scrutiny of the trustee's accounts may constitute laches sufficient to release the trustee from such liabilities.[11] A cause of action against a trustee for breaches of the duty of loyalty, however, is not barred by laches until a reasonable time after *all* beneficiaries become aware of the breach and fail to take appropriate action.[12] What constitutes laches depends upon the circumstances of each case, but the mere lapse of time alone will not bar the beneficiary where the position of others has not been changed.[13] Circumstances indicating an intention to abandon one's equitable remedies, along with a lapse of time, will be sufficient to bar a recovery.[14] A beneficiary with a contingent remainder interest may interfere to protect the estate during the life tenancy but is not guilty of laches or acquiescence until the estate comes into the beneficiary's possession. Even the contingent remaindermen are well advised to take action immediately upon receiving notice of a breach, whether or not prior interests have terminated.[15]

[7] 3 Scott on Trusts §216.2.
[8] *See* Bogert, Trusts and Trustees §1007 n.9 and accompanying text.
[9] Rounds, Protections Afforded to Massachusetts' Ancient Burial Grounds, 73 Mass. L. Rev. 176 (1988).
[10] *See* 3 Scott on Trusts §216.2.
[11] *See* id. §219; *see also* Bogert, Trusts and Trustees §964.
[12] *See* Lawson v. Haynes, 170 F.2d 741 (10th Cir. 1948); Bogert, Trusts and Trustees §543(u); *see also* §6.1.3.5.
[13] *See* Bogert, Trusts and Trustees §§948, 949.
[14] Id. §949 n.36 and accompanying text.
[15] *See* id. §949 n.66 and accompanying text; 3 Scott on Trusts §219.4.

§5.6   Liabilities of the Beneficiary

With the possible exception of those trusts under which the beneficiary for all intents and purposes controls the trustee (*e.g.*, the revocable inter vivos trust, the realty trust, the nominee trust), the beneficiary incurs no liabilities arising inherently out of ownership of the beneficial interest, except for taxes.[1] In the absence of agreement, the beneficiary is not personally bound to indemnify the trustee for trust administration expenses.[2] The beneficiary may voluntarily undertake to make himself liable to the trustee by, for example, furnishing funds to enable the trustee to improve the trust estate or by litigating in order to collect insurance proceeds.

If a beneficiary wrongfully deals with trust property, any loss can be made up from the beneficiary's interest;[3] in the case of overpayment, the beneficiary may be personally liable.[4] Where an innocent overpayment has been made, there may be a change of position by the beneficiary which makes it inequitable to compel repayment.[5] A trustee makes distribution at his peril: An overpayment that is not repaid by the beneficiary is a personal obligation of the trustee.

A beneficiary is liable to the same extent as any other person for participation or collusion in a breach of trust.[6] If beneficiary *X* persuades the trustee improperly to lend or distribute to him trust property, *X* may be liable to beneficiaries *Y* and *Z*.[7] *X*'s own interest in the trust estate may be subjected to an equitable lien in their favor.[8]

The beneficiary would be ill advised to instruct the trustee in matters concerning management of the trust estate.[9] The trustee

§5.6   [1] *See* 3A Scott on Trusts §274.
[2] *See* Bogert, Trusts and Trustees §718.
[3] Restatement (Second) of Trusts §253 (1959).
[4] Id. §254.
[5] Id.
[6] Id. §256.
[7] Id.
[8] Id.
[9] Id. §216.

would be equally ill-advised to blindly follow the beneficiary's instructions.[10] The trustee is in no way excused from liability merely because some of the beneficiaries insisted upon an improper action — except perhaps as to a claim presented by those who did the insisting.[11] Moreover, the interfering beneficiaries may be held to have colluded in the breach of trust.[12] If a beneficiary engages in frivolous litigation against the trustee or the trust, that beneficiary's interest may be charged with payment of the costs.[13]

Except perhaps in certain cases where the beneficiary controls the trustee, the beneficiary will not be held liable as the owner of the trust estate.[14] Thus in matters involving the trust estate, the beneficiary is liable neither in contract[15] nor in tort;[16] neither criminally for a nuisance on the trust property,[17] for a trustee's unlawful acts of discrimination,[18] nor as a stockholder.[19] The beneficiary may not be forced to contribute personal funds in order to prevent the trust property from being taken by foreclosure.[20] Nor is the trustee "entitled to a charge on the beneficiary's interest in the trust to secure a liability of the beneficiary to the trustee not connected with the administration of the trust, unless the beneficiary contracts to give him such a charge."[21]

---

[10]Id. §256(2) (one beneficiary's consent to a breach of trust will not relieve trustee from liability to the other beneficiaries); 1 Scott on Trusts §8 (trustee not an agent of the beneficiary).

[11]Restatement (Second) of Trusts §216 comment *g* (1959).

[12]Id. §256.

[13]*See* 3 Scott on Trusts §188.4 n.13 and accompanying text.

[14]*See* 3A Scott on Trusts §274.

[15]*See* id. §275.

[16]*See* id. §276.

[17]*See* id. §265.3.

[18]*See* Bogert, Trusts and Trustees §731.

[19]*See* 3A Scott on Trusts §265.2.

[20]*See* 2A Scott on Trusts §176.

[21]Restatement (Second) of Trusts §250 (1959).

The Trustee's Duties

§6.1   The Trustee's General Duties

When property is transferred from one person to another, the transferee's legal status with respect to the property will depend in large part on the transferor's intent. If the intent is to make a gift, then the transferor imposes no duties on the transferee with respect to the property. If the intent is to create a contract, bailment, or trust, then the transferor imposes certain enforceable duties on the transferee. A trust relationship brings with it five fundamental duties:

1. the duty to be generally prudent
2. the duty to carry out the terms of the trust

3. the duty to be loyal to the trust
4. the duty to give personal attention to the affairs of the trust
5. the duty to account to the beneficiary

If any one of these duties is lacking, there is a good chance that the transferee's legal status with respect to the property is something other than that of a trustee.

§6.1.1 *Duty to Be Generally Prudent*

The trustee has a duty to act reasonably and competently in all matters of trust administration, not just in investment matters.[1] With respect to investments, this standard of prudence is a standard of *conduct*, not *performance*.[2] A trustee's action or inaction will not be judged in hindsight. As a general rule, the amateur trustee must exercise "such care and skill as a man of ordinary prudence would exercise in dealing with his own property."[3] On the other hand, one who holds oneself out as a professional with special skills is under a duty to employ those skills.[4] Thus the trustee's administration had better be as advertised.

---

§6.1 [1] A distinction should be drawn here between this overarching duty to act reasonably and competently in all matters of trust administration and the so-called *prudent man rule* that provides the trustee with a standard of conduct for the investment of trust assets. *See* §6.2.2.1. The more general duty to act reasonably and competently in all matters of trust administration requires the trustee to exercise caution, reasonable care, and at least the skill of a person of ordinary intelligence in the fulfillment of all duties arising under the trust; the "prudent man rule" is a more specific application of this general duty.

[2] Harvard College v. Amory, 26 Mass. (9 Pick.) 446, 461 (1830); Restatement (Third) of Trusts §§204, 227 (1992); 3 Scott on Trusts §§204, 227.

[3] Restatement (Second) of Trusts §174 comment *a* (1959); 2A Scott on Trusts §174; *Harvard College, supra* at 461; *but see* Uniform Probate Code §7-302, 8 U.L.A. 555 (1983) (holding trustee to standard of "a prudent man" dealing with the property of another).

[4] 2A Scott on Trusts §174.1; Uniform Probate Code §7-302, 8 U.L.A. 555 (1983).

§6.1.2 Duty to Carry Out the Terms of the Trust

The trustee has an overarching duty to carry out the intentions of the settlor as they have been communicated in the governing instrument.[5] The wishes of the beneficiaries are subordinate to those of the settlor. While legally the trustee is neither an agent of the settlor nor an agent of the beneficiary,[6] it can do no harm for trustees to consider themselves agents of their settlors. Take for example a spendthrift trust. Let us assume that notwithstanding its antialienation provisions, the beneficiary intends to assign the beneficial interest. Moreover it may be in the beneficiary's interest to do so. The trustee's first and foremost duty, however, is to the intentions of the settlor as they have been set forth in the governing instrument. The assignment must not be honored;[7] the trustee is not an agent of the beneficiary.

If the trustee honors the assignment, the settlor ought to have recourse. Would not the trustee's obligation to carry out the settlor's intentions be an illusory one if only the beneficiary could seek its enforcement? Certainly the beneficiary will not be raising any objections in the situation just described. As for the settlor, the matter of what rights, if any, are lodged with the settlor is covered in Chapter 4.

§6.1.3 Duty to Be Loyal to the Trust

A trustee is held to something stricter than the morals of the marketplace. Not honesty alone, but the punctilio of an honor the most sensitive, is then the standard of behavior. As to this there has

---

[5]Restatement (Second) of Trusts §164 comment *a* (1959); 2A Scott on Trusts §164, 164.1. *But see* 2A Scott on Trusts §§165-168 (deviation from terms of trust permitted in cases of impossibility, illegality, or a change in circumstances). Unless the settlor has reserved a power to modify or revoke the trust, however, subsequent oral expressions of the settlor are not admissible to vary the terms of the trust. Id. §164.1.

[6]Restatement (Second) of Trusts §8 (1959); 1 Scott on Trusts §8.

[7]*See, e.g.,* Restatement (Second) of Trusts §§164 (1959).

developed a tradition that is unbending and inveterate. Uncompromising rigidity has been the attitude of courts of equity when petitioned to undermine the rule of undivided loyalty by the "disintegrating erosion" of particular exceptions.[8]

A trustee is under a duty to act solely in the interest of the beneficiaries as to matters that directly and indirectly involve the trust property.[9] This duty springs from the trust relationship rather than from any provision of the trust instrument. It is the bedrock of the trust relationship; it is a duty of undivided loyalty.

The trustee must not allow personal interests to compete with the interests of the beneficiaries arising under the trust.[10] The trustee who has an interest adverse to the trust that he intends to assert must resign the trust[11] unless all the beneficiaries are informed and consent to his retention of the office.[12] Likewise the trustee of a business may not enter into a competing business for personal benefit.[13] It is also the case that a trustee of land may not assert a claim of adverse possession against the trust.[14] A trustee of two trusts may sell property from one trust to the other only if neither trust is disadvantaged.[15]

The duty of loyalty, however, does not make the trustee an agent of the beneficiary. The trustee thus may not yield to a demand by the beneficiaries to commit a breach of trust, for that

---

[8]Meinhard v. Salmon, 249 N.Y. 458, 464, 164 N.E. 545, 546 (1928) (Cardoza, C.J.).

[9]*See* Restatement (Third) of Trusts §170(1) (1992); 2A Scott on Trusts §170; The Employee Retirement Income Security Act (ERISA), 29 U.S.C. §§1104(a)1, 404 (1974) codifies this duty for fiduciaries of employees' pension plans.

[10]*See* Restatement (Second) of Trusts §170 comment *p* (1959); 2A Scott on Trusts §170.23.

[11]*See* 2A Scott on Trusts §170.23.

[12]*See* Restatement (Second) of Trusts §216 comment *g* (1959); 3 Scott on Trusts §§216, 216.2.

[13]*See* Restatement (Third) of Trusts §§170 comment *p*, 206 comment *l* (1992); 2A Scott on Trusts §§170.23, 206.

[14]Railroad Co. v. Durant, 95 U.S. 576 (1877); Smith v. Dean, 240 S.W.2d 789 (Tex. Civ. Ct. App. 1951).

[15]*See* Restatement (Third) of Trusts §170 comment *r* (1992); 2A Scott on Trusts §170.16.

would be putting the interests of the trustee before the interests of the trust. [16]

The duty of loyalty is not a passive one. It requires affirmative action by the trustee, who must do all that can honestly be done for the furtherance of the interests of the trust. [17] The trustee cannot consent to a judgment invalidating the trust nor pay a creditor who has a claim that cannot be enforced by suit. All demands must be pressed, even to the extent of bringing suit, unless it is evident that it is useless to do so. The trustee must not unreasonably fail to appeal adverse decisions. [18] The trustee must defend the trust. If a successful action is brought by a third party against the trust, the trustee is under a duty to the beneficiary to appeal to a higher court if it is reasonable to do so. [19]

A trustee is entitled to take a reasonable fee from the trust estate for all fiduciary services. [20] This is an inherent conflict, but it is nonetheless permitted since it would be unreasonable to expect trustees to serve without compensation. (At early English common law the trustee did not have a right to compensation. [21])

The trustee is also entitled to reimbursement for reasonable expenses, [22] but the general rule is that, apart from the right to reasonable compensation, a trustee may not receive direct or indirect economic benefit from the trust estate, including acts of self-dealing unless authorized to do so by the settlor of a revocable trust, by the terms of the trust instrument, by the court, by statute, or by all of the beneficiaries including the remaindermen after full and fair disclosure. [23] As a practical matter, the trustee bent on

[16]In Estate of Carmean, Los Angeles Super. Ct. Civ. P374331 (1984) (unpublished), the court held that the duty of loyalty was breached when a trust officer imprudently diverted income from the maintenance of the trust property to the beneficiaries in order to keep them quiet, that is, in order to "rid herself of the burden of handling requests and listening to hard luck stories."
[17]See Restatement (Second) of Trusts §2 comment b, §170 (1959).
[18]See id. §177 comment d.
[19]See id. §178 comment a; 2A Scott on Trusts §178.
[20]See §3.5.2.4.
[21]See 3A Scott on Trusts §242.
[22]See §3.5.2.3.
[23]See Restatement (Third) of Trusts §§170 comment w, 206 (1992); 2A Scott on Trusts §170.

transacting with the trust estate "for his own account" seldom will find the last option (beneficiary consent in a nonjudicial setting) a viable one. Most trusts will have some beneficiaries who are un-born, unascertained, or under legal disabilities such as minority or mental incapacity, thereby making the consent of all the beneficia-ries unobtainable.

So rigorous is the duty of loyalty that an act of self-dealing will be regarded as constructively fraudulent and, at the option of the beneficiary, will be set aside.[24] The trustee is not given an opportunity to justify his action; an untrammelled choice of affirmance or rejection rests with the beneficiary.[25] If the benefi-ciary elects to affirm the transaction, the trustee must account for all profit; if the beneficiary disaffirms, the trustee must make good all losses.[26] Thus if a trustee, motivated by divided loyalties, imprudently acquires or retains on behalf of the trust a particu-lar investment, the trustee will be held liable for any resulting loss suffered by the trust whether or not the investment is a sound fiduciary investment. Moreover the trustee — at the elec-tion of the beneficiaries — may be liable even for the difference between the highest unrealized value of the investment and its realized value.[27]

It is obvious that the trustee should scrupulously avoid the assumption of so serious a risk; no intelligent person desires to become an insurer against loss under such circumstances. The trustee's invariable rule should be to avoid dealing with the trust property in this way.

This rule sounds almost unreasonably harsh, but it is required because of the demonstrated fallibility of humanity. There are no exceptions, although there are limits. Thus if the trustee honestly sells the trust property to a third person and *there is no scheme to*

---

[24]*See* Restatement (Second) of Trusts §206 comment *b* (1959); 3 Scott on Trusts §§206, 208.4.

[25]*See* 2A Scott on Trusts §170.2.

[26]*See* Restatement (Second) of Trusts §206 comment *b* (1959); 2A Scott on Trusts §§170.2, 206.

[27]*See* §§7.1, 7.2.3.1-7.2.3.2.

repurchase, the trustee is not conclusively forbidden to buy it back again.[28] So also after the trustee has stepped down.[29]

§6.1.3.1 Trustee Benefiting as Borrower and Lender

Nothing good can come of a trustee's borrowing from the trust estate no matter how competitive the interest rate may be and no matter how complete the paper trail, with perhaps the limited exception of the short-term deposit of funds awaiting distribution on the commercial side of the trustee bank.[30] The thief when caught asserts it is only a loan. Even when borrowing is duly authorized, it will always bring with it the appearance of impropriety, the trustee being on both sides of the transaction.[31] Was the

---

[28]*See* Restatement (Third) of Trusts §170 comment *e* (1959); 2A Scott on Trusts §170.6.

[29]*See* Restatement (Second) of Trusts §170 comment *g* (1959). But if the trustee steps down for the purpose of purchasing the trust property, then the sale can be set aside at the election of the beneficiary. 2A Scott on Trusts §170.8.

[30]Comptroller of the Currency Regulation 9.10, Funds Awaiting Investment or Distribution, 12 C.F.R. §9.10 (1963). The Employee Retirement Income Security Act (ERISA) permits the fiduciary ("a bank or similar financial institution supervised by the United States or a State") under an employee's pension plan to invest all or part of the plan's assets in deposits with itself that bear a reasonable rate of interest if either a provision of the plan expressly authorizes it to do so or the plan covers only employees of the fiduciary. ERISA §408, 29 U.S.C. §1108(b)(4) (1974). Most banks now have the operational capability of "sweeping" uninvested trust cash into short-term investments on a daily basis, thus reducing substantially the occasions when it would be appropriate for a bank trustee to deposit trust funds in noninterest-bearing accounts. *See, e.g.*, Upp v. Mellon Bank, N.A., 799 F. Supp. 540 (E.D. Pa. 1992), *rev'd*, 994 F.2d 1039 (1993).

[31]The case of John Zaccaro, husband of former Vice-Presidential candidate Geraldine Ferraro, and his handling of the estate of an elderly woman in New York illustrates the pitfalls of fiduciaries borrowing from their estates and trusts. Mr. Zaccaro had borrowed from the estate $175,000 which he paid back with interest. Nonetheless, he was removed as conservator of the woman's estate. The judge in the case, New York Supreme Court Justice Edwin Kassof, wrote, "Thus it is generally accepted that the fiduciary is not permitted to use estate funds for his own benefit or for investments in his own business. There is no necessity for finding malicious intent, deliberate wrongdoing or criminal conduct. The mere

authority fairly obtained? Why didn't the trustee go to the market-place? Who represented the trust in the transaction? Will the trust be thought of first if the trustee's personal financial situation begins to sour? Who will represent the trust in the event of default? What happens if the trustee goes bankrupt?

Moreover, from the perspective of the trustee, when a portion of the trust assets is invested in a personal obligation the trustee ventures outside the safe harbor of the Prudent Man Rule (which is a rule of conduct, not performance) to become an insurer of the value of the portion.[32]

The *no further inquiry rule*[33] should continue to apply to unauthorized trustee borrowings, and the courts should resist the temptation to recognize "fairness" and "benign intentions" as legitimate defenses to such activity. To do otherwise is to tempt the honest and afford avenues of escape to the dishonest. The law should be absolutely unambiguous in this regard and ignorance of it should never be a judicially recognized excuse.

On the other hand there is some social utility in allowing the trustee to lend *to* the trust if there is sensitivity to the loyalty considerations attendant even when funds flow from the trustee to the trust. A strict definition of self-dealing would encompass trustee lending in that the trustee receives from the trust estate not only fee compensation but also interest income.[34] Moreover, if for some reason the credit-worthiness of the trust erodes, does the duty of loyalty require some forbearance on the part of the lending trustee? The outcome of a particular case is likely to depend on its own set of facts and circumstances.[35] It is recommended, how-

---

appearance of impropriety must be assiduously avoided. This standard has been applied with uncompromising rigidity by the courts." Washington Post, Aug. 31, 1984, §1, at A1.

[32]*See* §§6.1.1, 6.2.1.

[33]*See* Estate of Rothko, 43 N.Y.2d 305, 372 N.E.2d 291 (1977), *aff'g* 56 A.D.2d 499, 392 N.Y.S.2d 870 (1977), *aff'g* 84 Misc. 2d 870, 379 N.Y.S.2d 923 (1975). *See generally* 3 Scott on Trusts §206.

[34]*But see* First Natl. Bank of Boston v. Slade, 379 Mass. 243, 399 N.E.2d 1047 (1979); Bullivant v. First Natl. Bank of Boston, 246 Mass. 324, 141 N.E. 41 (1923). *See generally* 2A Scott on Trusts §170.20; Bogert, Trusts and Trustees §543(L).

[35]*See generally Slade, supra* note 34; *Bullivant, supra* note 34; Bogert, Trusts and Trustees §543(L); 2A Scott on Trusts §§170.20, 170.23A, 170.24.

ever, that unless the trust instrument specifically permits the trustee to lend funds to the trust, the trustee should refrain from engaging in such activity.

In the context of the corporate fiduciary with general banking powers the trust should specifically permit the trustee to enter into a loan with its commercial department. Even if the trust specifically permits the trustee to lend funds to the trust, the terms of the loan must be competitive. With respect to a trustee's loan to a corporation that is owned and controlled by the trust, the law is somewhat ambiguous as to whether the trustee may protect its position to the detriment of the corporation and of course the trust.[36] What if the lending trustee calls the loan, driving the corporation into bankruptcy and the trust into oblivion?[37] In this context may the commercial side and the trust side of a bank be treated as separate entities? As the corporation has only one management pyramid and one set of shareholders, the answer has to be no.[38] Thus it is recommended that lenders attempt to avoid loans to corporations that are controlled by their trusts. As a practical matter, the attorney for the trust will find it a difficult task leading the lending trustee through a gauntlet of federal insider trading compliance requirements on one side and state-imposed fiduciary obligations on the other.

§6.1.3.2   Trustee Invests in Its Own Stock

When trustees lend to themselves without authority they breach the duty of loyalty. Are things any different if a corporate trustee invests trust assets in itself, in its own stock? This situation usually arises inadvertently when bank stock pours over by will into a trust of which the bank is a trustee or as an incident to the bank's merger with or acquisition of another bank. Again, nothing good can come of such entanglements. If the corporate entity is publicly traded, the entity as trustee may not exploit inside information on

---

[36]*See supra* note 35.
[37]*Id.*
[38]2A Scott on Trusts §170.18.

behalf of the trust.[39] Independent judgment in the voting of proxies is virtually impossible.[40] If the bank gets into trouble its trust department may be tempted to hold onto its own stock for any number of business considerations unrelated to the welfare of its trusts, such as supporting the stock's price in order to maintain the confidence of trust or commercial customers.[41] In either case, such nonfeasance constitutes a continuing act of self-dealing arising out of the bank's divided loyalties. Moreover even in the face of duly obtained authority the trustee is saddled with the over-arching obligation to be prudent. Thus express retention language in the governing instrument cannot relieve the trustee of its duty to monitor the investment.[42] Such entanglements never should be initiated by the trustee and when they inadvertently develop should be ended as soon as it is prudent to do so. If the stock is part of the holdings of a revocable trust and the donor wants the trustee to hold the trustee's stock, the trustee at a minimum should require a letter from the donor directing retention of the stock and holding the trustee harmless from the consequences of so doing.

§6.1.3.3   Trustee Benefiting as Buyer and Seller

Any act that appears to be in the interest of the trustee instead of the trust estate may constitute a breach of trust for which the remedies are as complete as the equity court can make them. The trustee cannot make any profit out of the use of the trust property or gain any advantage, direct or indirect, by its purchase or sale. The trustee — individual or institutional — must not sell trust property to himself personally,[43] sell his own property to the

---

[39]*See generally* §§7.3.3.3, 7.3.4.2(a).

[40]*See generally* Report, Voting by Corporate Trustee of Its Own Stock Held in Trust, 3 Real Prop. Prob. & Tr. J. 517 (1968); Barclay, Voting Bank's Own Stock Held in Trust (pts. 1-2), 106 Tr. & Est. 70, 678 (1967).

[41]*See generally* 2A Scott on Trusts §170.15.

[42]*See* Restatement (Second) of Trusts §231 comments *a, b* (1959); Mueller v. Mueller, 28 Wis. 2d 26, 135 N.W.2d 854 (1965).

[43]*See* Restatement (Third) of Trusts §170 comment *b* (1992).

trust,[44] sell property under circumstances where his personal interest might affect his judgment,[45] renew the trust lease in his own name,[46] buy property for himself which he ought to have bought for the trust,[47] or be guided by the interests of any third person including other trusts.[48]

A gray area has developed in the law, namely the selling by the trustee of legal, brokerage, and consulting services to the trust.[49] Again, as with the sale of goods such transactions fall within the strict definition of *self-dealing*, in that economic benefit is accruing to the trustee from the trust estate over and above the trustee fees. In England the practice is forbidden,[50] but in most American jurisdictions it is not.[51]

The practice is troubling. The trustee is on both sides of the service contract, so the arrangement on its face is the product of divided loyalties. At the very least such transactions put great stress on the trustee's independent judgment. Thus, to avoid even the appearance of impropriety, the trustee should not charge for routine legal or consulting tasks,[52] and should turn over to the

[44]*See* id. comments *h, i.*
[45]*See* id. comments *c, d, e.*
[46]*See generally* 2A Scott on Trusts §170.23.
[47]*See* Restatement (Third) of Trusts §170 comment *k* (1992).
[48]Id. comment *q.*
[49]*See* id. comment *o*; Restatement (Second) of Trusts §242 comment *d* (1959); 2A Scott on Trusts §§170.22, 242.2.
[50]*See* Robinson v. Pett, 3 P. Wms. 249 (1734). *See generally* Bogert, Trusts and Trustees §975.
[51]*See* Restatement (Second) of Trusts §242 comments *d, k* (1959); 3A Scott on Trusts §242.2; Bogert, Trusts and Trustees §975. *But cf.* Tellier, Annot., Right of Executor or Administrator to Extra Compensation for Legal Services Rendered by Him, 65 A.L.R.2d 809 (1959).
[52]The authors acknowledge that there is a divergence of opinion over whether the trustee who renders legal services to his or her trust is entitled to additional compensation. In recent years bills have been filed in both the California and New York legislatures aimed at what is perceived by the sponsors to be "double dipping." See Pollock, State Legislators Move to Curb Double Dipping by Estate Lawyers, Wall St. J., June 23, 1993, at B5, col. 1. The American Bar Association, however, has opposed any legislative initiatives to limit or regulate the practice of lawyer-trustees taking double compensation. *See* Link, Developments Regarding the Professional Responsibility of the Estate Administration Lawyer: The Effect of the Model Rules of Professional Conduct, 26 Real Prop. Prob. & Tr. J. 1 (1991); Bogert, Trusts and Trustees §975.

trust any routine brokerage commissions that are generated as a consequence of these transactions with the trust estate.[53] Extraordinary legal, consulting, and brokerage services should be purchased by the trust at arm's length from independent third parties.[54] When the trustee is also the service vendor, accountability is reduced: The trust is deprived of the benefit of independent advice, and the beneficiaries are deprived of the benefit of the checks and balances inherent in arm's-length contractual relationships.[55] When the trustee, for example, acts also as attorney, it must fall to the court or to the beneficiaries to monitor the quality of the legal work, the commitment to the expeditious resolution of the legal matter, and the reasonableness of the legal fees. Because court oversight is inefficient and beneficiary oversight often illusory, neither alternative is particularly satisfactory.

§6.1.3.4 Indirect Benefit Accruing to the Trustee

Vast wealth is concentrated in the hands of the nation's relatively small corps of trustees.[56] With wealth comes patronage and with patronage comes the opportunity and the temptation to benefit indirectly from its dispensation. The opportunities are virtually unlimited and the benefits to be gained subtle and often difficult to detect. Nevertheless the conscientious and ethical trustee resists the temptation to benefit personally from the economic power that comes with the right to control the property of others.

Trustees should think twice before selling or loaning trust property to — or purchasing goods and services with trust prop-

---

[53]*See* Restatement (Third) of Trusts §§170, comment *o* (1992); Restatement (Second) of Trusts §206 comment *k* (1959); 2A Scott on Trusts §170.22.

[54]*See generally* Brown, The Punctilio of an Honor the Most Sensitive, 131 Tr. & Est. 24 (1992). *See also* First Natl. Bank of Boston v. Brink, 372 Mass. 257, 268, 361 N.E.2d 406, 412 (1977) (Liacos, J., concurring in part and dissenting in part) (commenting on the perceived or actual conflicts of interest that can arise when an attorney and fiduciary are one in the same).

[55]*See* §§3.2.2-3.2.3.

[56]By government estimates, substantially more than $4.5 trillion worth of property was held in employee benefit and personal trusts alone in 1989.

erty from — their spouses, relatives, business associates, attorneys, as well as persons in a position to offer indirect considerations. Trustees should not accept benefits of a pecuniary or nonpecuniary nature from a service vendor,[57] and should always strive to avoid the hint of impropriety. Like Caesar's wife, the trustee must be above suspicion. When the trustee yields to these temptations it is not long before rationalizing takes over and the interests of the beneficiaries are compromised.

The practice of *social investing* illustrates how seductive this economic power can be. Social investing has been defined by Professor Langbein and Judge Posner as the "pursuit of an investment strategy that tempers the conventional objective of maximizing the investor's financial interests by seeking to promote nonfinancial social goals as well."[58] A trustee who voluntarily undertakes to practice social investing uses the trust estate to promote the trustee's own political and social goals — a clear case of indirect self-dealing.[59] The trustee who yields to third-party pressure to practice social investing is acting on divided loyalties; the trustee who seeks the acclaim of particular constituencies, or at least the cessation of their criticisms, may be subordinating the interest of the trust to the interest of the trustee.[60] If social investing has any place in the law of trusts, it is incumbent upon the courts and the legislatures to define this exception to the trustee's duty of undivided loyalty in a way that establishes reasonable limits

[57]*See, e.g.,* In re Estate of Rothko, 43 N.Y.2d 305, 372 N.E.2d 291 (1977), *aff'g* 56 A.D.2d 499, 392 N.Y.S.2d 870 (1977), *aff'g* 84 Misc. 2d 830, 379 N.Y.S.2d 923 (1975) (a case in which independent judgment was called into question because of professional advantages and financial opportunities that accrued to coexecutors from the sale of estate assets); Brown, *supra* note 54 (referring to a case, ultimately settled, involving an executor who selectively revealed information regarding real property in the estate in order to give an advantage to a friend participating in the subsequent auction of that piece of property).

[58]Langbein & Posner, Social Investing and the Law of Trusts, 79 Mich. L. Rev. 72, 73 (1980).

[59]*See* Rounds, Social Investing, IOLTA, and the Law of Trusts: The Settlor's Case Against the Political Use of Charitable and Client Funds, 22 Loy. U. Chi. L.J. 163, 170-172 nn.27, 31 (1990).

[60]Langbein & Posner, *supra* note 58, at 96-104. "We conclude that the duty of loyalty . . . forbid[s] social investing in its current form." Id. at 76.

on the trustee's right to promote with the trust estate personal political or social goals or the goals of third parties.

Florida's adoption in 1978 of an IOLTA program[61] has brought a state-imposed exception to the duty of loyalty. In furtherance of the IOLTA concept, the judiciaries of a number of states[62] are now authorizing or compelling attorney-trustees to apply the income earned by certain client trust accounts to charitable and professional organizations. In the First Circuit, the concept has recently withstood a challenge on First, Fifth, and Fourteenth Amendment grounds.[63] A similar challenge is underway in the Fifth Circuit.[64]

The corporate trustee (*e.g.*, a bank) is a collection of human beings performing a myriad of tasks in furtherance of a myriad of corporate purposes. Thus there is ample opportunity for the corporation and the individual employees to directly and indirectly self-deal. The breaches can be subtle. They are often hidden in a thicket of complicated financial transactions and thus difficult to sort out, let alone prevent and detect by those not privy to the inner workings of the institution.[65] As a general rule, neither the corporate trustee nor its employee should directly or indirectly

---

[61]*See generally* Comment, IOTA — Overcoming Its Current Obstacles, 18 Stetson L. Rev. 415 (1989). *See also* §9.4.2.

[62]See A.B.A. IOLTA Clearinghouse, IOLTA Profiles, 7 IOLTA Update 1, 4-7 (1991). It should be noted, however, that there is legislative involvement in the Maryland, New York, Ohio and Pennsylvania IOLTA programs. The IOLTA Update is a valuable resource for statistics relating to the various state programs.

[63]*See e.g.*, Washington Legal Found. v. Massachusetts Bar Found., 993 F.2d 962 (1st Cir. 1993) (holding in part that an IOLTA account is not a "formal" trust and that the "interest earned on IOLTA accounts belongs to no one"); *but see* Ritchie et al., Decedents' Estates and Trusts 1318 (8th ed. 1993) ("Funds received by a lawyer on behalf of a client are held in trust for the client."; Sinibaldi, The Taking Issue in California's Legal Services Trust Account Program, 12 Hastings Const. L.Q. 463 (1985) ("the laudable purpose of California's [IOLTA] program should not sustain it against a Takings Clause challenge").

[64]*See* Washington Legal Found. v. Texas Equal Access to Justice Found., No. 94-CA-081JN (W.D. Tex. Feb. 7, 1994).

[65]*See* Brown, The Punctilio of an Honor the Most Sensitive, 131 Tr. & Est. 24, 24-25 (1992). Author Peter O. Brown suggests a simple test to govern individual ethical conduct in trust administration to avoid any resulting conflicts: "If an intended act is even faintly suggestive of impropriety, don't do it." Id. at 26. *See also* Comptroller of the Currency Regulation, Self-Dealing, 12 C.F.R. §9.12 (1963) (list of prohibited transactions arising from conflict situations; for

transact with the trust property.[66] Unless authorized by the terms of the governing instrument or by statute, the corporate trustee should not direct trust business to its in-house real estate sales operation, its discount brokerage operation, or its proprietary mutual funds.[67] When the corporate trustee receives "soft dollars"[68] from its security trading activities or "financial incentives

---

example, §9.12(c) prohibits a trustee from "selling or otherwise transferring assets from its fiduciary account to itself, its employees or affiliates").

[66]The duty of loyalty extends to employees and agents of the trustee. The focus is on the functions performed, not the mere title of trustee. *See* Bogert, Trusts and Trustees §543 n.21 and accompanying text. *See, e.g.*, Matter of People (Bond & Mtge. Guar. Co.), 303 N.Y. 423, 103 N.E.2d 721 (1952).

[67]At the very least, a trust company should establish strong ethical policies to ensure compliance with both fiduciary and business ethics. Brown, *supra* note 65, at 31. *See* Comptroller of the Currency Trust Interpretation No. 273 (Sept. 25, 1992), concerning trust department purchase of securities through affiliated discount brokerage companies. The following states have enacted legislation allowing banks, under certain circumstances, to invest trust assets in mutual funds for which the banks act as investment advisors: Alabama (Ala. Code §19-3-120.1); Arizona (Ariz. Rev. Stat. Ann. §6-246); Arkansas (Ark. Code Ann. §28-71-104); Colorado (Colo. Rev. Stat. §11-10-107); Connecticut (Conn. Gen. Stat. Ann. §45a-209); Delaware (Del. Code Ann. tit. 12, §3312(a)); Florida (Fla. Stat. Ann. §660-417); Georgia (Ga. Code Ann. §53-8-2(e)); Idaho (Idaho Code §68-404(A)); Illinois (Ill. Ann. Stat. ch. 760, para. 5/5.20); Indiana (Ind. Code Ann. §28-1-12-3(i)); Iowa (Iowa Code Ann. §633.123(2)); Kentucky (Ky. Rev. Stat. Ann. §386.020(1)(g)); Louisiana (La. Rev. Stat. Ann. §9:2127(c)); Maine (Me. Rev. Stat. Ann. tit. 18-A, §7-408); Maryland (Md. Code Ann., Est. & Trusts §15-106(c)(1)); Massachusetts (Mass. Ann. Laws ch. 167G, §3(11)); Michigan (Mich. Stat. Ann. §23.710(185)); Minnesota (Minn. Stat. Ann. §48.38(6)); Mississippi (Miss. Code Ann. §81-5-33); Missouri (Mo. Rev. Stat. §362.550(11)); Nebraska (Neb. Rev. Stat. Ann. §30-3205(2)); Nevada (Nev. Rev. Stat. §669.225); New Jersey (N.J. Rev. Stat. Ann. §3B:14-23(w)); New York (N.Y. Est. Powers & Trusts Law §11.2.2(b)(1)); North Carolina (N.C. Gen. Stat. §36A-66.2); Ohio (Ohio Rev. Code Ann. §1109.10(11)); Oklahoma (Okla. Stat. Ann. tit. 60, §175.55); Oregon (Or. Rev. Stat. §709.175(2)); Pennsylvania (20 Pa. Cons. Stat. Ann. §7314.1); Rhode Island (R.I. Gen. Laws §19-9-16); South Carolina (S.C. Code Ann. §62-7-302(a)(6)); South Dakota (S.D. Codified Laws Ann. §55-1A-9); Tennessee (Tenn. Code Ann. §35-3-117(h)); Texas (Tex. Prop. Code Ann. §113.053(g)); Utah (Utah Code Ann. §75.7-402); Virginia (Va. Code Ann. §26-44.1); West Virginia (W. Va. Code §44-6-9(b)); Wisconsin (Wis. Stat. Ann. §881.01(4)).

[68]*Soft dollar purchases* occur when "a national bank chooses to purchase products or services and pay for them with brokerage commissions arising from securities transactions for trust accounts. . . ." Comptroller of the Currency Regulation TBC-17 Banking Issuance 267 (1990). *See generally* Pickard, Institutional Portfolio Execution: Soft Dollar Arrangements, 8 Prentice Hall L. & Bus. 22 (1990).

for doing business on behalf of fiduciary accounts with third-party vendors,"[69] issues of indirect self-dealing present themselves.

Soft dollar issues are covered by §28(e) of the Securities Exchange Act.[70] Section 28(e) is designed to create a safe harbor for money managers, including fiduciaries, who receive investment research as a result of commissions they pay to a broker.[71] The practice of using commission dollars to also purchase investment research is known as *soft dollar arrangements*. The potential abuse is that the fiduciary is using client funds to not only make trades but also to receive investment research. Prior to May 1, 1975, commissions on securities trades were generally fixed, hence the receipt of investment research along with the execution of trades was not an issue.[72] With the abolition of the fixed commission structure and the ability to negotiate commissions the question arose whether it was appropriate to allow a fiduciary to pay more to place trades with a broker who also provides investment research.[73] Since a fiduciary could lower costs by paying for the execution of trades alone, isn't there a duty to do so? Section 28(e) allows a fiduciary to pay a higher commission as long as the commission is reasonable in relation to the brokerage and research services provided.[74] It also overrides any other state or federal law unless the state or Congress passes a contrary law after the date of enactment of §28(e).[75]

In investment matters, the trust officer, as an employee of the trustee, has a common law duty of loyalty to the trust, which coexists with the 1934 Securities Exchange Act's narrow insider trading proscriptions.[76] The nature and scope of these proscrip-

---

[69]Brown, *supra* note 65, at 27.

[70]Securities Exchange Act §28(e), 15 U.S.C. §78(a) (1988). For the SEC safe harbor rules governing soft dollar transactions by fiduciaries, see Securities, Brokerage and Research Services, 51 Fed. Reg. 16004 (1986).

[71]Id.

[72]For an analysis of the impact of the change from the fixed commission structure of the U.S. capital market, which existed prior to May 1, 1975, to the deregulated environment in effect thereafter, see Note, Problem of Fiduciaries Under the Securities Laws, 20 Real Prop. Prob. & Tr. J. 503, 570 (1985).

[73]Id. at 570-571.

[74]Id.

[75]Id. at 573.

[76]*See* §7.3.4.2(a).

tions[77] have been poorly explained by securities lawyers to the fiduciary community, with the result that trust officers have been frightened into an obsessive concern with avoiding the act's criminal sanctions. In fact, this obsession has led to allegations of breaches of the common law duty of loyalty.[78] The " '34 Act," for example, does not abrogate the trust officer's common law duty to exploit public information (even information derived from colleagues on the commercial side) in furtherance of the interests of the trust.[79] The failure to utilize such information out of an irrational fear of criminal sanction is in itself a breach of the duty of loyalty.

On the other hand, the trust officer may not exploit any inside information relating to the trust itself directly or indirectly for personal benefit. The general rule is that as much relevant information as is legally permissible should flow to the trust and as little as possible should flow out of the trust.[80] Confidential information, as with light in a black hole, stays in the trust officer's file. The

---

[77]*See* §7.3.3.3.

[78]In a suit against the FDIC by the beneficiaries of a testamentary trust containing a large concentration of stock in the insolvent parent corporation of the bank cotrustee, it was alleged that the bank breached its fiduciary duty by failing to evaluate, manage, or analyze the stock during a period when the stock went from a high of $6,030,726 in June 1986 to a low of $260,605 in August 1990. The Bank in its answer had suggested that the Bank lawfully "could not" have evaluated, managed, or analyzed the stock and accordingly had not done so. The case was settled before trial. *See* Godfrey v. FDIC, Civil No. 90-0290-B-C (D. Me. 1990).

[79]*See* Comptroller of the Currency Regulation, 12 C.F.R. §9.7(d) (1963):

> The Chinese Wall provision [embodied in 12 C.F.R. §9.7(d)] has been misinterpreted at times as an absolute barrier. The doctrine does not require the total separation of trust and commercial functions within the bank. Neither does it prohibit the integration of joint marketing and servicing of fiduciary and commercial department customers. The original and continuing intent of the Chinese Wall was to prevent the passage of material inside information between a bank's fiduciary and commercial departments in violation of securities laws and regulations.

Comptroller's Handbook for National Trust Examiners, Conflicts of Interest, Introduction §701.1 (July 1984).

[80]*See* §6.2.3.

trust officer conducting an auction of trust property, for example, violates the duty of loyalty by disclosing nonpublic information relating to asset value to certain bidders with whom the officer has a direct or indirect relationship and not to the others.[81]

Moreover, as with the trust company itself, the trust officer should refrain from directly or indirectly transacting with the trust property.[82] This will usually take the form of contracting on behalf of the trust for goods and services with persons in a position to directly or indirectly further the personal interests of the trust officer.

§6.1.3.5 Duty of Loyalty to the Beneficiary

As we have seen, a trustee is under a duty to act solely in the interest of the beneficiaries as to matters that directly and indirectly relate to the trust property.[83] The trustee, however, may have occasion to deal with a beneficiary in matters *unrelated to the trust property*, such as selling the beneficiary life insurance or providing the beneficiary with brokerage or legal services. Such activity is permissible, but the trustee must be scrupulously fair.[84] While such dealings may not be forbidden per se, they carry with them the presumption, albeit rebuttable, of undue influence.[85] This is because the trustee-beneficiary relationship is a confidential one, as solemn as that of priest-penitent, physician-patient, and attorney-client.[86] A judicial finding of undue influence, at the very least, would entitle the beneficiary to disaffirm the transaction.[87]

Nor may the trustee through abuse of confidence gain a

[81]*See* Brown, *supra* note 65, at 24-25. *See also* note 79 (Administration of Fiduciary Powers).

[82]*See* Bogert, Trusts and Trustees §543 n.21.

[83]*See supra* note 9 and accompanying text.

[84]*See* Restatement (Third) of Trusts §170(2) (1992); Bogert, Trusts and Trustees §544.

[85]*See* Bogert, Trusts and Trustees §544.

[86]*See* Restatement (Second) of Trusts §2 comment *b* (1959); Bogert, Trusts and Trustees §544 nn.15-23.

[87]*See supra* note 86.

direct or indirect advantage in outside transactions with beneficiaries.[88] Unlike dealing with a stranger, the trustee may not take advantage of his peculiar knowledge or position, either for personal gain or for the profit of some of the beneficiaries to the exclusion of others.[89]

The best course is for the trustee to avoid commercial and financial dealings with the beneficiaries altogether; if such activity must be pursued, it should be done only after full disclosure of all relevant information and only after they have obtained competent independent advice on those matters that directly and indirectly relate to the activity.[90] The trustee always has the burden of showing that the beneficiaries were fully informed and thoroughly understood the matter and that no advantage of position or influence was taken,[91] or face the consequences of abusing the confidential relationship.

It goes without saying that the trustee should never solicit gifts or other favors from beneficiaries. At the very least such solicitations would have the appearance of extortion. Nor should the trustee accept unsolicited gifts or favors from the beneficiaries, for to do so cannot help but cloud independent judgment — particularly should the wishes of the settlor as manifested in the governing instrument and the wishes of the beneficiaries come in conflict. Matters are worsened if unsolicited gifts or favors from fewer than all beneficiaries are accepted, because then the trustee's ability to be impartial is called into question.[92] The trustee's duty of impartiality in matters relating to the beneficiaries is an incident of the general duty of loyalty, so it goes without saying that the trustee ought not to act as an agent (*e.g.*, as attorney-at-law) for a beneficiary whose interests are in conflict with the interests of the other trust beneficiaries, whether or not the conflicting interests are trust-related.[93]

---

[88]*See* Bogert, Trusts and Trustees §544.
[89]Id.
[90]Id.
[91]Id. *See* §7.2.3.
[92]*See* Restatement (Third) of Trusts §183 (1992); 2A Scott on Trusts §183.
[93]Id.

§6.1.4   Duty to Give Personal Attention (Not to Delegate)

Because the trustee's relationship with the trust beneficiaries is a personal one, the administration of the trust may not be delegated.[94] If the trustee can avoid responsibility by delegating fundamental duties to a third party, then the settlor's intention in selecting a particular trustee will be thwarted. On the other hand, the trustee has a fiduciary obligation to seek whatever assistance necessary to execute the efficient and competent administration of the trust.[95] As a general rule, the trustee may never delegate to others the responsibility to coordinate the trust's administration and to supervise agents.[96] Moreover some specific functions are nondelegable no matter how intense the supervision,[97] such as discretion as to how income and principal may be used in furtherance of the purposes of the trust.[98] The consequences of improper delegation are severe: The trustee becomes liable for the errors and omissions of his agents.[99]

On the other hand, asset custody, record keeping, and other such ministerial tasks generally may be delegated to others.[100] An agent may be allowed to collect dividends and rents, keep the books, and act for the trustee where a "prudent man of business" would employ an agent.[101] Thus the trustee employs a stockbrokerage to purchase stocks and pays for the same through it.[102] In such cases, the trustee will not be held liable for the default of an

---

[94]*See* Restatement (Third) of Trusts §171 (1992); 2A Scott on Trusts §171.

[95]*See* Restatement (Third) of Trusts §§171 comment *a*, 227 comment *j* (1992); 2A Scott on Trusts §§171.2, 227.1.

[96]*See* Restatement (Third) of Trusts §171 comments *e*, *k* (1992); 2A Scott on Trusts §171.1.

[97]*See* Restatement (Third) of Trusts §171, comment *e* (1992); 2A Scott on Trusts §171.1; Bogert, Trusts and Trustees §555.

[98]2A Scott on Trusts §171.2.

[99]*See* Restatement (Second) of Trusts, §225(2)(b) (1959); 2A Scott on Trusts §§171.1, 225.1.

[100]*See* Restatement (Third) of Trusts §171 comment *f* (1992); 2A Scott on Trusts §171.2; Bogert, Trusts and Trustees §555.

[101]Id.

[102]*See* 2A Scott on Trusts §171.2.

agent, unless due care in selecting that agent was not exercised.[103] Likewise a trustee who has employed a reputable conveyancer is not responsible for a flaw in the title that the conveyancer overlooked. If, however, a loss occurs through the careless failure of the trustee to see that the agent uses due diligence, it really is the trustee's own negligence that triggers liability. The trustee may vote stock by proxy at shareholder meetings, unless the block of stock represents a controlling interest or there are other than routine matters on the table.[104] Many states have statutes to that effect.[105] As to controlling interests or nonroutine matters, delegation by means of a general proxy is inappropriate.[106]

In the gray area is the matter of asset selection. In the past, investment discretion was considered a nondelegable function.[107] The principle was best illustrated by the sale of real estate or personal property: The trustees could not delegate the essential matters of the sale (i.e., the determination of the price and terms and the central question whether the sale had best be made).[108] Similarly, the trustees could not give a general power of attorney to make sales or purchases of trust securities, but having reached a decision to sell certain trust securities they ordinarily would deliver a special power of transfer, thus employing an agent to perform a purely ministerial act.[109]

The modern trend is to permit the trustee to delegate some investment discretion to investment advisers and others, provided there is adequate supervision by the trustee.[110] This allows the trustee to retain an investment advisor and to pay for the advisor's

[103]It would be unreasonable to require the trustee to be a guarantor of the conduct of the agent where the delegation was proper and the trustee has otherwise acted prudently. *See* Restatement (Second) of Trusts §225(2)(c) (1959); 2A Scott on Trusts §§171.2, 225.1; Bogert, Trusts and Trustees §557.

[104]*See* Restatement (Second) of Trusts §193 comment *b* (1959); 3 Scott on Trusts §193.3; Bogert, Trusts and Trustees §556.

[105]3 Scott on Trusts §193.3.

[106]Id.

[107]*See* Restatement (Second) of Trusts §171 comment *h* (1959); 2A Scott on Trusts §§171.2, 227.9A.

[108]*See* Restatement (Second) of Trusts §171 comment *g* (1959); 2A Scott on Trusts §171.2; Bogert, Trusts and Trustees §556.

[109]Id.

[110]*See* Restatement (Third) of Trusts §171 comment *f* (1992).

services from the trust. The theory of the early common law that the trustee needs no assistance in investment matters has been discarded. This relaxation of the prohibition against delegation in the investment context is embodied in §171 of the Restatement (Third) of Trusts (the *Prudent Investor Rule*), which recognizes that some "fiduciary authority" may with adequate supervision be delegated.[111] "The trustee," however, "personally must define at least the trust's investment objectives."[112] The trustee must also make the decisions that establish the trust's investment strategies and programs, at least to the extent of approving plans developed by agents and advisers.[113] Section 171 thus gives trustees the flexibility to carry out their investment duties and does away with the general prohibition against trustees' delegating investment discretion.[114] As long as trustees are prudent in selecting their advisors, participate in setting trust investment objectives, and routinely monitor the advisors' performance, they should not be liable for delegating to advisors.[115]

It is now settled law that a trustee may prudently invest in a mutual fund without breaching the duty not to delegate.[116] But what about the practice of incorporating the trust estate itself? The argument has been advanced that if the trust estate is incorporated, the trustees are thereafter freed from the inherent limitations of the trust and even from their liability for the continued administration. A trust, however, is a personal confidence. Thus, the better view is that the corporation will act simply as an agency to carry out the trust[117] and that the trustees are in no way liberated from their responsibility in the premises.[118] A trustee who holds the working control of the stock is accountable as a fiduciary for the administration of corporate affairs absent express language in the governing instrument to

[111]Id.
[112]Id. comment *h*.
[113]Id.
[114]Id. comment *f*.
[115]Id.
[116]Id. §227 comment *m*; 3 Scott on Trusts §227.9A; Bogert, Trusts and Trustees §673.
[117]*See generally* 3 Scott on Trusts §190.9A.
[118]Id. *See also* 3 Scott on Trusts §225.

the contrary. Corporate transactions will be treated as though they were the trustee's.[119]

As stated above, the trustee has an affirmative fiduciary obligation — and therefore the implied authority — to seek out the advice of experts if it is prudent to do so. If the specialized services of lawyers, accountants, genealogists, private investigators, and the like are necessary for the proper administration of the trust, then the trustee has a duty to consult them at trust expense on behalf of the trust.[120] As can be seen, the trustee must walk the fine line between improper delegation and improper failure to delegate. The "amateur" trustee, for example, should guard against the natural inclination to turn over the entire administration of the trust to "experts" such as lawyers, investment advisors, brokers, financial planners, and institutions acting as agents for fiduciaries.[121] There is more to trust administration than a series of legal tasks; than making investment decisions; than security custody and record keeping. Conscientious and reasonable "amateurs" make excellent trustees, provided they actively coordinate and supervise.

A trustee should not only guard against delegating the entire administration to "experts" and others but also to the cotrustee.[122] Cotrustees hold the trust property in joint tenancy;[123] accordingly there is authority that one of them alone may de-

---

[119]*See* 2A Scott on Trusts §§171.1, 171.4; Annot., Trustee's Power to Exchange Trust Property for Share of Corporation Organized to Hold the Property, 20 A.L.R.3d 841 (1968); *see also* Uniform Trustees' Power Act §3(c)(3), 7 U.L.A. 746 (1988), which provides that a trustee has the power "to continue or participate in the operation of any business or other enterprise, and to effect incorporation, dissolution, or other change in the form of the organization of the business enterprise."

[120]*See generally* Restatement (Third) of Trusts §171 (1992); 2A Scott on Trusts §171.2.

[121]*See* Restatement (Third) of Trusts §227 comment *j* (1992). *See, e.g.*, Shriners Hospitals v. Gardiner, 152 Ariz. 527, 733 P.2d 1110 (1987) (holding that express authority to employ and compensate attorneys, accountants, agents and brokers merely a recognition of the trustee's obligation to obtain expert advice, not a license to remove himself from the role as trustee).

[122]*See* Restatement (Third) of Trusts §184 (1992); 2A Scott on Trusts §184; Bogert, Trusts and Trustees §555.

[123]*See* Bogert, Trusts and Trustees §145, 554.

mand and receive interests, rents, dividends, and other sums of money due the trust.[124] It has been stated to be the rule, in the absence of any knowledge of unfitness, that the "other" trustees may permit one of their number to exercise the trust powers and will not be liable if the designee abuses them.[125] It also has been said that in cases where the trust duties cannot conveniently be exercised by joint action, the trustees may make a reasonable apportionment of them and that an individual trustee will not, under these circumstances, be liable for the loss of funds caused by the neglect of the other.[126] Although the rule forbidding delegation has thus been relaxed, there are distinct limitations. In fact it is very dangerous for one cotrustee to fall into the habit of leaving the trust business to another. It is the duty of all trustees, unless excused by the instrument,[127] to participate in the trust administration.[128] May one cotrustee allow the other cotrustee to make and execute investment decisions without prior consultation or approval? Typically, this issue arises when a trust has a professional cotrustee and a nonprofessional cotrustee. In the context of a nonprofessional delegating to a professional cotrustee, the answer is probably yes. The Prudent Investor Rule would now seem to permit this delegation, but this may not be the rule in all jurisdictions.[129]

The question which is difficult, in practice, is the extent to which one of several cotrustees may be subject to surcharge as a result of allowing one or more of the others to assume custody and control of part or all of the trust property. These cases ordinarily do not involve an active participation in a wrongful act. Neverthe-

---

[124]"If the performance of an act may be properly delegated by the trustee he may give such power to a co-trustee as well as to any other qualified person." Bogert, Trusts and Trustees §555. *See also* id. §554; Restatement (Second) of Trusts §194 comment *b* (1959); 3 Scott on Trusts §194.

[125]*See* Restatement (Second) of Trusts §224 (1959); 3 Scott on Trusts §224.

[126]*See* Bogert, Trusts and Trustees §589.

[127]*See* Restatement (Third) of Trusts §184 comment *c* (1992); 2A Scott on Trusts §184.

[128]*See* Restatement (Third) of Trusts §184 (1992); 2A Scott on Trusts §184; Bogert, Trusts and Trustees §584.

[129]*See* Restatement (Third) of Trusts §171 comment *f* (1992).

less the ensuing loss may well have been "made possible" by the "neglect" of the inactive trustee. [130] It is improper for a trustee to allow a cotrustee to act generally as the trustee's agent [131] and to do alone what ought to have been done jointly (*e.g.*, allowing the cotrustee to invest the trust funds without consultation or supervision [132] or by standing by and allowing the cotrustee to commit a breach of trust). [133] If one trustee commits a breach of trust, the cotrustee is liable if redress is not sought. [134]

As may be expected, it is doubly dangerous for one trustee to allow a cotrustee to have exclusive management of the trust estate after the latter has proved unreliable. Thus in one case the trust instrument provided that each trustee was to be held liable for his own defaults only (a fairly common clause). The active management of the estate was entrusted to a person who had been the testator's financial advisor. This person collected and embezzled $30,000, which the inactive trustee discovered. The inactive trustee nevertheless allowed the cotrustee to continue to manage the estate, and the latter then embezzled additional monies from the trust estate. The inactive trustee was not held liable for the first embezzlement but was surcharged with the amount of the second. [135]

A delegation issue is raised by the practice, now commonly followed by corporate cotrustees, of retaining exclusive possession of the trust property and of issuing checks and making distributions without signature of the remaining trustees. It is probable that the courts will approve this practice under most

[130]*See* Restatement (Second) of Trusts §224(2)(d) (1959); 3 Scott on Trusts §224.3.
[131]*See* Restatement (Second) of Trusts §224(2)(b) (1959); 3 Scott on Trusts §224.2.
[132]*See* Restatement (Third) of Trusts §171 comments *f, k* (1992); 3 Scott on Trusts §224.3.
[133]*See* Restatement (Second) of Trusts §224(2)(d) (1959); 3 Scott on Trusts §224.3.
[134]*See* Restatement (Second) of Trusts §224(2)(e) (1959); 3 Scott on Trusts §224.5.
[135]In re Matter of Mallon's Estate, 43 Misc. 569, 89 N.Y. Supp. 554 (1904), *aff'd sub nom.* Matter of Howard, 110 App. Div. 61, 97 N.Y. Supp. 23 (1905), *aff'd*, 185 N.Y. 539, 77 N.E. 1189 (1906).

circumstances.[136] Yet the principle remains unshaken that the trustee will be liable if the trust property is unjustifiably left in the exclusive control of the cotrustee and is lost.[137] The representations of the cotrustee as to the status of the property may not be relied upon; personal investigation is required.[138] It is not clear whether trustees may delegate access to a safe deposit box to one of their number. Professor Scott cites several state statutes which indicate approval.[139] Good practice suggests access by more than one person, as by one trustee and a deputy or agent of another.

Occasionally trustees adopt a program of divided custody and responsibility. Thus a trustee who is particularly skilled in real estate matters is given charge of that part of the trust portfolio or one who lives near a fraction of the trust property is expected to manage that fraction. It is, of course, possible to make these arrangements and yet to avoid criticism, if all of the trustees keep themselves informed of the facts and problems as they arise and participate in all decisions of significance. The habit is not a salutary one in the absence of express permission.

There has been developing in the law a principle that the professional or corporate fiduciary is held to a standard higher than that of an amateur. This concept of a higher standard for professional trustees has matured to the point where it is now a part of the Restatement:

> On the other hand, it follows from the requirement of care as well as sound policy that, if the trustee possesses a degree of skill greater than that of an individual of ordinary intelligence, the trustee is liable for a loss that results from failure to make reasonably diligent use of that skill. So also, if a trustee, such as a corporate or professional fiduciary, procured appointment as trustee by expressly or impliedly representing that it possessed greater skill than that of an individual of ordinary intelligence, or if the trustee has or repre-

---

[136]*See* Restatement (Second) of Trusts §194 comment *b* (1959); 3 Scott on Trusts §194; Bogert, Trusts and Trustees §555.

[137]*See* Restatement (Second) of Trusts §224(2)(d) (1959); 3 Scott on Trusts §224.3.

[138]*See* Restatement (Third) of Trusts §227 comment *j* (1992).

[139]3 Scott on Trusts §224.2.

sents that it has special facilities for investment management, the trustee is liable for a loss that results from failure to make reasonably diligent use of that skill or of those special facilities.[140]

The professional should take heed; the amateur should behave as if there is only one standard: the highest one.

Express allocations of fiduciary responsibilities can raise troubling issues. If, for example, the governing instrument allocates investment discretion to one trustee, to what extent does the "other" trustee have a fiduciary obligation to monitor the activities of the investing trustee? The California courts were asked to consider this perplexing issue in *Kirkbride v. First Western Bank.*[141] In *Kirkbride* a corporate fiduciary was held liable for the speculative investments of a cotrustee, even in the face of explicit allocations of investment responsibilities to the cotrustee.[142] The speculations with trust assets were made when the trust was revocable by the settlor who at all relevant times was of full age and legal capacity and fully informed. To be sure the California legislature responded to *Kirkbride* by amending the California Probate Code to provide trustees some limited prospective relief from the holding.[143] It now provides that "a trustee of a revocable trust is not liable to a beneficiary for any act performed or permitted pursuant to written directions from the person holding the power to revoke, including a person to whom the power to direct the trustee is delegated."[144] Nevertheless, the message of the California courts and legislature is clear: In the face of express allocation of certain responsibilities to one trustee, the "other" trustee should be careful not to inadvertently delegate coordinating and supervising functions, regardless of how protective and exculpatory the language in the governing instrument. This is particularly necessary when the trust is irrevocable. If a prospective "other"

---

[140]Restatement (Third) of Trusts §227 comment *d* (1992); *see also* Bogert, Trusts and Trustees §612.

[141]Civ. No. 58254, Super. Ct. No. 101232 (Cal. App. 2d 1981) (unpublished).

[142]Id.

[143]Cal. Prob. Code §16462 (West 1991).

[144]Id.

trustee practically or politically would be unable to supervise the acting trustee and appropriately respond to any breaches of trust, including if necessary the solicitation of judicial involvement, or if the prospective "other" trustee could not be adequately compensated for the extra effort and liability attendant with such divisions of responsibility, then serious consideration should be given to declining the business.

This discussion of delegation would be incomplete without reference to the ultimate delegation breach: the resignation of the trustee without a qualified successor in place, even when the governing instrument purports to grant the trustee such authority.[145] A resignation provision is never a license to abandon a trust once accepted.

§6.1.5   Duty to Account to the Beneficiary

The trustee assumes enforceable obligations. Without enforceability, there is no trust; beneficiaries would be unable to protect their interests. Thus the trustee's general duty to account to someone other than himself is an indispensable one.

§6.1.5.1   Duty to Provide Information

An incident of the trustee's general duty to account is the duty to provide the beneficiary with all the information which is needed to protect the beneficiary's equitable interest.[146] Secrecy and accountability are incompatible.

§6.1.5.2   Duty to Keep and Render Accounts

An incident of the trustee's general duty to account and the trustee's particular duty to provide information is the trustee's

---

[145]*See* Bogert, Trusts and Trustees §511; 2A Scott on Trusts §171.1.
[146]*See* Restatement (Second) of Trusts §173 (1959); 2A Scott on Trusts §173.

duty to keep written accounts that show the nature, amount, and administration of the trust property.[147] All doubts are resolved against the trustee who does not keep accurate accounts.[148] A trust provision that states that the trustee does not have to account will not be enforced.[149] The courts consider such a provision as being against public policy, so it is without effect. Jurisdictions will vary as to the necessary form of an account, but in every trust account there should be a clear showing of seven fundamental sets of facts: income received, income paid, balance of income, additions to principal, deductions from principal, principal on hand, and changes in investments. The account will ordinarily be presented with debtor and creditor sides.

The statutes of nearly all states require the testamentary trustee to file an inventory with the court soon after appointment. The trustee of a testamentary trust should take care to ensure that the inventory is accurate. The balance of personal and real property set forth on the inventory will be the beginning balances of a testamentary trustee's first account. Also, the values of the property on the inventory establish the trustee's financial responsibility for those assets. Even in the case of the inter vivos trust where there is usually no court involvement, the inventory is indispensable from every standpoint. It is the starting point for all subsequent accounts.

To reiterate, on failure to keep adequate accounts, all doubts are resolved against the trustee, and the trustee may be denied compensation.[150] The beneficiary may demand an accounting.[151] Compelling an accounting is within the jurisdiction of a court of equity.[152]

The trustee is entitled periodically to a discharge of liability by

[147]See Restatement (Second) of Trusts §172 (1959); 2A Scott on Trusts §172; Bogert, Trusts and Trustees §962.

[148]See Restatement (Second) of Trusts §172 comment b (1959); 2A Scott on Trusts §172; Bogert, Trusts and Trustees §962.

[149]See 2A Scott on Trusts §172 n.16 and accompanying text.

[150]See Restatement (Second) of Trusts §243 (1959); 2A Scott on Trusts §§172, 243; Bogert, Trusts and Trustees §962.

[151]See Restatement (Second) of Trusts §172 comment c (1959); 2A Scott on Trusts §172.

[152]See 2A Scott on Trusts §172; Bogert, Trusts and Trustees §963.

means of the judicial settlement of accounts [153] (*allowance of the account*). The trustee is discharged of any liability for transactions covered by the account. [154] A careful examination of local statute and case law should be made to determine the extent to which the judicial allowance of the trustee's account acts as a discharge from further obligation for the transaction covered thereby. Commonly the statutes require notification of the interested parties, either by personal service, mailing, or publication. [155] The procedure followed in most states provides for the appointment of a guardian ad litem to represent persons unborn or unascertained and often to represent persons under some legal disability.

The final decree allowing a trustee's account can be reopened only under circumstances that would allow the reopening of an ordinary decree of the equity or probate court (*e.g.*, to correct fraud). [156] Finality in the settlement of accounts furthers the public interest that there be honest people willing to serve as trustees. Thus a decree allowing an account ordinarily cannot be questioned in a collateral proceeding in law or in equity. [157] Of course, for a decree to be final the court must have jurisdiction to make the decree, and the machinery for giving notice must satisfy due process. [158]

Inter vivos trust instruments often provide for periodic ac-

[153]*See* Bogert, Trusts and Trustees §970.

[154]*See* id. §974.

[155]*See* Restatement (Second) of Trusts §220 comment *d* (1959); 3 Scott on Trusts §220; Bogert, Trusts and Trustees §974.

[156]*See* Restatement (Second) of Trusts §220 comment *a* (1959); 3 Scott on Trusts §220; Bogert, Trusts and Trustees §974. For a case involving the reopening of allowed accounts for "constructive fraud," see National Academy of Sciences v. Cambridge Trust Co., 370 Mass. 303, 346 N.E.2d 876 (1976), which involved a trustee's good faith representation on its accountings that a widow had not remarried and thus was entitled to income payments when in fact she had remarried and under the governing instrument was not so entitled. The court found that the trustee had made "no reasonable efforts to ascertain the true state of the facts it [had] misrepresented in the accounts."

[157]*See* 3 Scott on Trusts §220.

[158]*See* Restatement (Second) of Trusts §220 comment *c* (1959); 3 Scott on Trusts §220. *See, e.g.*, Mullane v. Central Hanover Bank & Trust Co., 339 U.S. 306 (1950).

countings in a nonjudicial setting,[159] with discharge of further liability upon assent of certain adult beneficiaries.[160] Some provide for release upon the beneficiary's failure to object within a certain period, usually within 60 days of receipt.[161] It is unsettled whether, in a nonjudicial setting, the assent of present beneficiaries can bind future beneficiaries, remaindermen, and others including minors, the unborn and the unascertained. In this regard, the law is particularly uncertain when it comes to the nonjudicial settlement of accounts that reflect a shifting of beneficial interests. Given this uncertainty, it may be unwise for a trustee to place too much reliance on these provisions. From the perspective of the beneficiary, however, the privacy attendant with a nonjudicial settlement is preferable to the publicity, time, and expense attendant with a judicial proceeding.

§6.2   Specific Duties Incident to General Duties

The trustee has a myriad of duties that are offshoots of the general duties to be prudent, to carry out the terms of the trust, to be loyal to the trust, to give personal attention, and to account.[1] Some particular duties are offshoots of other particular duties. The duty to follow the Prudent Man Rule, for example, is not only an offshoot of the general duty to be prudent, but also of the specific duty to protect the trust property, the specific duty to make the trust property productive, and the specific duty to balance the interests of income beneficiaries and remaindermen.

[159]*See generally* Westfall, Nonjudicial Settlement of Trustees' Accounts, 71 Harv. L. Rev. 40 (1957).
[160]Id. at 60-63.
[161]Id.
§6.2   [1]*See* §6.1.

§6.2.1   Duties to Take Active Control of, Segregate, Earmark, and Protect Trust Property

The trustee's duty to take active control of, segregate, earmark, and protect the trust property is implicit in all the trustee's general duties. If the trust is to do its job, the trust property must be kept safe.

It is axiomatic that the trustee must take reasonable steps to take control of all property due the trust,[2] and face liability for loss that occurs during or because of delay in so doing.[3] This duty includes redressing breaches of trust by predecessor fiduciaries,[4] including executors of pour-over wills,[5] and may even include the trustee's suing to collect insurance proceeds. The trustee however has no obligation to fund such litigation personally unless indemnified by the trust beneficiaries, although there may be an affirmative duty to solicit their voluntary indemnity.[6] The trustee takes control of the trust property by re-registration, through agents, or by acquiring physical possession, as appropriate.[7] For example, it is now a standard practice of mutual funds to evidence ownership by means of the computer-generated account statement rather than a paper certificate. Re-registration would therefore be enough. On the other hand, with respect to closely held corporations where paper certificates remain the standard means of evidencing ownership, physical possession would be required as well.[8]

It is the duty of the trustee to earmark the trust property and to keep it separate from the trustee's own property and from other property not subject to the trust (including funds of different

---

[2]*See generally* Restatement (Second) of Trusts §175 (1959).

[3]*See generally* 2A Scott on Trusts §175; Bogert, Trusts and Trustees §§583, 594.

[4]*See* Restatement (Second) of Trusts §223(2)(a) (1959); 2A Scott on Trusts §177; Bogert, Trusts and Trustees §583.

[5]*See, e.g.*, Pepper v. Zions First Natl. Bank, N.A., 801 P.2d 144 (Utah 1990).

[6]*See generally* Bogert, Trusts and Trustees §582; 2A Scott on Trusts §175.

[7]*See generally* Bogert, Trusts and Trustees §583; 2A Scott on Trusts §175.

[8]*See generally* Bogert, Trusts and Trustees §583; 2A Scott on Trusts §175.

trusts).[9] Most of the evils of trust mismanagement will be avoided if this rule is strictly observed. Unless authorized by statute, decision, or the governing instrument, the trustee should not commingle.

Mingling the trust funds with funds belonging to the individual trustee generally is held to be a breach of trust.[10] Many states have statutes covering such activity, which is a *criminal act* in some states.[11] Even if commingling is not a per se breach of trust, the trustee nevertheless invites full personal responsibility if anything goes wrong.[12] Additions to a trust fund, whether by the settlor or others, ought to be permissible as not the type of commingling contemplated by the prohibition.[13] Separate management of additions seems unnecessary and in most cases not in the economic interest of the beneficiaries.

The trustee should deposit trust funds only in a properly identified trust account.[14] If the deposit is made in the individual name of the trustee, however, the trustee will be treated as a guarantor of the solvency of the bank even though due care was used in the choice of the bank and the funds were not in any way misused.[15]

All negotiable securities, and even partially negotiable securities such as registered coupon bonds, should be deposited in a safe deposit vault.[16] If that is inconvenient, they should be kept in a

---

[9]*See generally* Restatement (Second) of Trusts §179 (1959); 2A Scott on Trusts §179.3; Bogert, Trusts and Trustees §596.

[10]*See generally* Restatement (Second) of Trusts §§179 comment *d*, 205 comment *f*; Bogert, Trusts and Trustees §§596, 707.

[11]*See* 2A Scott on Trusts §179.1 n.5 for a collection of state statutes criminalizing the commingling of trust funds.

[12]*See, e.g.*, Kirby v. Frank, 132 N.J. Eq. 378, 28 A.2d 267 (1942) (a trustee is held strictly accountable when he commingles trust funds with those of his own, and any doubt will be resolved against him).

[13]*See* 2A Scott on Trusts §179.2; Smith v. Stranahan, 314 Mass. 329, 50 N.E.2d 397 (1943) ("The futility of having two or more parallel trusts in the hands of the same trustee to accomplish the same objects in the same way is plainly apparent.").

[14]*See generally* Bogert, Trusts and Trustees §598; Restatement (Second) of Trusts §180 (1959).

[15]*See generally* 2A Scott on Trusts §180.2; Bogert, Trusts and Trustees §596.

[16]*See generally* Bogert, Trusts and Trustees §598.

separate strongbox and properly identified as trust property. Trust securities ought not be kept in the trustee's personal safe-deposit box even if they are in a separate envelope. The particular danger to be avoided here is the commingling of assets of the trust estate with the trustee's own property.[17]

More often than not, a single trust instrument will provide for the creation of more than one trust. A single discretionary trust, for example, might be established at the outset under the terms of the instrument, and there might then be a provision for the trust to divide into separate trust shares at some future time, perhaps when no child of the settlor is alive and under the age of 21. It is likely that the terms of the trust would then authorize the trustee to manage the properties of the various separate trust shares as a common fund[18] — not to be confused of course with a common trust fund[19] — in order to reduce the administrative costs of running separate trusts. Despite the existence of this permissive provision, however, there is a practical downside: The effectiveness of the trustee's defense against an allegation of breach of trust may depend upon the faithful and productive management of each of the individual trust shares. Thus managing separate trusts as a common fund might cause a problem involving only one trust to spread throughout the instrument's entire system of trusts.

Over the years, it has become apparent that it is in the economic interest of trustees and beneficiaries alike that some commingling be permitted.[20] Legislatures and courts from time to time have responded by relaxing somewhat the general prohibi-

---

[17]See Bogert, Trusts and Trustees §596, providing the following reasons for the duty to earmark: (1) to facilitate identification of trust property were the trustee to die in office; (2) to deter a trustee from using trust funds for personal benefit; (3) to facilitate an equitable enforcement action by beneficiaries or creditors against a trustee who is uncooperative, disloyal, or insolvent.

[18]See generally 2A Scott on Trusts §179.2; Maxwell, Comment, Statutory Procedures for the Combination or Division of Trusts, 21 Real Prop. Prob. & Tr. J. 561 (1986).

[19]See generally Bogert, Trusts and Trustees §677; 2A Scott on Trusts §227.9.

[20]See generally Bogert, Trusts and Trustees §677.

tion against commingling.[21] The most obvious example of this relaxation is the *common trust fund*.[22]

From the beneficiary's standpoint, a small fund, whether initially small or the tag end of a trust, offers little possibility of diversification or of yield and would be better off commingled with other trust funds similarly situated.[23] Thus in the early part of the twentieth century was born the concept of the common trust fund.[24] As time went on, many states were prepared through legislation to exempt the arrangement from the common law prohibition against commingling.[25] Aside from the segregation duty, however, rose the question whether a common trust fund would be deemed an association for federal income tax purposes.[26] Beginning in 1936 the tax roadblock was removed: The Federal Revenue Act of 1936 (now §584 of the 1986 Code) allows a pass-through of the income tax liability to the participating trusts.[27] Today thousands of common trust funds are administered by hundreds of banks across the country.[28]

The Internal Revenue Code defines a common trust fund as a fund maintained by a bank exclusively for the collective investment and reinvestment of monies contributed thereto by the bank in its capacity as a trustee, executor, administrator, or guardian and in conformity with federal rules and regulations.[29] The Comptroller of the Currency regulates national banks in the exercise of their trust powers. This includes the administration of their common trust funds.[30] The compilation of the regulations applicable to the fiduciary activities of national banks is known in the trade as "Regu-

---

[21]Id.

[22]Id.

[23]*See generally* Bogert, Trusts and Trustees §677.

[24]*See* Bogert, Trusts and Trustees §677.

[25]Id.

[26]*See* Brooklyn Trust Co. v. Commissioner of Internal Revenue, 80 F.2d 865 (2d Cir. 1936), *cert. denied*, 298 U.S. 659 (1936) (holding that a common trust fund was essentially conducting an investment business for profit, and thus, is "taxable as an association").

[27]*See generally* Bogert, Trusts and Trustees §261.

[28]*See* id. §677 n.34.

[29]*See* 2A Scott on Trusts §227.9.

[30]*See* Bogert, Trusts and Trustees §§677, 270.25.

lation 9" or simply "Reg 9."[31] Since no common trust fund gains the §584 income tax advantage unless it conforms to the requirements of federal law, common trust funds administered by state banks, as a practical matter, must also comply with Reg 9.[32]

The common trust fund itself is a trust with its own governing instrument.[33] Its trustee is a bank, and can only be a bank.[34] When the bank's own trust accounts — its fiduciary customers if you will — invest or participate in the common trust fund, funds from a number of trusts come together. The resulting commingling would place the bank, as trustee of the various participating trusts, in breach of its duty to segregate were it not entitled to the statutory common trust fund exemption.

Over the years, the cost of generating, storing, and transferring paper stock and bond certificates has prompted courts and legislatures, in furtherance of the economic interests of trustees and beneficiaries alike, to relax somewhat the common law duty to earmark.[35] The practice of holding certificates in bulk with book entry, in special purpose depository institutions, and in the name of third persons or nominees, has been the result.[36] Moreover, it is clear that electronic data entry will make paper certificates go the way of the carbon copy.[37] The law of trusts should be able to accommodate most such innovations, with the exception of those that entail the commingling of trust property with the personal assets of the trustee or the nominee. Thus the trustee should still think twice before placing trust property in "street name" with a broker.[38]

---

[31]*See generally* id. §134; 2 Scott on Trusts §96.5.

[32]*See generally* Bogert, Trusts and Trustees §677.

[33]*See* Comptroller of the Currency Fiduciary Powers of National Banks and Collective Investment Funds, 12 C.F.R. 9 (1992).

[34]*See* Bogert, Trusts and Trustees §677.

[35]*See* id. §596.

[36]*See generally* 1 Whitney, Trust Department Administration and Operations §3.01[11] (1992).

[37]*See generally* Group of 30, Clearance and Settlement Systems in the World's Securities Markets (1988) (recommending a worldwide move to "dematerialize" securities).

[38]Id. at iii.

The trustee must take all reasonable steps to protect the trust property.[39] This duty is not delegable.[40] A necessary part of this general duty encompasses vigilant protection of the trust property against deterioration or loss.[41] Thus it is implicit in the so-called *prudent man rule* in all its manifestations, including the Restatement's recently adopted *prudent investor rule*, that the trustee, in investing the trust estate, must strive to protect trust principal from the ravages of inflation.[42] The trustee at trust expense should insure the trust property to the extent it is reasonable to do so.[43] Property taxes should be paid in a timely fashion to avoid a tax sale.[44] Also, the trustee may be liable if he permits stock subscription rights to expire.[45]

Claims owned by the trust estate must be enforced whether against strangers or against a predecessor trustee or the settlor's estate.[46] Thus a trustee who has reason to suspect that a cotrustee is depleting or about to deplete the trust property must take reasonable steps to prevent him from doing so.[47]

It is the duty of the trustee to defend actions affecting the trust estate.[48] Pursuant to this duty, the trustee has full power to sue on behalf of the trust estate and to defend suits in which it is involved or in which the trustee is involved as trustee.[49] All demands must be pressed, even to the extent of bringing suit,[50] or else the trustee will be liable for any loss caused by unjustified forbearance.[51] Under some circumstances, it may be in the economic interest of the beneficiaries, and therefore prudent and reasonable, to forbear or to compromise a claim or submit it to

[39]*See* Bogert, Trusts and Trustees §582; 2A Scott on Trusts §176.
[40]*See generally* 2A Scott on Trusts §171.
[41]*See* Restatement (Second) of Trusts §176 comments *b, c* (1959).
[42]*See* Restatement (Third) of Trusts §227 comment *e* (1992).
[43]*See* Bogert, Trusts and Trustees §599.
[44]*See id.* §602; 2A Scott on Trusts §176.
[45]*See* 2A Scott on Trusts §176 n.28 and accompanying text.
[46]*See id.* §177; Bogert, Trusts and Trustees §§592, 594.
[47]*See* Restatement (Third) of Trusts §184 comment *a* (1992).
[48]*See* 2A Scott on Trusts §178; Bogert, Trusts and Trustees §581.
[49]*See* Bogert, Trusts and Trustees §§594, 869.
[50]*See* 2A Scott on Trusts §177.
[51]Id.

arbitration.[52] Because of the attendant expense to the trust, the patently futile prosecution of a claim itself can constitute a breach of the specific duty to protect the trust property.[53] State statutes authorize a trustee to compromise, usually with court approval.[54]

§6.2.2 Duty to Make Trust Property Productive

The trustee has a specific duty to make the trust property productive, unless the settlor intended otherwise or it is impractical to do so.[55] This specific duty is an offshoot of the trustee's general duty to be prudent and the general duty to carry out the terms of the trust, particularly if the terms make provision for income beneficiaries.[56] Inherent in the duty to make the trust property productive is the duty, as well as right, to invest the trust property.[57] The "prudent man rule" in its original manifestation,[58] and as it has evolved in the various jurisdictions by statute and decision,[59] is designed to provide a safe harbor for the trustee carrying out investment responsibilities by holding the trustee to a standard of *conduct* rather than *performance*.[60]

---

[52]*See* Restatement (Second) of Trusts §192 (1959).

[53]*See* Restatement (Second) of Trusts §192 comment *c* (1959); 3 Scott on Trusts §192.

[54]*See* 3 Scott on Trusts §192.

[55]Restatement (Third) of Trusts §§181 comment *a*, 227 comment *a* (1992). *See generally* Bogert, Trusts and Trustees §611.

[56]Restatement (Third) of Trusts §227 comment *i* (1992).

[57]Id. comment *a*.

[58]Harvard College v. Amory, 26 Mass. (9 Pick.) 446, 461 (1830).

[59]*See generally* 3 Scott on Trusts §227.13.

[60]Restatement (Third) of Trusts §227 comment *b* (1992) (the Prudent Investor Rule). *See also* Bogert, Trusts and Trustees §612 n.23 and accompanying text. *But see* Washington Legal Found. v. Massachusetts Bar Found., 795 F. Supp. 50, 53 (D. Mass. 1992) ("[under Massachusetts law] the extent of a putative beneficiary's property interest is limited by the so-called 'prudent man doctrine' ").

§6.2.2.1   The *Harvard College* Prudent
Man Rule and Its Progeny

In *Harvard College v. Amory*,[61] the Supreme Judicial Court of Massachusetts set forth the following rule:

> All that can be required of a trustee to invest, is, that he shall conduct himself faithfully and exercise a sound discretion. He is to observe how men of prudence, discretion and intelligence manage their own affairs, not in regard to speculation, but in regard to the permanent disposition of their funds, considering the probable income, as well as the probable safety of the capital to be invested.[62]

Essentially, the trustee is to strike a reasonable balance between the extreme of the nonincome producing speculation that subverts the interests of the income beneficiary and the extreme of the wasting asset that subverts the interests of the remainderman. A middle ground, that allows for a reasonable flow of income and a reasonable rate of growth is the goal. Down through the years, many jurisdictions, either judicially or legislatively, have adopted some form of the rule. Some have adopted the rule almost verbatim;[63] others have tinkered with its language.[64] A few have rejected the rule in favor of the *legal list* and then returned to the rule with a renewed appreciation for its flexibility.[65]

The *Harvard College* Prudent Man Rule has proved remarkably adaptable to changing economic environments.[66] In 1974 Congress included a modified version of the rule in the Employee Retirement Income Security Act (the *Federal Prudent Man Rule*).[67]

Concern has been expressed that "much of the apparent and

---

[61]26 Mass. (9 Pick.) 446 (1830).

[62]Id. at 461.

[63]*See generally* 3 Scott on Trusts §227.5; Restatement (Third) of Trusts topic 5 (Investment of Trust Funds) introduction 3 (1992); Bogert, Trusts and Trustees §§612-613.

[64]*See, e.g.*, Bogert, Trusts and Trustees §§612 n.17 comment, 613 n.14.

[65]*See* 3 Scott on Trusts §227.13 (New York is a good example).

[66]*See* Berquist, The Prudent Man Rule in Massachusetts Today, 122 Tr. & Est. 44 (Dec. 1983).

[67]*See* Bogert, Trusts and Trustees §612 n.20.

initially intended generality and adaptability of the *Harvard College* prudent man rule [has been] lost as it [has been] elaborated in the courts and applied case by case."[68] To be sure, certain investment practices, as a practical matter, have come to be off-limits to even the most careful, skillful, and cautious of trustees (*e.g.*, engaging in futures and option trading and venture capital programs).[69] Moreover the clear distinction between income and principal implicit in the *Harvard College* Prudent Man Rule is being blurred by two relatively recent developments: (1) the eclipse of the income-only trust by the discretionary trust, and (2) the widespread acceptance of the *total return concept*.[70] Certainly a consensus is emerging that investment prudence should be judged not on the basis of each individual security in isolation but on the basis of the portfolio as a whole.[71] In 1992, the American Law Institute, in an effort to respond to these concerns and developments, published its *Prudent Investor Rule*:

§277 General Standard of Prudent Investment

The trustee is under a duty to the beneficiaries to invest and manage the funds of the trust as a prudent investor would, in light of the purposes, terms, distribution requirements, and other circumstances of the trust.

(a) This standard requires the exercise of reasonable care, skill, and caution, and it is to be applied to investments not in isolation but in the context of the trust portfolio and as a part of an overall investment strategy, which should incorporate risk and return objectives reasonably suitable to the trust. . . .[72]

What specific investments, then, are suitable for a trustee? That is a subject beyond the scope of this handbook and far better covered by others.[73] Suffice it to say that the traditional trust portfolio consists of a mix of equities (common stock) and indebt-

---

[68]*See* Restatement (Third) of Trusts topic 5 (Investment of Trust Funds) introduction 3 (1992).
[69]*See* id. §227 comment *f.*
[70]*See* id. §227 comment *i.*
[71]Id.
[72]Id. §227.
[73]Id. §227 comment *k.*

edness (*e.g.*, bonds, debentures, promissory notes, and money market instruments). [74] At one time, the prevailing practice was to weight the mix in favor of fixed income securities; today, the prevailing practice is to weight the mix in favor of equities. [75]

While investing in fixed income securities presumably generates a predictable stream of income, they can lose some of their real value in periods of inflation. [76] Equities, on the other hand, tend to keep pace with inflation but can lose their value in periods when the market is down. [77] "Do what you will, the capital is at hazard." [78] Thus the prudent trustee not only calls for a reasonable balance between equities and fixed income securities, but also diversification among economic sectors, geographical areas, and maturity dates, of course taking into account in the formulation of investment objectives the settlor's intentions. [79] In this regard, the trustee should be particularly careful to not improperly retain property received from the settlor or a prior fiduciary; the closely held business, the stock with sentimental value, and the unproductive real estate holding are common traps for the unwary. [80]

What specific investments are then improper for trustees? The drafters of the Prudent Investor Rule would say that it depends on the facts and circumstances of the particular trust [81] — *no* investment is considered per se imprudent or prudent. [82] It must be noted that the Restatement's rule has been adopted only by Illinois, [83] although six states have independently updated their rules of prudent investing to accommodate concepts of modern portfolio theory. Up to now, at least, some investments have been deemed per se imprudent: enterprises lacking in seasoned perfor-

---

[74]Id. *See also* comments *l* and *m*.

[75]Id. comment *l*.

[76]Id.

[77]Id.

[78]*Harvard College*, 26 Mass. at 461.

[79]*See* Restatement (Third) of Trusts §227 comments *e-h* (1992).

[80]*See generally* 3 Scott on Trusts §230.

[81]*See* Restatement (Third) of Trusts §227 comment *k* (1992).

[82]*See* id.

[83]*See* Ill. Ann. Stat. ch. 760, 5/5 (1973), as amended by P.A. 87-715 (1992); Restatement (Third) of Trusts §227 reporter's note (1992).

mance as to safety and yield;[84] junior mortgages;[85] wasting assets (*e.g.*, leaseholds, royalties, patents, oil wells, natural gas wells, timberlands, and coal mines);[86] most family businesses;[87] other speculations of one sort or another.[88] It goes without saying that under any rule, investments in any enterprise in which the trustee has a personal interest is off-limits.[89]

Once the trust property is well invested, the investments should not be changed without good reason. The trustee should strive to assess market panics or dramatic inflations in market values with professional detachment. It is not the duty of the trustee to follow the ticker as might a speculator, but when a company in which trust funds are invested shows a threatened lack of earnings or there is an actual suspension of interest or dividends, the investment should be liquidated.

If a trust security has acquired a speculative value much above its true value as an investment, it is obviously time to reduce the trust's position in that investment, if not sell out altogether.[90] And yet a mere increase in market value is not enough, for the doctrine "can readily be pressed so far as to sanction a practice of trading and trafficking in trust securities, which would be attended with dangerous results to the trust fund."[91]

§6.2.2.2   The Prudent Investor's Code of Conduct

The *Harvard College* Prudent Man Rule and its progeny are rules of conduct, not performance. While the prudence of the

---

[84]*See generally* Bogert, Trusts and Trustees §§612, 679. *But see* Restatement (Third) of Trusts §227 comment *l* (1992).
[85]*See* Bogert, Trusts and Trustees §674. *But see* Restatement (Third) of Trusts §227 comment *n* (1992).
[86]*See* Bogert, Trusts and Trustees §827.
[87]Id. §§571-577.
[88]Id. §612.
[89]Id. §543.
[90]*See* 3 Scott on Trusts §231.
[91]New England Trust Co. v. Eaton, 140 Mass. 532, 537, 4 N.E. 69, 72 (1886).

trustee's conduct will be judged in light of the facts and circumstances applicable in a given situation, there are some long-accepted indicia of prudent conduct. At minimum the trustee should always:

(1) decide whether to accept a trust only after making an exhaustive examination of the trust portfolio and only after a thorough audit of the accountings of the prior fiduciary is completed;[92]

(2) require, before taking on a trusteeship, that a predecessor fiduciary remedy any breaches of fiduciary duty and cleanse the portfolio of improper investments, absent compelling reasons to do otherwise;[93]

(3) upon accepting a trusteeship, immediately take control of all property belonging to the trust and set about cleansing the portfolio of improper investments;[94]

(4) understand the intentions of the settlor as they are expressed in the governing instrument and invest accordingly;[95]

(5) investigate each investment, personally monitor the portfolio on a regular basis, and respond to changed circumstances in a timely fashion to the extent a response is deemed appropriate;[96]

(6) obtain expert investment advice as appropriate;[97]

(7) maintain reasonable diversification at all times, unless it is clearly the intention of the settlor that this not be done;[98]

(8) maintain an adequate cushion of liquidity so that the

---

[92]*See generally* Bogert, Trusts and Trustees §684.

[93]*See generally* Restatement (Second) of Trusts §223 (1959).

[94]Bogert, Trusts and Trustees §583.

[95]Id. §683.

[96]Id. §612.

[97]Id. *See also* §§555, 556, 701. *See generally* Restatement (Third) of Trusts §171 (1992).

[98]*See* 3 Scott on Trusts §228.

cash needs of the trust may be accommodated in an orderly fashion;[99]

(9) understand that no capital is risk-free and that even insured bank accounts and fixed income government issues are "at hazard" in that their value erodes with inflation, and act upon that understanding;[100]

(10) invest for the long term unless there is a legitimate reason not to do so;[101]

(11) keep all trust property invested at all times unless there is a legitimate reason not to do so;[102]

(12) keep meticulous permanent records of all investment research, deliberations, and decisions.[103]

(13) assess in advance the tax consequences of contemplated investment changes.

Adherence to this code of conduct does not mean that the trustee will be immune from suit for improper investing, but it will help to show that the trustee's conduct was prudent.

§6.2.3   Duty of Confidentiality

An offshoot of the trustee's general duty of loyalty is the specific duty to keep all the affairs of the trust confidential.[104] The trustee's duty to act solely in the interest of the beneficiaries means that third parties are told only what the law requires the trustee to divulge or what furthers the interests of all the beneficiaries.[105] An unauthorized disclosure of information pertaining to the trust or pertaining to a beneficiary is a breach of the duty of loyalty and, at minimum, grounds for removal.[106]

---

[99]*See generally* Bogert, Trusts and Trustees §612.

[100]*See* id. §612 n.90. *See also* Restatement (Third) of Trusts §227 comment *e* (1992).

[101]*See generally* Bogert, Trusts and Trustees §612.

[102]*See generally* id. §611.

[103]*See generally* id. §962.

[104]*See* Restatement (Third) of Trusts §170 comment *s* (1992).

[105]Id. §170; *see also* 2A Scott on Trusts §170.

[106]*See* Bogert, Trusts and Trustees §527.

§6.2.4   Duty to Separate Income from Principal and the Right to Income

Unless a contrary intention is expressed in the governing instrument, one class of beneficiaries will get the income or use of the trust property and another will ultimately get the principal free of trust.[107] As a matter of law, unless the settlor intended otherwise, a life beneficiary is entitled to the net income as it accrues.[108] It must be distributed periodically at reasonable intervals.[109] Thus, one offshoot of the trustee's general duty to carry out the terms of the trust will likely be the specific duty to separately account for income and principal.[110]

This is a critical duty. The determination where to credit a receipt or debit an expense directly affects the property interests of the life beneficiary and the remainderman: A receipt credited to income will benefit the life beneficiary whereas a receipt credited to principal will benefit the remainderman.

A trustee is also under a duty to act impartially. Thus, the trustee must be careful to distinguish between principal and income with regard both to receipts and expenditures so that neither the life beneficiary nor the remainderman will be deprived of what is due to each.

The trustee must decide what qualifies as income and what

---

[107]*See generally* 3A Scott on Trusts §232.

[108]Note, however, that a life beneficiary is entitled to income in the form of corporate distributions to stockholders once the distribution becomes payable to shareholders of record on a designated date after the creation of the beneficial interest. *See generally* Restatement (Second) of Trusts §236. Income in the form of periodic payments such as interest and rents, however, is treated as accruing from day to day. *See generally* Restatement (Second) of Trusts §235 comment *a* (1959). *See also* Revised Uniform Principal and Income Act §4, 7B U.L.A. 157 (1985).

[109]Although the trustee is not obligated to distribute income upon receipt, it is reasonable, where the trust does not specify the frequency of income payments, to distribute income semiannually or quarterly. *See generally* 2A Scott on Trusts §182; Bogert, Trusts and Trustees §814. It might in fact be reasonable in certain instances for the trustee to withhold income to build up a reserve for payment of future expenditures. Id.

[110]*See generally* 2A Scott on Trusts §183. *See also* Bogert, Trusts and Trustees §816.

qualifies as principal for trust accounting purposes. For guidance the trustee should look to the law that governs the administration of the trust.[111] Some jurisdictions have comprehensive legislation that, unless contrary to the governing instrument, determines allocation issues and apportionment issues.[112] Others rely less on a statutory framework and more on the common law and the generally accepted practices of the jurisdiction.[113] Of course if the terms of the trust direct where a receipt is to be credited or where an expense is to be debited, then the trust term controls.[114] Deviation by the trustee, without any special circumstances or prior court approval, would be a breach of trust. Above all the trustee must understand that the rules governing what is income for tax purposes are separate from the rules governing what is allocated to income for trust accounting purposes.[115] An IRD receipt, for example, may be income for tax purposes but principal for trust accounting purposes.[116]

[111]When the terms of the trust provide neither for the allocation of receipts and expenses nor for the applicable law, a conflict of laws question may arise. *See* 4A Scott on Trusts §586. The trustee or court may resolve such questions by ascertaining the intention of the settlor. Otherwise, matters of administration might be resolved through application of the law of the place of administration, and matters of construction might be resolved through application of the law of the settlor's domicile. Id. *See generally* J. A. Schoenblum, 1 Multistate and Multinational Estate Planning §17 (1982).

[112]For a catalog of state legislation applicable to the allocation of income and principal and the apportionment of expenses, see Bogert, Trusts and Trustees §816 nn.64-66.

[113]*See generally* Bogert, Trusts and Trustees §816 n.67 and accompanying text.

[114]*See generally* 2A Scott on Trusts §164.

[115]*See* Bogert, Trusts and Trustees §816. The trustee should note that the economic theories that form the basis for principles of accounting for tax purposes and of accounting for trust purposes differ substantially. *See* Bogert, Trusts and Trustees §816 n.63 and accompanying text.

[116]Receipt of income in respect of a decedent (*IRD receipt*) is income received to which a decedent had rights prior to death but which was not payable or collected until after death. *See generally* M. C. Ferguson et al., Federal Income Taxation of Estates, Trusts, and Beneficiaries §3.3 (2d ed. 1993). Once the receipt is paid, it must be included in the gross income of the estate or trust of the decedent for the taxable year when received. I.R.C. §691(a)(1) (1992). For trust accounting purposes, however, the receipt is treated as principal. *See* Revised Uniform Principal and Income Act §4(b)(1), 7B U.L.A. 157 (1985) ("receipts due but not paid at the date of death of the testator are principal").

§6.2.4.1   What Receipts Are Allocated to Income for Trust Accounting Purposes?

The ordinary current receipts of a trust are income. They should be credited to the income account and distributed, after making provision for ordinary expenses, to the beneficiary who is entitled to receive income.[117] This includes: routine rents; ordinary and extraordinary cash dividends; items of current interest;[118] accrued increment on bonds or other obligations issued at discount;[119] shares in a corporation other than the distributing corporation;[120] a pro rata share of the income earned during administration of the settlor's estate.[121] As to extraordinary cash dividends, the majority rule is that they belong to income, although some jurisdictions have held that they are apportionable between income and principal.[122]

§6.2.4.2   What Receipts Are Allocated to Principal for Trust Accounting Purposes?

Proceeds from the sale of trust property are considered principal; thus, realized capital gains, although income for tax pur-

---

[117]Ordinary current receipts will generally include the earnings, profits, and products that result from use or investment of the trust corpus. See 3A Scott on Trusts §233.1. Ordinary receipts that indicate merely a change in the form of the corpus, however, are not to be credited to the income account but are retained as principal. Id. See also Bogert, The Law of Trusts and Trustees §816. The Revised Uniform Principal and Income Act provides rules for the allocation of most receipts. Revised Uniform Principal and Income Act §3, 7B U.L.A. 154 (1985). For a catalog of states where the Act has been adopted, see Bogert, Trusts and Trustees §816 nn.64, 65.

[118]See 3A Scott on Trusts §233.1.

[119]Id. See also Revised Uniform Principal and Income Act §7, 7B U.L.A. 165 (1985).

[120]A dividend in the form of shares in a corporation other than the distributing corporation is generally allocable as income unless the dividend is declared out of capital. 3A Scott on Trusts §236.5.

[121]See 3A Scott on Trusts §234.4.

[122]See id. §236.4.

poses, are considered items of principal for trust accounting purposes.[123] So also are most distributions of stock, including ordinary and extraordinary stock dividends, subscription rights, and dividends in liquidation.[124] Additional shares resulting from stock splits are of course items of principal, as are capital gain distributions from mutual funds.[125]

§6.2.4.3   What Receipts Are Apportioned Between the Income and Principal Accounts?

The money received by way of "yield" from a wasting investment presents a peculiar problem.[126] Such a yield involves a continuing dissipation of principal to the economic detriment of the remainderman.[127] In order to be impartial, therefore, the trustee should set aside some part of the yield to protect the remainderman from this gradual loss.[128] Examples of wasting investments

---

[123]Bogert, Trusts and Trustees §§822-823 (1984).

[124]For a discussion of the rules of allocation for ordinary and extraordinary stock dividends, including the distinction between the "Massachusetts rule" and the "Pennsylvania rule," see 3A Scott on Trusts §§236.3-236.8. For a discussion of the treatment of rights to subscribe to shares of stock and the treatment of dividends in liquidation, see id., §§236.9-236.10.

[125]The recent trend among jurisdictions has been adoption of the "Massachusetts rule" which holds that stock dividends, whether announced as stock dividends or as stock splits, are principal. See 3A Scott on Trusts §236.3. There are, however, some jurisdictions where legislation provides guidelines for apportionment. See id. §236.3 n.7 (citing New York and Pennsylvania legislation that provides that both stock splits and stock dividends are treated as income if made at the rate of six percent or less of the existing shares).

[126]A *wasting asset* is one whose value will depreciate or be destroyed in time because it currently benefits the life beneficiary at the expense of the remainderman, leaving the remainderman with an asset of little or no value. See generally 3A Scott on Trusts §239; Bogert, Trusts and Trustees §827; Revised Uniform Principal and Income Act §§9-11, 7B U.L.A. 168 (1985).

[127]See 3A Scott on Trusts §239.

[128]Id. The Revised Uniform Principal and Income Act sets specific guidelines for apportioning receipts from wasting assets such as minerals and other natural resources, timber, royalties, patents, and so forth. See Revised Uniform Principal and Income Act §§9-11, 7B U.L.A. 168 (1985).

are copyrights, patents, royalties, leaseholds, and property subject to depletion.[129]

The apportionment of wasting assets is purely a matter of calculation. It may be done by fixing the value of the property at the time of creation of the trust and paying the life tenant from time to time that part of the yield which would equal the usual rate of return in trust investments.[130] It also may be done by apportioning the proceeds of sale when the property is sold.[131] The decisions in cases involving mining operations, quarries, and oil wells are numerous and diverse in their holdings.[132] Obviously if the instrument shows that the life beneficiary is to enjoy all benefits of wasting property, neither amortization of receipts nor apportionment of proceeds is necessary.[133]

Under the common law, the trustee had a duty to the remainderman to amortize bond premiums.[134] Thus, the purchase of a bond at a price in excess of its face amount called for the allocation of some of the bond income, as it was received, to the principal account.[135] The Revised Uniform Principal and Income Act has relieved the trustee of this duty.[136] It should be noted that, for purposes of tax accounting, premiums on purchases on tax-exempt bonds must be amortized.[137]

The Act treats the matter of wasting assets in this way:

> Except as provided in sections 9 and 10, if the principal consists of property subject to depletion, including leaseholds, patents, copyrights, royalty rights, and rights to receive payments on a contract

[129]*See generally* 3A Scott on Trusts §239.

[130]*See* id. §§239 n.4, 241.4.

[131]*See* id.

[132]For a general discussion of the wide range of holdings among the jurisdictions in this area, see 3A Scott on Trusts §239.3.

[133]*See generally* id. §239.1.

[134]Id. §239.2.

[135]Id.

[136]The Act provides that no provision is required for amortization of bond premiums except for bonds payable in the future in accordance with a fixed appreciation schedule. Revised Uniform Principal and Income Act §7, 7B U.L.A. 165 (1985).

[137]For the federal tax treatment of premiums paid in purchasing tax-exempt bonds, see I.R.C. §171 (1992).

for deferred compensation, receipts from the property, not in excess of 5% per year of its inventory value, are income, and the balance is principal. [138]

Sometimes the trust property includes a building that generates income. Should a trustee apportion some of this income to principal to establish a depreciation reserve? The majority of cases on this issue hold that a trustee is not required to establish a reserve for depreciation. [139] Furthermore some cases hold that it is not proper for the trustee to establish a reserve. [140] Thus, absent a contrary intention, it appears a trustee has no power to establish a reserve. [141]

On the other hand, nonincome producing property works a hardship on the beneficiary. [142] Thus, upon the sale of such property, an appropriate portion of the proceeds should be allocated to the income account unless a fair reading of the governing instrument suggests that the settlor intended otherwise. [143] Likewise the proceeds from the settlement of a note long in default should be appropriately apportioned between both accounts. [144] When the proceeds are brought into the hands of the trustee, a

[138]Revised Uniform Principal and Income Act §11, 7B U.L.A. 172 (1985).

[139]For a catalog of cases that hold that the trustee has no duty to establish a reserve for depreciation of a building held by a trust, see 3A Scott on Trusts §239.4 n.2.

[140]For a catalog of cases that hold it improper for a trustee to establish a reserve for the depreciation of a building held by a trust, see 3A Scott on Trusts §239.4 n.4.

[141]See id. §239.4.

[142]Id. §240.

[143]As a general rule, where unproductive property is held by the trust due to direction by the settlor or a delay in the sale of the nonproductive asset, the net proceeds are apportioned between principal and income by determining the principal amount that, when earning interest at the current rate of return on trust investments for the amount of time during which the nonproductive asset was held by the trust, will yield interest equal to the net proceeds minus that principal amount. See id. §241.1. See also Bogert, Trusts and Trustees §824; Restatement (Second) of Trusts §241(2) (1959). Cf. Revised Uniform Principal and Income Act §12, 7B U.L.A. 173 (1985) (income should be determined as if principal had been invested to yield four percent per annum).

[144]A default in interest payment on a bond may be an example of a productive asset which becomes nonproductive. See generally 3A Scott on Trusts §§240.3, 241.3-241.3A.

calculation is made which attempts to award to the life tenant the income which would have been received if the unproductive property actually had produced at a current rate of return.[145] In the case of unproductive property, an income allocation is appropriate even when a particular investment has resulted in a capital loss.[146]

Absent a contrary intention expressed in the instrument, a trustee is under a duty to the income beneficiary to sell the unproductive property within a reasonable time.[147] The rules expressed herein also apply to *under*productive property.[148] Thus if property that produces income substantially less than the current rate of return on trust investments is held, the trustee, absent a contrary intention, should make an apportionment when the property is sold.[149] Also, absent a contrary intention, the trustee should within a reasonable time sell underproductive property.[150]

§6.2.4.4   What Expenses Are Allocated Entirely to Income, Entirely to Principal, and Apportioned Between Income and Principal?

Expenses that are connected with the everyday administration of the trust property are chargeable entirely to income. Examples include ordinary repairs to real estate, annual real property taxes, insurance premiums, and legal expenses in-

---

[145]*See supra* note 143.

[146]Restatement (Second) of Trusts §241 comment *b* (1959).

[147]3A Scott on Trusts §240; *see also* Restatement (Second) of Trusts §240 (1959).

[148]*See* 3A Scott on Trusts §240; Restatement (Second) of Trusts §240 comment *b* (1959).

[149]The trustee, when allocating proceeds from the sale of underproductive property, must modify the general rule for allocating proceeds from the sale of unproductive property (as explained *supra* note 143) to account for the small income received as well as for the associated carrying charges of the underproductive asset. *See* 3A Scott on Trusts §241.1.

[150]*See supra* note 147.

curred in collecting income.[151] Income taxes attributable to trust accounting income are charged to income.[152]

Expenses incurred primarily for the protection and preservation of the principal are chargeable entirely to principal. This includes legal expenses that relate to the interpretation of the trust or the behavior of the trustee; alterations and additions to real estate; expenses for preparation of property for rental or sale; income taxes on capital gains; brokers' commissions; the costs of a guardian ad litem appointed to represent remainder interests; and the expenses of making final distribution.[153]

Some expenses are chargeable in part to income and in part to principal, such as trustee's fees and costs of periodic accountings that pertain both to the income and the remainder interests.[154]

The trust may include property that does not produce any current income. Where should the expenses of the unproductive property be charged? The answer to this difficult question depends upon the terms of the trust. Generally, the current as well as extraordinary expenses of unproductive property are payable from principal unless the terms of the trust provide otherwise.[155]

---

[151]The Revised Uniform Principal and Income Act provides that "ordinary expenses" are chargeable against income. Revised Uniform Principal and Income Act §13(a), 7B U.L.A. 175 (1985). *See generally* 3A Scott on Trusts §233.2; Bogert, Trusts and Trustees §802.

[152]Revised Uniform Principal and Income Act §13(a)(6), 7B U.L.A. 176 (1985).

[153]Id. §13(c). *See generally* 3A Scott on Trusts §233.3.

[154]Revised Uniform Principal and Income Act §13(a)(3), 7B U.L.A. 176 (1985). Ordinary practice is to pay the trustee a commission on income earned that is chargeable against income. *See* 3A Scott on Trusts §233.3. The trustee is also ordinarily paid a commission, either upon acceptance of the trust or upon the distribution of principal, which is chargeable against principal. Id. To determine how any other service is to be charged, the nature of the service must be considered. Id. *See also* Bogert, Trusts and Trustees §975. *Cf.* Revised Uniform Principal and Income Act §13(a)(5), 7B U.L.A. 176 (1985) ("one half of trustee's regular compensation, whether a percentage of principal or income, and all expenses reasonably incurred for current management of principal and application of income" are chargeable against income).

[155]Where the trustee by terms of the trust is directed to sell unproductive property, and the property is not immediately sold, the ordinary expenses of carrying the property should generally be charged to principal. *See* 3A Scott on Trusts §233.4. *See also* Restatement (Second) of Trusts §233 comment *m*

It should be noted that some jurisdictions require a trustee to adjust the income and principal amounts when certain tax elections upset the equilibrium between the competing equitable interests.[156] Let us take a residuary testamentary trust, for example. Administration expenses paid from the principal of the probate estate are elected to be taken as an income tax deduction, rather than as an estate tax deduction. This reduces the taxable income of, but not the income actually paid to, the life beneficiary. Some jurisdictions require that some income be transferred to the principal account so that the trust remainderman is compensated for not benefitting from an estate tax deduction (and so that the income beneficiary is not given a free ride.)[157]

§6.2.4.5   When Does Income Begin and What Happens to Accrued But Undistributed Income When the Trust's Term Expires or the Beneficiary Dies?

The beneficiary of a trust is entitled to income earned on the trust property computed back to the date the trust is deemed to arise.[158] Thus, in the case of a trust that will receive a portion or all of the residue of the settlor's estate, income will accrue to the trust beneficiary from the date of the settlor's death even though there will be some time thereafter before the trust actually receives a distribution from the settlor's estate.[159]

In most states this includes income earned on funds used to pay enforceable debts, taxes, and expenses of administration.[160]

(1959). However, if the terms of the trust direct the trustee to retain unproductive property, it is assumed that the settlor intended carrying costs to be paid out of income. 3A Scott on Trusts §233.4.

[156]*See, e.g.,* Matter of Warms, 140 N.Y.S.2d 169 (Sur. Ct. 1955).

[157]*See generally* M. L. Ferguson et al., Federal Income Taxation of Estates, Trusts and Beneficiaries §4.2.6 (1993).

[158]*See* 3A Scott on Trusts §234.

[159]Id.

[160]For a catalog of states where income earned by the assets of the estate used to pay debts, taxes, and administrative expenses is payable to the life

A specific devise of property or a specific legacy of property to a trustee carries with it the income earned on the property.[161] In some cases the settlor will create a trust by a general pecuniary legacy. When the executor distributes the pecuniary legacy to the trustee, the general rule is the trustee is entitled to a proportionate share of the income earned by the estate during its administration.[162] When estate property is transferred to a trustee by the settlor's executor the trustee has a duty to review the executor's account to determine that the trust has received its share of income.[163] Periodic rental, interest, and annuity payments that continue after the testator's death accrue on a daily basis.[164] Thus periodic payments accruing to the testator before his or her death are items of trust principal, and payments accruing afterward are items of trust income.[165] "In all other cases, any receipt from an income producing asset is income even though the receipt was earned or accrued in whole or in part before the date when the asset became subject to the trust."[166]

On termination of an income interest under a trust that is up and running, the beneficiary or his estate receives income then having been earned but undistributed.[167] If the day fixed by a corporation for determining which stockholders of record are entitled to a dividend comes before the termination date of the trust, the dividend goes to the beneficiary or the beneficiary's estate even though the dividend is not mailed out until after the termination date.[168] Unpaid rents, interest, and annuities accrue on a daily basis to the beneficiary up to the date of termination.[169] If the beneficiary's death triggers the termination, then

---

beneficiary, see 3A Scott on Trusts §234.4 n.1. *See generally* Revised Uniform Principal and Income Act §5, 7B U.L.A. 160 (1985).

[161]*See* 3A Scott on Trusts §234.1.

[162]*See* id. §234.2.

[163]*See generally* id. §177. *See also* Bogert, Trusts and Trustees §817 n.11.

[164]Revised Uniform Principal and Income Act §4(b)(2), 7B U.L.A. 157 (1985).

[165]Id.

[166]Id. §4(c).

[167]Id. §4(d).

[168]Id. §4(e).

[169]Id. §4(d).

accrued income will be paid to the beneficiary's estate.[170] These income accrual rules apply unless the settlor expressed a contrary intention in the governing instrument.[171] As most modern trust instruments will address the matter of undistributed and accrued income, the trustee is likely to find the answers to most accrual questions simply by reading the governing instrument.

§6.2.5   Duty of Impartiality

A difficult aspect of the trustee's general duty of loyalty is the specific duty to treat all beneficiaries impartially, that is, not to favor one beneficiary over another unless authorized to do so by the governing instrument.[172] And even when so authorized the trustee's discretionary acts favoring one beneficiary over another must be in furtherance of the intentions of the settlor, not in furtherance of the trustee's own biases and predilections.[173] However, the greatest risk of breaching the duty of impartiality is run not in the context of discretionary distributions but in the context of the competing interests of income beneficiaries and remaindermen.[174]

In the absence of the settlor's contrary intention, the trustee has a duty to separate income from principal and then to distribute the net income to the income beneficiary and eventually to turn over the principal free of trust to the remaindermen.[175] This is implied by the trustee's general duty to carry out the terms of the trust. The general duty of loyalty however, requires that the trustee balance the interests of the income beneficiaries and the remaindermen — in other words, *the trustee must be impartial when dealing with those with conflicting equitable interests.*[176]

---

[170]Restatement (Second) of Trusts §235A (1959).

[171]*See generally* 3A Scott on Trusts §234.

[172]2A Scott on Trusts §183; Restatement (Third) of Trusts §183 (1992).

[173]*Supra* note 172.

[174]3A Scott on Trusts §232; Restatement (Third) of Trusts §232 comment *b* (1992).

[175]*See* §6.2.4.

[176]2A Scott on Trusts §183; Restatement (Third) of Trusts §183 (1992).

This is easier said than done: For example, who should bear the burden of the insurance premium, the income account or the principal account?[177] The difficulty in balancing competing equitable interests manifests itself most dramatically, however, in matters of *investment* and of *disclosure of information.*

With respect to investments, the trustee has traditionally walked a tightrope. Investing for maximum income may sacrifice growth, to the displeasure of the remainderman;[178] investing for maximum growth may cause the income beneficiary to complain.[179] This is an inevitable outgrowth of the traditional distinction between income and principal, a trust accounting concept that takes no account of the investment concept of *total return.*[180]

The *Harvard College* Prudent Man Rule and its progeny[181] acknowledge these conflicting interests and attempt to balance them. It was first enunciated at a time when the psychological wall between the income beneficiary and the remainderman was higher than it is today. Then, income-only trusts and use-only trusts involving land were the rule;[182] now, settlors tend to bestow on their trustees considerable discretionary authority, particularly the authority to invade principal for the benefit of the life beneficiary and to accumulate income for the benefit of the remaindermen.[183] Also, in the last 50 years the discretionary trust has come into its

[177]*See* §6.2.4.4.

[178]*See* Dennis v. Rhode Island Hosp. Trust Natl. Bank, 744 F.2d 893, 897 (1st Cir. 1984) (In holding the trustee liable to the remaindermen the court said: "[T]here is evidence that the trustee did little more than routinely agree to the requests of the trust's income beneficiaries that it manage the trust corpus to produce the largest possible income.").

[179]In in re Francis M. Johnson Trust, 211 Neb. 750, 320 N.W.2d 466, 469 (1982), the trustees held onto stock in a corporation that paid no dividends and upon dissolution of the corporation allocated a part of the gain to income. A minor beneficiary challenged the allocation. Although the court held the allocation to be a proper exercise of discretion, it did say: "Trustees may not, however, sacrifice income for the purpose of increasing the value of the principal of the trust."

[180]*See* Restatement (Third) of Trusts §227 comment *e* (1992).

[181]*See* id.; Harvard College v. Amory, 26 Mass. (9 Pick.) 446, 461 (1830). *See also* 3 Scott on Trusts §227.

[182]Bogert, Trusts and Trustees §§5-8.

[183]*See generally* Restatement (Third) of Trusts §227 comment *i* (1992).

own,[184] bringing about some practical blurring of the distinctions between the life beneficiary and the remainderman. However it remains the general rule that a trustee has a duty to be impartial in investment matters.

When it comes to the disclosure of information, the conflicting interests of the income class and the remainder class can put the trustee between a rock and a hard place. As we have seen, an incident of the trustee's general duty to account is the specific duty of disclosure,[185] while at the same time an incident of the trustee's general duty of loyalty is the specific duty of confidentiality.[186] What is a trustee to do if disclosures to the remainderman would violate the confidences of the income beneficiary? Suppose the income beneficiary's alcoholism was the basis for a proper exercise of the trustee's discretion to invade principal. Should the income beneficiary's medical history be disclosed to the remainderman? In theory the answer lies in another specific duty: the duty to balance the interests of the life beneficiary and the remainderman. Probably the best way out of this impasse is for the trustee to provide the remaindermen with only so much information about the income beneficiary as they need to protect their interest, in this case to determine whether the trustee has committed an abuse of discretion.[187] In the example at hand, what this means is harder to say. They are certainly not entitled to the medical file, but they should not be stonewalled either.

§6.3   Governmental Reporting Obligations

The trustee must be attentive to federal and state governmental reporting obligations. In addition to those obligations arising

[184]2A Scott on Trusts §155.

[185]*See* §6.1.5.

[186]*See* §6.2.3.

[187]*See generally* Bogert, Trusts and Trustees §961; 2A Scott on Trusts §173.

under the tax and securities laws, the trustee of a pension trust may be required to file periodic reports with the Department of Labor; the trustee of a charitable trust with the state attorney general; the corporate trustee with the Comptroller of the Currency or state banking commissioner; and so forth. Do not forget property tax filings with City Hall and of course abatement notices. The list of governmental reports and filings is long and will vary from jurisdiction to jurisdiction. A caution is therefore in order: This handbook presents only a few of the more common reports and filings.

§6.3.1   Tax Filings

After a trust becomes irrevocable it is likely to be treated as a separate taxable entity for federal and state tax purposes.[1] If the trust does not already have an Employer Identification Number at that time one must be applied for on Form SS-4.[2] For any year in which the trust has taxable income or gross income exceeding $600 the trustee must file a federal fiduciary income tax return, Form 1041, on April 15 of the following year.[3] Beneficiaries are notified of taxable and nontaxable distributions on the form's Schedule K-1. While the K-1 must be in the hands of the beneficiaries by April 15, it is good practice for the trustee to do so sooner in order that the beneficiaries may prepare their own tax returns in a timely fashion. The trust's estimated tax payments are due April 15, June 15, September 15, and January 15.[4] The trust's federal income tax must be carefully estimated, since the trustee who substantially and negligently overpays may be personally liable for interest on the overpayment, while the consequences of substantially and negligently underpaying taxes

---

§6.3 [1]In matters involving the income taxation of trusts, the trustee is referred to Ferguson, Freeland & Ascher, Federal Income Taxation of Estates, Trusts, and Beneficiaries (2d ed. 1993).

[2]*See* 26 C.F.R. §301.6109-1 (1992).

[3]*See* Bogert, Trusts and Trustees §265.

[4]Id.

include personal liability for any penalties that may be assessed as a result of the underpayment. Further, many states impose a tax on the trust's taxable income. This may impose certain state tax reporting and payment obligations on the trustee.

The generation-skipping tax on certain transfers is a relatively new tax which places additional tax-reporting burdens on trustees.[5] A federal GST tax payment obligation may arise upon one or more of the following events: (1) a trust's creation, (2) a trust's termination, and (3) a distribution of principal or income from a trust.[6] If either the trust itself or the recipient of the property interest enjoys an exemption, a federal GST tax may *not* be due.[7] The tax is generally separate from and independent of the federal estate, gift, and income tax. Under certain circumstances, the trustee may be obliged to file a GST tax return[8] as well as pay the tax due. For some GSTs, the trustee files an informational return and provides the recipient with data that the recipient will need to prepare the GST tax return and pay the tax. In matters related to the GST tax the prudent trustee communicates and coordinates with the settlor's executor and the trust beneficiaries as appropriate, and raises any cash needed to pay the tax in an orderly and timely fashion.

The trustee of an Individual Retirement Account or Simplified Employee Plan IRA (SEP-IRA) is required to make yearly reports to the IRS and to the taxpayer on the status of the account.[9] Employee benefit plan trustees must report distributions to participants on Form 1099-R.[10]

---

[5] I.R.C. §2601; *see generally* Stephens et al., Federal Estate and Gift Taxation ¶12.03[1] (6th ed. 1991).

[6] Id. at ¶13.02.

[7] Id.

[8] Id. at ¶18.02. For information on when and under what circumstances such returns must be filed, as well as other matters related to the federal generation-skipping-transfer tax, the trustee is referred to Stephens et al., *supra* note 5.

[9] *See* Treas. Reg. §§1.408-5–1.408-9.

[10] A complete list of federal tax forms (as well as the forms themselves) may be found in *IRS Forms*, published by Tax Management Inc., a subsidiary of the Bureau of National Affairs, Inc., 1231 25th St. NW, Washington DC 20037-1197.

§6.3.2   SEC Filings

When the trust acquires voting rights or a power of disposition over more than five percent of a class of registered securities, the trustee *may* have to report the event to the Securities and Exchange Commission, the issuer, and each exchange on which the security is traded.[11] The same may be necessary when the trust acquires voting rights or a power of disposition over more than ten percent of a class of registered securities.[12]

§6.3.3   Bank Regulatory Filings

Each national bank that exercises fiduciary powers must periodically submit reports to a myriad of governmental agencies,[13] including the Comptroller of the Currency.

---

[11]*See generally* Victor P. Whitney, 2 Trust Dept. Admin. & Operations §15.10 (1993).

[12]In matters relating to the trustee's SEC reporting obligations, the trustee is referred to Louis Loss's and Joel Seligman's Securities Regulation (3d ed. 1992).

[13]See Whitney, *supra* note 11, for a list of these reports.

CHAPTER 7

The Trustee's Liabilities

§7.1 Trustee's Liabilities Generally

The trustee is liable to the beneficiary for injury caused by negligent and intentional breaches of trust. There are some breaches, however, for which the trustee may be held absolutely liable even when acting in good faith. The trustee, for example, is absolutely liable for injury to the beneficiary's equitable interest occasioned by misdelivery[1] or by the trustee's misconstruing the nature and extent of the trustee's powers.[2] There are also some breaches for which the trustee may be held liable even in the

---

§7.1 [1]*See* Restatement (Second) of Trusts §226 comments *a, b* (1959).
[2]*See* Restatement (Second) of Trusts §201 comment *b* (1959).

absence of a causal connection between the injury and the breach,[3] such as the failure to segregate and earmark[4] and engaging in unauthorized acts of self-dealing. As a general rule, however, the trustee is not liable to the beneficiary if the trust sustains economic injury (*e.g.,* investment losses or poor investment performance) unless there has been a breach of trust.

Under the common law, the trustee, as holder of the legal title to the trust property, is liable in contract and in tort to nonbeneficiaries as if the trustee were the absolute owner of the property,[5] although under certain circumstances indemnification and reimbursement from the trust estate for such third-party liability may be possible.[6]

§7.2 Trustee's Liability as Fiduciary to the Beneficiary

The trustee is accountable to the beneficiary for breaches of fiduciary duties. These duties are enumerated and discussed in Chapter 6 of this handbook. Much difficulty could be avoided if the trustee took the time to learn each of these many duties. Specificity is the key. A general uninformed concern about "fiduciary duty" will not keep the trustee out of trouble. On the other hand, the beneficiary who puts forth the general allegation of "breach of fiduciary duty" should be called upon to elaborate. Which duty? How was it breached? Was the breach intentional or negligent?

The remedies available to the beneficiary are not available to a stranger to the trust. They are available, however, to anyone hav-

---

[3]*See generally* 3 Scott on Trusts §205.1.

[4]*See* Restatement (Third) of Trusts §205 comment *f* (1992).

[5]*See generally* Bogert, Trusts and Trustees §712 (contractual liability), §731 (tort liability); Restatement (Second) of Trusts §261 (1959); 3A Scott on Trusts §261.

[6]*See* §3.5.2.3.

ing a right to represent the interest of the beneficiary, including an assignee or a creditor with a lien.[1] Even persons to whom income or principal is payable at the discretion of the trustee would have standing to bring the matter of the trustee's abuse of discretion before the court.[2] If the trustee refuses to sue or defend on behalf of the trust estate, the beneficiary may proceed against the trustee and the third party as codefendants, but the trustee must be shown to be in default.[3]

§7.2.1 Intentional Breaches

In the world of trusts, an intentional breach is usually two breaches: a breach of the duty of loyalty coupled with some other breach. For example, when a trustee without authority borrows from the trust estate at no interest, both the duty of loyalty *and* the duty to make the trust property productive have been breached, as well as the duty to segregate and earmark. The breach of the duty of loyalty never travels alone. Moreover, the element of self-dealing tends to make the associated breach a continuing one. Thus the self-dealing menu of damage theories may be more extensive than the negligence menu.[4]

§7.2.2 Negligent Breaches

Like the intentional breach, the negligent breach is actually two or more breaches: a breach of the duty to be generally prudent in conducting the affairs of the trust coupled with some other breach. Let us assume, for example, that the trustee negligently makes an unauthorized distribution of principal to an income

---

§7.2 [1]*See* Bogert, Trusts and Trustees §970 (creditor of beneficiary or of trust itself has standing to demand an accounting); 3 Scott on Trusts §200.

[2]*See* Bogert, Trusts and Trustees §871 n.4 and accompanying text; *see generally* 2 Scott on Trusts §128.3.

[3]*See* Bogert, Trusts and Trustees §869 n.20 and accompanying text.

[4]*See* 3 Scott on Trusts §205.1.

beneficiary. Here the trustee has breached both the duty to be prudent and the duty to carry out the terms of the trust.

§7.2.3   Types of Relief

If the trustee commits an intentional breach or falls below the required standard of care, the law seeks to place the beneficiary at least in the position that would have been occupied had there been no breach of trust. The liabilities imposed upon the defaulting trustee are designed to attain this objective and are not necessarily mutually exclusive.

§7.2.3.1   Tracing and Accounting for Proceeds and Profits

It is fundamental that the trust property and any income earned on it be kept within the trustee's control.[5] This obligation extends not only to the property in its original form but to any new form into which it has been changed or converted. For example, if the trustee, in breach of trust, allows the trust property to pass to a purchaser for value who is innocently unaware of the beneficiary's equitable interest in the property, then the purchaser is entitled to keep the property.[6] The trustee may be accountable to the beneficiary for the proceeds and liable for damages, but if the transferee is not a bona fide purchaser for value, then the beneficiary is entitled to have the property (if traceable) returned to the trust.[7] If the property is not traceable, then the trust is entitled to a recovery of the proceeds. Recovery is usually effected judicially by the imposition of a constructive trust upon the proceeds.

A plaintiff seeking relief for the misappropriation of property may prefer a return to the status quo to money damages and thus may assert that the wrongdoer is a constructive trustee in the hopes of having the property traced and retrieved. Even if the

[5]*See generally* 2A Scott on Trusts §175.
[6]*See* Restatement (Second) of Trusts §284 (1959).
[7]*See generally* Bogert, Trusts and Trustees §866.

plaintiff is successful in asserting a trust relationship, however, the property must still be identified with reasonable precision if tracing is to be an available option.[8] If by ordinary accounting methods the beneficiary can show that trust cash has been deposited to the personal bank account of the trustee a lien may be placed upon all the funds in the account.[9]

All profits gained by use of the trust fund belong to the trust estate and not to the trustee. This is true whether the profits have been gained rightfully or wrongfully. "The principle is that, in the management of a trust, the trustee may lose but cannot gain."[10]

§7.2.3.2 Damages

The wronged beneficiary is not necessarily limited to the remedy of tracing and recovery. If tracing is impractical, damages from the trustee's personal assets may be sought.[11] As a general rule, damages would be computed on the basis of any loss occasioned by a breach to include the value of any subsequent earnings and gains which would have accrued to the trust were it not for the breach. An improper delay on the part of the trustee in liquidating an investment is the type of breach for which the remedy of damages may be appropriate.

The matter of improper delay in selling provides a useful illustration of how the introduction of an element of self-dealing into a fact pattern could provide the plaintiff-beneficiary with a theory of damages more generous than would otherwise be available in a simple negligence context. Let us assume that the trust owns 20 percent of the stock of a company and the trustee personally owns 10 percent of the same stock. Let us also assume that there is a rising market and the trustee negligently allows the stock to ride up in value to the point where it comprises 50 percent of the trust's portfolio. It is clear that, as the stock grows as an ever-larger percentage of the value of the trust portfolio, a prudent

---

[8]*See* id. §921.
[9]*See generally* id. §924.
[10]Baker v. Disbrow, 18 Hun 29, 30 (1879), *aff'd mem.* 79 N.Y. 631 (1880).
[11]*See generally* Bogert, Trusts and Trustees §862.

trustee, concerned about inadequate diversification, would have been chipping away at the stock unless the settlor had given clear express or implied retention instructions.[12]

Suppose the stock then gradually loses its value, with the company eventually going bankrupt at the bottom of the value curve. The portfolio has lost 50 percent of its value. A trustee who negligently (or in trust parlance, imprudently) retains a certain stock in a declining market is liable for the difference between the depressed value of the stock and the economic value that would have accrued to the trust if the stock were prudently liquidated and the proceeds then prudently invested.[13] This hypothetical "prudent liquidation" point is likely to be fixed somewhere between the highest and lowest point on the stock's value curve. If, on the other hand, the improper retention is occasioned by an act of self-dealing — perhaps part of the trustee's effort to buttress the price of the trustee's own holding in the stock — then the hypothetical "prudent liquidation" point might be fixed on the value line closer to the top of the curve.[14] If the trustee intentionally declined to diversify when the stock reached its highest price because of the effect sales would have on the trustee's own holding, then the beneficiary is entitled to damages computed as if the stock were sold at its highest price. After all, if the trustee had liquidated the stock and embezzled the proceeds, then the trustee would be expected to return the economic value that was lost to the trust at the time of the embezzlement; can it not be said that our hypothetical trustee has appropriated the trust's stock to his own use when — in order to protect the price of his personal holding — the trustee fails to diversify?

Trustees may not reduce their liability for a breach of trust with a gain from a separate and distinct breach of trust.[15] If, however, a trustee makes a profit and also suffers a loss through the *same* breach of trust, the beneficiaries are entitled only to the

[12]*But see* 3 Scott on Trusts §231.

[13]*See generally* 3 Scott on Trusts §§209, 230.

[14]*Cf.* Restatement (Second) of Trusts §179 comment *d* (1959) (trustee absolutely liable for any losses occasioned trust during period when trustee failed in bad faith to earmark).

[15]*See* Restatement (Third) of Trusts §213 (1992).

amount of the profit less the amount of the loss or they may charge the trustee with the loss reduced by the amount of the profit.[16]

§7.2.3.3   Punitive or Exemplary Damages

The courts of equity had no power to award punitive damages. It therefore followed that an award of damages for breach of fiduciary duty could not have a punitive element to it, the office of trustee itself being a creature of equity.[17] The absence of any mention of punitive damages in the Restatement of Trusts would tend to suggest that this is the modern state of the law as well. Recently, however, courts have begun to assess punitive damages against trustees and these assessments are being upheld, particularly in cases where the breach of fiduciary duty involves fraud or malice.[18] Courts, however, have always considered it within their equitable powers to reduce or deny compensation — and reimbursement for expenses as well — to trustees who are held to be in breach of trust.[19]

§7.2.3.4   Injunction and Specific Enforcement

The beneficiaries' rights are fundamentally equitable; their remedies are correspondingly broad. They include: the right to a decree of specific performance, injunction, restitution, general accounting, the appointment of a receiver, and removal of the trustee.[20] Moreover, equity will impel a court that has taken jurisdiction to retain jurisdiction until the entire matter is "cleaned up" once and for all.

---

[16]Id.

[17]*See generally* 22 Am. Jur. 2d *Equity* §738 (1990).

[18]*See* Bogert, Trusts and Trustees §862 n.12 and accompanying text.

[19]*See generally* Bogert, Trusts and Trustees §861; *see also* Restatement (Third) of Trusts §205 comment *a* (1992).

[20]*See generally* Bogert, Trusts and Trustees §861.

§7.2.3.5   Statutory Penalties Accruing to Beneficiaries

The trustee must monitor not only developments in the common law of trusts but also in the judicial construction of certain criminal and civil statutes that perhaps were not written with the personal trust in mind. The racketeering and consumer protection statutes should be of particular concern because of their generous treble damage provisions. Such provisions provide the trial bar with an economic incentive to take on the smaller breach of fiduciary duty cases.

(a) **Consumer protection.** In suits by beneficiaries against professional trustees,[21] it is now common practice to allege violations of the consumer protection statutes, which in some jurisdictions can bring treble damage recoveries to successful consumer-beneficiaries.[22] The defendant professional trustee should take such allegations particularly seriously when they are made by settlors of funded revocable trusts. This is because the professional trustee of such a trust is likely to have, or have had, a contractual relationship with the settlor and because the professional trustee advertises fiduciary services to the public.

Apart from matters of litigation, there are innumerable consumer-oriented laws and regulations governing transactions between the trustee and the settlor and the trustee and beneficiary. At the point when a trust is established, for example, the trustee may be required to make certain disclosures to the settlor such as the trustee's prevailing fee structure.

(b) **RICO.** In suits by beneficiaries against trustees for breaches of fiduciary duty, it is now not unusual to see a count alleging that the trustee engaged in a pattern of racketeering

---

[21]*See* §7.3.3.1; *see generally* 17 Am. Jur. 2d *Consumer Protection* §§280-305 (1990).

[22]*See generally* Sovern, Deceptive Trade Practices, 52 Ohio St. L.J. 437, 448 n.66 and accompanying text (1991).

activity in violation of Title IX of the Organized Crime Control Act of 1970 (the "RICO Statute").[23] A successful civil RICO action against a trustee could result in the beneficiary being awarded treble damages.[24] In addition to the federal RICO statute, over 20 states now have "little RICO" statutes.[25]

§7.2.3.6   Removal

The court will remove a trustee if it is in the interest of the trust to do so.[26] Removal may be ordered because of hostility between the trustee and a beneficiary or a cotrustee, although relief has been denied if the trustee's duties are essentially ministerial or if the proper administration of the trust would not be hampered.[27] Hostility alone, however, is not grounds for removal.[28]

The court has removed trustees, or said that it would do so, for the following reasons: insanity, habitual drunkenness, criminality involving moral turpitude, failure to obey trust-related court orders, thwarting the purposes of the trust, chronic inactivity, unauthorized commingling, failure to account, a personal interest adverse to the trust, the taking of excessive and unauthorized compensation, and embezzlement, as well as a myriad of other serious and material breaches of trust too numerous to mention here.[29] Most jurisdictions have statutes covering one or more of the above cases.[30]

The court has declined to remove trustees for the following causes: irregularity in the way a trustee was appointed, personal

---

[23]"Racketeer-Influenced and Corrupt Organizations," 18 U.S.C. §§1961-1968 (1988); *see generally* D. Abrams, The Law of Civil RICO (1991).

[24]18 U.S.C. §1964; *see generally* 31A Am. Jur. 2d *Extortion, Blackmail* §227 (1989).

[25]*See generally* id. §§241-259.

[26]*See* Restatement (Second) of Trusts §107 comment *a* (1959). *See also* 2 Scott on Trusts §107.

[27]*See* Bogert, Trusts and Trustees §527.

[28]*See generally* id. §527.

[29]Id.; 2 Scott on Trusts §107.

[30]*See generally* Bogert, Trusts and Trustees §527 nn.7, 8; 2 Scott on Trusts §107 n.22.

insolvency, nonresidency, good faith error in judgment, and isolated acts of negligence.[31]

By the terms of the trust instrument, power to remove the trustee may be lodged in one or more individuals. A power granted to a beneficiary or some other person to terminate the trust has been said to involve a power to remove the trustee.[32] The trustee of an irrevocable trust should be aware that the retained power in a settlor (or the power in a beneficiary) to remove and replace the trustee may, under certain circumstances, subject the trust property to estate taxes upon the power holder's death.[33]

§7.2.4   Cofiduciary and Predecessor Liability and Contribution

The trustee will be liable for an improper delegation of a duty;[34] on the other hand, it is well settled that a trustee is not responsible for a cotrustee's breach of trust unless the trustee participated in, approved, acquiesced in, or concealed the breach, or failed to take what steps were necessary to compel the cotrustee to redress the breach.[35] If several trustees unite in a breach of trust, they are jointly and severally liable, and the entire claim of the beneficiary may be satisfied from the property of one trustee.[36] A trustee who has made good a loss occasioned by a breach of trust is entitled to contribution from those cotrustees participating in the wrong,[37] but in this day and age a professional trustee may well find it difficult to persuade a court to order a participating "amateur" cotrustee to make contribution.[38]

---

[31]*See generally* Bogert, Trusts and Trustees §527.

[32]*See* 2 Scott on Trusts §107.3. *See also* Restatement (Second) of Trusts §107 comment *i* (1959).

[33]*See generally* Wall Estate v. Commissioner, No. 15311-91, 101 T.C. No. 21 (Oct. 12, 1993) (Nims, J.); Rev. Rul. 79-353, 1979-2 C.B. 325; Priv. Ltr. Rul. 89-160-32 (May 1, 1989).

[34]*See* Restatement (Third) of Trusts §171 (1992).

[35]*See* Restatement (Second) of Trusts §224 (1959).

[36]Bogert, Trusts and Trustees §862 n.3 and accompanying text.

[37]Id. §862 n.7 and accompanying text.

[38]*See generally* Restatement (Third) of Trusts §227 comment *d* (1992).

It long has been stated as the general rule that the successor trustee is in no way liable for the acts of the predecessor.[39] This statement undoubtedly is correct, but there is an equally well-settled rule that the successor trustee has a positive duty, upon taking over the trust estate, to see that the predecessor has properly accounted for the whole of it. Indeed, failure to prosecute any claim that may exist against the predecessor may constitute a breach of trust on the part of the successor.[40] Moreover, with the array of criminal statutes on the books covering everything from money laundering to hazardous waste, the successor trustee now more than ever cannot afford to dispense with an examination into the doings of his predecessor in office and into the condition of the trust property, particularly if it is real property. Due diligence is the order of the day.

At minimum, the successor should require an accounting if one has not been formally made. Copies of the fiduciary income tax returns for the previous three years should be scrutinized. If the property is coming from the settlor's estate the successor should also obtain copies of federal and state estate tax returns. This matter is of growing practical importance especially since so many inter vivos trusts are conducted without formal accountings. The person proposed as successor trustee should insist, whenever it is reasonably possible, that accounts of the predecessor be made up and allowed or the assents obtained as provided in the trust instrument. Furthermore, it is often possible (and always desirable) to require that unsuitable holdings in the trust portfolio be removed before the succession is completed, or at least marked for very early removal after the succession. It is of little importance to a successor trustee whether the theoretical basis for surcharge is the predecessor's malfeasance or the successor's nonfeasance in prosecuting the trust's just claims against the predecessor. Moreover the bringing of a suit against a predecessor may have unpleasant collateral social and financial consequences for the successor, particularly if the predecessor is a relative, friend, business associate, or customer of the successor. The prudent person makes

---

[39] *See* Restatement (Second) of Trusts §223 (1959).
[40] *See* id. §223 comment *d*.

certain, before succeeding to the trust office, that all things are in order, and does not rely on any express language in the governing instrument purporting to relieve a successor of the duty to investigate the acts of the predecessor.

§7.2.5   Insurance and Indemnification for Liability Arising Out of a Breach of Fiduciary Duty to the Beneficiary

Unless the trustee is an attorney, fiduciary liability insurance will be exceedingly difficult, if not impossible, to obtain for coverage for breaches of fiduciary duty; if it *is* obtained, the premium costs must be borne personally by the trustee[41] and not by the trust estate. Moreover, it goes without saying that a trustee may not be indemnified from the trust estate for an adverse judgment arising out of a breach of fiduciary duty.

§7.2.6   Exculpatory Provisions Covering Breach of Fiduciary Duties to the Beneficiary

Many trust instruments contain provisions that purport to limit the trustee's liabilities to the beneficiary. In some jurisdictions such provisions are void as against public policy.[42] In those jurisdictions where they are not, courts will go only so far in giving them force and effect.[43] As a general rule, anything beyond exculpation for ordinary negligence is of doubtful validity.[44] No provision, for example, can relieve a trustee from liability for a breach of the duty of loyalty. Nor can a trustee hide behind a provision that has been improperly inserted.

---

[41]*See* §3.5.4.2. *See also* Bogert, Trusts and Trustees §599.

[42]*See generally* Whitman, Exoneration Clauses in Wills and Trust Instruments, 4 Hofstra Prop. L.J. 123 (1992); Bogert, Trusts and Trustees §542.

[43]Id.

[44]Id.

An issue of the improper insertion of an exculpatory provision is likely to come up when the drafting attorney is also the named trustee.[45] When the attorney-trustee drafts into the instrument a provision limiting liability, there is at best an appearance of impropriety and conflict of interest. After all, he has a duty to represent the interests of the settlor, his client — not his own interests. In situations where the drafting attorney is the named trustee, the best practice is for the attorney to insist that the settlor seek competent, independent legal advice on the matter of trustee exculpation.[46] The benefit to the settlor is self-evident; the benefit to the trustee is that the exculpation is less vulnerable to attack than it would be otherwise. The next best practice is for the attorney to fully disclose to the settlor the existence and import of such a provision.[47] In no event should the drafting attorney casually dismiss as mere boilerplate an exculpatory provision — neither in practice nor in response to client inquiries.[48] That practice is unacceptable.

§7.2.7 Beneficiary Consent, Ratification, and Release

The beneficiary's informed consent, ratification, or release is sufficient to discharge the trustee from liability to the beneficiary for breaches of trust.[49] The trustee must understand that the term *beneficiary* means *all* the beneficiaries: those with remainder interests as well as those with income interests; those with contingent interests as well as those whose interests have vested.[50] The matter of the limitation of a trustee's liability to the beneficiary through

---

[45]*See* Restatement (Second) of Trusts §222, comment *d* (1959).
[46]Id.
[47]*See* Marsman v. Nasca, 30 Mass. App. 789, 573 N.E.2d 1025 (1991), *review denied*, 411 Mass. 1102, 579 N.E.2d 1361 (1991) (exculpatory clause upheld in face of unrefuted testimony that the settlor asked the attorney-trustee to insert the clause).
[48]*See* Jonathan v. Irving Trust Co., 151 Misc. 107, 270 N.Y. Supp. 721 (1934), *aff'd*, 243 A.D. 691, 277 N.Y.S. 955 (1935).
[49]*See* Restatement (Second) of Trusts §§216-218 (1959).
[50]*See generally* 3 Scott on Trusts §216.2.

the beneficiary's own actions or inactions is covered elsewhere in this handbook.[51]

§7.2.8 Liability Without Economic Injury to the Beneficiary

A trustee is liable for intentional breaches of trust, whether or not the breach caused economic injury to the trust. This is particularly the case when it comes to breaches of the duty of loyalty. Lack of economic injury is no more a defense to a trustee's breach of the duty of loyalty than is the failure to steal a defense to the crime of breaking and entering. While money damages may not be an available remedy in the absence of economic harm, there is always injunction, removal, and assessment of costs — and possibly even criminal sanction.[52]

Negligent breaches also can bring liability without economic injury. Let us take, for example, the trustee who negligently concentrates the trust estate in only one stock. Last year the stock's performance was well below the market average; this year its performance is, and continues to be, well above the market average. The beneficiary, concerned that the portfolio is at an unacceptable level of risk, retains counsel who finally manages either by litigation or negotiation to get the trustee to diversify. While ultimately the trust suffered no resulting economic injury, the trustee nonetheless was in breach of the duty to diversify. Thus while money damages may be inappropriate, it would be appropriate for the trustee personally to bear the burden of all legal fees and associated costs incurred by the beneficiary and others in getting the trustee to prudently diversify. Had the trustee sold when the stock was down, there would have been realized losses that could have formed the basis for an assessment of damages.[53] There is some irony here. Had the stock been sold in a down market in a conscientious — albeit belated — effort to

[51]See §5.5.
[52]But see Bogert, Trusts and Trustees §861 n.10 and accompanying text.
[53]See Restatement (Third) of Trusts §205 (1992).

carry out the duty to diversify, the trustee's liability could well be keyed to those losses.[54]

§7.2.9   Personal Liability of Trust Officers

There are instances where trust officers have been sued personally, along with their corporate employers, for breaches of fiduciary duty, notwithstanding the fact that the corporate employer was the named trustee. True, the trust company may be held liable for the acts of the trust officer under the doctrine of respondeat superior. It does not follow from this, however, that the trust officer is then relieved of liability.[55] A trust officer is at some financial risk if the trust company does not carry employee liability insurance; the trust company is financially weak, bankrupt or otherwise unable or unwilling to indemnify the trust officer; or the trust officer's homeowner's policy does not cover acts performed in the course of employment.

§7.3   Trustee's Liability as Legal Owner to Nonbeneficiaries

It has been seen that the trustee, so far as concerns the outside world, is the owner of the trust property and that the duty to account to the beneficiary is primarily an internal matter.[1] It follows that in dealing with strangers the trustee is the responsible

---

[54]In one case, a bank trustee was held liable for the failure to diversify even though "the value of the trust principal increased and 'substantial income' was earned throughout the bank's tenure as trustee." First Alabama Bank of Huntsville, N.A. v. Spragins, 515 So. 2d 962 (Ala. 1987). Liability was based on the difference between the actual increase and the increase that might have been achieved with a diversified portfolio. See also Restatement (Third) of Trusts §§209-211 (1992).

[55]See Bogert, Trusts and Trustees §901 n.9 and accompanying text.

§7.3 [1]See §3.5.1.

party, even though the trustee has no beneficial interest in the trust property. It is entirely erroneous to regard the trustee as an agent or to assume that the trust estate or beneficiary will be primarily liable; the trustee has full and primary liability.[2] The beneficiary ordinarily has no liability, except in the case where the trustee has been stripped of substantial control over management of the trust property and the law of the jurisdiction finds the essence of the relationship to be that of principal-agent.[3]

Because the trustee must bear this burden of full personal responsibility and because all gains must accrue to the trust estate, the trustee who has acted properly is given certain rights against the trust estate. These rights are equitable in nature and include the right of reimbursement and exoneration.[4] In cases where the creditor, whether in contract or in tort, finds difficulty in collecting directly from the trustee, may the trust estate be reached instead? Or should the creditor be limited, by subrogation, to whatever rights of indemnity the trustee may have? These and other such questions are considered below. However, it should be noted:

> Where a liability to third persons is imposed upon a person, not as a result of a contract made by him or a tort committed by him but because he is the holder of the title to the trust property, a trustee as holder of the title to the trust property is subject to personal liability, but only to the extent to which the trust estate is sufficient to indemnify him.[5]

§7.3.1   Liability as Legal Owner in Contract to Nonbeneficiaries

Under the common law, when the trustee enters into a contract with a nonbeneficiary, even though he does so rightfully and

---

[2]*See generally* Restatement (Second) of Trusts §261 (1959).

[3]*See* Bogert, Trusts and Trustees §§247E-247F (discussing the liability of beneficiaries of certain business trusts).

[4]*See* Restatement (Second) of Trusts §244 (1959).

[5]Id. §265.

on behalf of the trust estate, it nevertheless is the trustee's contract and not that of the trust estate.[6] Thus, a suit at law upon the contract is against the trustee personally; judgment issues against the trustee individually;[7] execution upon such a judgment cannot issue against the trust assets.[8] Trust assets can be reached upon execution only through subrogation to whatever equitable rights of indemnity the trustee may have against the trust estate.[9] In some jurisdictions, however, either by statute or on different theories of law, the trust assets may be reached directly.[10]

The creditor's access to the trust estate will be measured strictly by the extent of the trustee's authority to act.[11] It follows that a creditor who intends to contract with the trustee should ascertain that the trustee has the authority to enter into the transaction on behalf of the trust. In the absence of such authority, the creditor may only look to the trustee's personal assets. Thus the prudent prospective creditor calls for the trust instrument and examines its provisions. Even when the trustee lacks the authority to enter into a particular contract on behalf of the trust, however, the creditor may look to the trust estate to the extent the trust benefits from the transaction.[12]

§7.3.2   Agreements with Nonbeneficiaries to Limit Contractual Liability

The trustee may contractually limit personal liability in matters involving nonbeneficiaries[13] or have it limited to the extent of the trust estate.[14]

Thus, a trustee may contract in such a way as to preclude

---

[6]Bogert, Trusts and Trustees §712.
[7]Id.
[8]Id.
[9]Id. §716.
[10]Id. §712.
[11]See 3A Scott on Trusts §268.2.
[12]See id. §269.1.
[13]Id. §263.
[14]See generally Bogert, Trusts and Trustees §714 (rev. 2d ed. 1984). But see Restatement (Second) of Trusts §263, comment a (1959) (words "as trustee" or

personal liability by adding after his signature the qualification "as trustee, but not individually."[15] With respect to negotiable instruments, however, a duly authorized trustee is not personally liable even if he simply signs "as trustee," provided the instrument identifies the trust.[16] Trust instruments sometimes are recorded and often contain clauses exempting the trustee from personal liability;[17] in such cases a reference to the trust in the contract may suffice to do away with the trustee's liability.[18] Any creditor who is on actual notice of the existence of such a clause should be taken to have excused the trustee.[19] It will not do, however, in the present state of the law, for a trustee to rely upon a provision in the instrument of which the creditor has no notice.[20]

§7.3.3 Liability as Legal Owner in Tort to Nonbeneficiaries

The trustee is as responsible for the torts which he commits in the course of administering the trust estate as he would be for those committed in the course of administering his own affairs.[21] Thus the trustee is personally liable to nonbeneficiaries for any injury to them occasioned by a failure to keep the trust property in proper repair.[22] Moreover, if servants are employed on behalf of the trust, the trustee's personal liability for their torts is determined exactly as though they were employed for the trustee's own affairs.[23] This liability is personal to the trustee; execution therefore runs against the trustee irrespective of whether he has a right

---

"as trustee for" without more may not be enough to limit the trustee's contractual personal liability).

[15] Restatement (Second) of Trusts §263 comment *a* (1959).
[16] *But see* 3A Scott on Trusts §263.1 n.2 and accompanying text.
[17] *See generally* Bogert, Trusts and Trustees §714.
[18] Id.
[19] Id.
[20] *See generally* 3A Scott on Trusts §263.2.
[21] *See* Restatement (Second) of Trusts §264 (1959).
[22] *See* 3A Scott on Trusts §264.
[23] *See* Restatement (Second) of Trusts §264 comment *b* (1959).

to indemnity from the trust fund.[24] On the other hand, successor trustees do not succeed to this liability[25] nor is a trustee in bankruptcy liable for the torts of his agents.[26]

The right of the tort creditor to reach the trust estate has been a matter of great confusion in the cases. The principal difficulty lies in the fact that the trustee's right of indemnity is not clear. It seems to be settled that if the trustee was not personally at fault *and* was not negligent in the selection of his agents, he has a right to exonerate himself from the trust estate, and the tort creditor has the right to levy against the trust property.[27] If a tort is committed while the trustee is acting beyond the scope of his duties, trust assets cannot be reached and judgment will be against the trustee personally.[28]

In jurisdictions that have adopted §7-306(b) of the Uniform Probate Code, the trustee would be liable to nonbeneficiaries in tort "only if he is personally at fault."[29] While the section is intended to offer some protection to the trustee, it is difficult to see the practical advantage of the section's adoption. The careful plaintiff will not only sue the trustee in his representative capacity but also sue the trustee in his individual capacity. The plaintiff need only allege "personal fault." Moreover, it will be the rare case where a judgment for the nonbeneficiary plaintiff contains no finding whatsoever of "personal fault" on the part of the trustee. Even when the wrongful acts were committed by the trustee's agents, there is the matter of their negligent selection and supervision.[30]

As a matter of practice, the wise trustee insures himself both as an individual and as trustee against nonbeneficiary claims in tort arising from the ownership or operation of the trust estate. The

---

[24]*See generally* 3A Scott on Trusts §264.
[25]*See generally* Bogert, Trusts and Trustees §731 n.19 and accompanying text.
[26]*See generally* 3A Scott on Trusts §264.
[27]Id.
[28]Id. §271A.2.
[29]*See generally* Bogert, Trusts and Trustees §732.
[30]Id. §731.

expense of such insurance is a proper charge against the trust estate.[31]

In the past 30 years a number of federal and state statutes have been enacted into law that are designed to protect consumers and redress acts of discrimination against certain classes of individuals. The trustee who deals with nonbeneficiaries on behalf of the trust estate may be bound by the requirements of these statutes and personally subject to their sanctions.

§7.3.3.1 Consumer Protection

A substantial majority of the states have enacted, in one form or another, statutes designed to protect consumers from unfair or deceptive trade practices.[32] Most if not all of these consumer protection statutes will cover trustees who render goods and services to the public on behalf of their trusts.[33] If an unincorporated automobile dealership, for example, were operated out of a trust, the trustee might be held personally liable to customers for statements by employees of the trust that the automobiles are of a particular quality when they are not, that repairs may be needed when they are not, or that there is a specific price advantage when there is not.[34] Under some state statutes, consumers have a private right of action,[35] while under others the attorney general must bring the action on behalf of the consumers.[36] In some states both options are available.[37] Private relief usually takes the form of rescission, restitution, and consequential damages.[38] In a number of jurisdictions, customers are entitled to treble damages and the recovery of attorneys' fees.[39]

---

[31]Id. §803.
[32]See generally 17 Am. Jur. 2d Consumer Protection §280 (1990).
[33]Id. §285.
[34]Id. §297.
[35]Id. §302.
[36]Id. §300.
[37]Id. §301.
[38]See generally J. Sovern, Deceptive Trade Practices, 52 Ohio St. L.J. 437 (1991).
[39]Id. n.66. (1991).

If the dealership were incorporated, legal liability for damages under the statute might run in the first instance to the corporate enterprise. The trust beneficiaries however would have a right in equity to compel the trustee personally to make good any loss to the trust occasioned by the assessment of damages against the dealership, provided the loss could be tied to a breach of trust.

Not all consumer protection statutes cast the broad "unfair and deceptive" net. Some target specific activities such as odometer tampering, pyramid schemes, and telephone sales solicitations.[40]

§7.3.3.2   Discrimination Based on Race, Color, Religion, Sex, Age, or Disability

As a general rule, the trustee may not discriminate on the basis of race, color, religion, sex, age, or disability in transactions with nonbeneficiaries on behalf of the trust.[41] This includes not only discrimination in the sale of goods and services to the public but also in matters relating to the hiring and employment of the trust's servants.[42] There are numerous exceptions and exemptions, which are beyond the scope of this handbook. Persons subject to unlawful discrimination may recover compensatory damages from the trustee, and in some cases punitive damages.[43]

The trustee's liability to nonbeneficiaries for intentional acts of discrimination is not indemnifiable from the trust estate.[44] If liability runs to a corporation held in the trust, the trustee may be compelled in equity to reimburse the trust estate for any resulting economic loss to the extent the loss is attributable to a breach of trust.

---

[40]*See generally* 17 Am. Jur. 2d *Consumer Protection* §299 (1990).
[41]*See generally* 14 C.J.S. *Civil Rights* §§43-101 (1991).
[42]Id. §§143-217.
[43]Id. §§222-475.
[44]*See generally* Bogert, Trusts and Trustees §734.

§7.3.3.3　Registration and Sale of Securities

The trustee may not engage in the interstate sale of securities held in the trust — or of securities representing beneficial interests in the trust itself — unless the securities are registered under the Federal Securities Act of 1933 or unless the sale falls under one or more of a number of statutory exemptions.[45] The determination of whether a particular interest constitutes a security and, if it does, whether it needs to be registered requires the specialized expertise of a securities lawyer. It certainly is not a job for the layman. The trustee who sells securities representing interests held by the trust, or beneficial interests in the trust itself, in violation of the registration requirements of federal law could be held personally liable to purchasers for their investment losses.[46] There are state registration requirements as well; known collectively as *Blue Sky Laws*, they carry their own private rights of action.[47]

The trustee also could incur personal civil liability to nonbeneficiaries for the unlawful insider trading of securities held in the trust estate.[48] This is the case even when the trustee acts solely in the interests of the beneficiaries, that is, when the trustee in no way profits personally.[49] *Insider trading* is trading in the securities markets while in possession of nonpublic information that would be important to a reasonable investor in making a decision to buy or sell a security.[50] Section 10(b) of the Securities Exchange Act of 1934 and Rule 10(b)(5) provide the legal frame-

---

[45]*See generally* L. Loss & J. Seligman, Securities Regulation (1993); 69A Am. Jur. 2d *Securities Regulation — Federal* §§934-1479 (1993); Problems of Fiduciaries Under the Securities Laws, 20 Real Prop. Prob. & Tr. J. 503 (1985).

[46]Id.

[47]*See generally* Bogert, Trusts and Trustees §247R.

[48]*See supra* note 45. *See also* M. P. Malloy, Can 10b-5 for the Banks? The Effect of an Antifraud Rule on the Regulation of Banks, 61 Fordham L. Rev. 523 (1993).

[49]Id.

[50]Id.

work for private rights of action in the insider trading context.[51] The trustee must make the trust whole for any losses to it occasioned by running afoul of the securities laws; and of course the trustee, not the trust, must bear the burden of attorneys' fees and other litigation costs that are a consequence of the illegal activities.[52]

§7.3.4   Liability as Legal Owner to the Sovereign

The trustee as titleholder has certain duties and obligations not only to the beneficiaries and to third parties but also to the city, the state, and the United States.

§7.3.4.1   Liability for Property Taxes

In the absence of statute, the trustee as legal owner would be personally liable for any taxes owed on tangible, intangible, and real property held in the trust.[53] In most cases, however, the trustee, as legal owner, is relieved by statute of personal liability either through the imposition of such liability on the beneficiary or on the property itself.[54] Consequently, as a practical matter, most property tax obligations are now directly imposed by statute on the trust estate.[55] Even if the trustee could not resort to a statute relieving him of personal liability for property taxes, he would have an equitable right to reimbursement from the trust estate.[56]

---

[51]Id.
[52]See Bogert, Trusts and Trustees §801 n.15 and accompanying text.
[53]See generally 3A Scott on Trusts §265.
[54]Id. §265.1.
[55]Id.
[56]See generally Bogert, Trusts and Trustees §807.

§7.3.4.2   Criminal and Civil Liability as Legal Owner

It has always been the case that the trustee may be held criminally liable for misappropriation of the trust funds.[57] This century, however, has seen a proliferation of statutes designed to regulate the advertising and sale of products and services to the public. These statutes have broadened substantially the trustee's opportunity to incur criminal liability in the course of administering a trust.

(a) Securities laws. The trustee as holder of the title to the trust portfolio has ample opportunity to run afoul of the criminal laws pertaining to the issuance, acquisition, and transfer of securities.[58]

(1) *Insider Trading (SEC).* The trustee may be held criminally liable for insider trading in violation of the federal securities laws even in those cases where the trustee does not profit personally.[59] Conviction can result in substantial fines being levied against the trustee — and this would include the corporate trustee and its officers, directors, and supervisory personnel. In addition, conviction can bring long jail terms.[60] The key, however, is that the information must be nonpublic. The trustee, however, may — and has a duty to — use public information in furtherance of the interests of the trust.

(2) *Securities Registration.* The trustee who transfers unregistered or restricted securities held in the trust in violation

---

[57]*See generally* 2A Scott on Trusts §179.1 (intentional misappropriation constitutes the crime of embezzlement).

[58]*See generally* S. Miller, Warning: Do Not Violate Insider Trading Rules, 129 Trusts & Estates 46 (1990); 69A Am. Jur. 2d *Securities Regulation — Federal* §§1724-1752 (1993).

[59]Id. *See also* Problems of Fiduciaries Under the Securities Laws, 20 Real Prop. Prob. & Tr. J. 503 (1985) (hereinafter "Problems").

[60]*See* Miller, *supra* note 58.

of the securities laws may be criminally liable.[61] Moreover a transferable share of beneficial interest in the trust itself may be a "security" subject to regulation.[62]

(3) *Ownership Disclosure.* When a trust acquires more than five percent of a class of registered securities, the trustee may be required to file certain disclosure forms with the Securities and Exchange Commission and with the Exchanges.[63] Determining who is and what securities are subject to these disclosure obligations is a complicated matter. It is a topic that falls beyond the scope of this handbook and beyond the ken of most trust attorneys as well. However, because the cost of noncompliance could be criminal sanctions, the trustee should consult a qualified securities lawyer if there is reason to believe that a holding is approaching (or has exceeded) the five-percent point.

(b) Environmental protection. As holder of the title to the trust property, the trustee is likely to face criminal sanctions if he intentionally or negligently, in the course of his administration, violates environmental statutes. In addition to a number of major federal environmental statutes on the books, each state as well has its own set of environmental laws.

While most environmental statutes require intent or negligence on the part of the trustee, under the federal Comprehensive Environmental Response, Compensation, and Liability Act (CERCLA),[64] an innocent trustee's liability as the "owner" for the clean-up of hazardous waste on or within the trust property may not be limited by the trust's ability to indemnify the trustee *except*

---

[61]*See generally* Problems, *supra* note 59; 69A Am. Jur. 2d *Securities Regulation — Federal* §§1724-1752 (1993).

[62]Id. *See also* Bogert, Trusts and Trustees §247R (registration of beneficial interests under state securities laws).

[63]*See generally* Problems, *supra* note 59; V. P. Whitney, Trust Department Administration and Operations §15.10 (1993); 69A Am. Jur. 2d *Securities Regulation — Federal* §§629-631 (1993).

[64]42 U.S.C. §9601 et seq. (1983). *See* S. Ferrey, The Law of Independent Power §6.05[3][c] (1993).

when the property is contaminated at the time of acquisition and the trustee undertakes promptly to correct the situation or *when the trustee has no control over the use of the trust property* — at least one federal district court has so held.[65] In other words, the trustee under certain circumstances may well be held strictly (and personally) liable for the full clean-up costs even if those costs *exceed* the value of the trust estate. Certainly the prudent prospective trustee should commission an exhaustive and comprehensive CERCLA inspection of any land comprising the trust estate before deciding whether to accept the trusteeship.

(c) Unauthorized practice of law. The nonlawyer-trustee, whether a corporation or an individual, should leave the drafting of the trust instrument to the settlor's lawyer. To be sure, practicing law without a license is a crime in some jurisdictions.[66] But what is perhaps of greater practical concern is that the nonlawyer-trustee (be it an individual or an institution like a bank) will be held to the standard of a competent trust lawyer in any *civil* action brought for negligent drafting.[67] Unlike the licensed attorney, however, the nonlawyer-trustee will have no legal malpractice insurance to fall back on.

---

[65]*See* City of Phoenix, Ariz. v. Garbage Servs. Co., 827 F. Supp. 600 (D. Ariz. 1993).

[66]*See generally* Rhode, Policing the Professional Monopoly: A Constitutional and Empirical Analysis of Unauthorized Practice Prohibitions, 34 Stan. L. Rev. 1, 11 n.39 (1981).

[67]Harper, James & Gray, 3 The Law of Torts §16.6 (1986).

CHAPTER 8

Miscellaneous Topics of General Interest to the Trustee

§8.1   Powers of Appointment

§8.1.1   In General

A power of appointment is a power of disposition.[1] It is a power given by the settlor to someone — usually a beneficiary, sometimes a third party — to short circuit, alter, or extend the terms of the trust. A power of appointment, as it is usually under-

---

§8.1   [1]Restatement (Second) of Property §11.1 (1986) (Donative Transfers).

stood, is not a discretionary power *in* a trustee to invade principal for the benefit of the beneficiary.[2] For purposes of this handbook, a power of appointment is not a power *in the trustee*; it is a power *to give directions to* the trustee.

The settlor determines the nature and extent of the power and how it is to be exercised by the power holder. For example, a general inter vivos power would give the power holder the right while alive to direct the trustee to turn over the trust property to the holder, the holder's creditors, or to anyone else.[3] A general testamentary power would give the power holder the right by will to direct the trustee to turn over the trust property to the power holder's estate, the estate's creditors, or to anyone else.[4] On the other hand, the holder of a limited inter vivos or testamentary power may appoint only to the members of a class of permissible takers.[5] This class can be large enough to include everyone in the world except the power holder, his creditors, his estate, and the creditors of his estate; otherwise for all intents and purposes the power would be a general one.[6]

The trustee should keep in mind that a power of appointment is not always labeled as such in the governing instrument. It sometimes travels in disguise. For example, a general inter vivos power might take the form of a reserved right of revocation, a beneficiary's right to have his debts satisfied from the trust estate, or simply an unrestricted right in someone to demand principal.[7]

A prospective trustee should make sure there are provisions in default of exercise. Let us take as an example the following trust: *A* to *B* for *C* for life, with *C* possessing a general testamentary power of appointment. What happens if *C* were to die intestate? The instrument being silent, it is likely that the death of *C* would

---

[2]*But see* id. §11.1 comment *d*.
[3]*See* id. §11.4.
[4]Id.
[5]Id. §11.4 comment *b*.
[6]Id.
[7]Id. §12.1 comment *a* & Reporter's Note to §12.1.

trigger a resulting trust in favor of *A* or *A*'s estate.[8] Were *C* to possess instead a limited power, there is a split of authority as to whether a resulting trust is triggered or whether the property passes in equal shares to the permissible appointees.[9] In any case, the settlor's counsel should have supplied the trust with terms that would become operative in the event *C* fails in whole or in part effectively to exercise the power.[10]

When a settlor makes himself a beneficiary *and* bestows on himself a *general* inter vivos power to appoint the trust property (*e.g.,* a reserved right of revocation), his creditors may have access to the property whether or not the power is ever exercised.[11] This is consistent with the longstanding public policy that one may not place property beyond the reach of one's creditors and still retain the right to enjoy it.[12] It is the settlor's *right* of exercise which makes the property vulnerable; not the fact of exercise. The right of exercise is treated as equivalent to an ownership interest in the property subject to the power. On the other hand, if the holder of the general inter vivos power is not the settlor and absent a statute to the contrary, the property is creditor-accessible only to the extent that the holder in fact exercises the power.[13] This restriction on access may not apply to the trustee in bankruptcy.[14] With respect to a *limited* power to appoint trust property, the holder is treated as though an agent of the settlor; thus the holder's creditors would have no access to the property whether the limited power is ever exercised.[15]

---

[8]Id. §24.1.

[9]*See generally* 1 Scott on Trusts §27.

[10]See Bogert, Trusts and Trustees §1064 for a sample provision in default of the exercise of a power of appointment (art. fourth, section 3).

[11]2A Scott on Trusts §156; *see also* §5.3.3. *But see* 4 Scott §330.12 (suggesting that property subject to an unexercised naked reserved right of revocation may not be reachable by the settlor's creditors).

[12]*See generally* 2A Scott on Trusts §156.

[13]*See generally* id. §147.3.

[14]Id.

[15]*See* id.; Restatement (Second) of Property §13.1 (1986) (Donative Transfers).

§8.1.2   Exercises of Power of Appointment in Further Trust

If the governing instrument is silent on the issue, may the holder of a *general* power of appointment exercise it in further trust (*e.g.*, instead of appointing the property outright and free of trust to X, appoint it to a trustee for the benefit of X)? The answer is yes.[16] This is inherent in the holder's overarching right to appoint to anyone, including himself. Even if the holder of a general power were not entitled to appoint in further trust, the same result could still be achieved in two steps: by first appointing to himself and then by impressing a trust upon the property for the benefit of X.

Authority is split over whether, absent express authority in the governing instrument, the holder of a *limited* power may appoint in further trust.[17] If the holder may appoint to members of a class comprised of X, Y, and Z, some courts would hold an exercise in further trust to be impermissible, because title would pass to the trustee who would be someone other than a designated member of the class.[18] The matter of appointments in further trust should be addressed in the governing instrument. When it is not, the trustee should next check for an applicable statute before turning to the cases.[19]

If a *general* power is exercised in further trust, is a new trust created or are the terms of the original trust merely altered or extended? Unfortunately, the question is not susceptible of any easy answer.[20] It may well depend upon who wants to know. Let us assume, for example, that A transfers property inter vivos to B in trust for C, who is given a *general* testamentary power of appointment. C exercises the power by providing in his or her will that B shall continue to hold the property in trust for the benefit of X. In this case C has expressed the intention that no new trust be created and that the terms of the original trust are

---

[16]*See generally* 1 Scott on Trusts §§17.2, 21.
[17]*See generally* id. §17.2.
[18]*See* id. §17.2 n.5 and accompanying text.
[19]*See* id. §17.2 n.7 and accompanying text.
[20]*See generally* id. §17.2.

merely to be extended. On the other hand, the creditors of C might demand that B turn the trust property over to C's estate so that it may be available to satisfy their claims. Once the claims are satisfied, a new trust presumably would arise for the benefit of X. Moreover, the court having jurisdiction over C's estate might assert that this new trust is now a testamentary trust requiring its continuing supervision.

Regardless of the form of the arrangement, that is to say, whether there is a continuing trust or the termination of one and the starting up of another, when it comes to substantive rights there are two trusts. The exerciser of the general power for all intents and purposes is the settlor of a new trust to which his or her creditors, spouse, the taxing authorities — perhaps even the welfare department — all may have access.[21] Even for purposes of the Rule Against Perpetuities, the holder of a general inter vivos power is deemed to have a vested interest in the property subject to the power.[22]

The form of the arrangement seems to be up to the settlor. If the settlor expresses an intention that the power holder may appoint new trustees upon an exercise in further trust, then such an appointment will be honored. But could the exercise of a *general* testamentary power of appointment have the effect of converting an inter vivos trust into a testamentary trust requiring subsequent periodic accountings to the court?[23] The attendant publicity and expense would make this an unfortunate result. Moreover it would fly in the face of the very concept of the power of appointment — a power of disposition, a power to direct. The holder who exercises the general testamentary power in further trust is either directing that the property stay with the current trustee or directing one trustee to transfer title to another. In neither case is it expected that the estate of the exerciser will take unto itself more of an interest in the property (nor that the court will acquire more supervision over the new arrangement) than is reasonably neces-

---

[21] *See generally* 2A Scott on Trusts §147.3.

[22] Leach, Perpetuities in a Nutshell, 51 Harv. L. Rev. 638, 654 (1938).

[23] *See generally* Restatement (Second) of Property §11.1 comment *b*, §13.4 comment *b* (1986) (Donative Transfers).

sary to accommodate the interests of those having a claim against the estate.[24]

With respect to the exercise of a *limited* testamentary power of appointment in further trust, there should be no excuse whatsoever for a court's converting an inter vivos trust into a testamentary trust. The deceased holder is for all intents and purposes no more than an agent of the settlor, the holder's estate having no ownership interest, constructive or otherwise, in the property subject to the power.

On the other hand, the exercise in further trust of a general testamentary power created under a *testamentary* trust as a practical matter might bring about a transfer of jurisdiction over the testamentary trust to the court supervising the administration of the power holder's estate. This however is as much a conflict of laws issue as it is an issue rooted in the nature of the power of appointment itself.

If the holder of a *general* power of appointment attempts to exercise the power in further trust and the "new" trust fails at the outset (or is established but some time thereafter fails), the property passes as a resulting trust to the power holder or his estate. It does *not* pass back to the settlor of the "original" trust or his estate, unless the "original" trust instrument provides for a different disposition or unless the power holder provided otherwise.[25] It is said that the property has been *captured* by the power holder or his estate.

If the holder of a *limited* power of appointment attempts to exercise the power in further trust and the "new" trust fails at the outset (or is established but some time thereafter fails), there is no capture. There are instead three possibilities, depending on the terms of the original trust: the property passes (1) to the takers in default, (2) in equal shares to the class of permissible appointees,

---

[24]Id.; *see also* In re Estate of Wylie, 342 So. 2d 996 (Fla. Dist. Ct. App. 1977); Aurora Natl. Bank v. Old Second Natl. Bank, 59 Ill. App. 3d 384, 375 N.E.2d 544 (1978).
[25]5 Scott on Trusts §426.

and (3) back to the settlor of the "original" trust or his estate.[26] In no event can the trustee keep the property.

As the above discussion suggests, the subject of powers of appointment in multijurisdictional settings is too complex to discuss in a book of this scope. It would be equally impractical to attempt a discussion of what exercises in further trust will and will not violate the Rule Against Perpetuities.[27] Suffice it to say that the trustee confronted with these issues should consult with counsel.

§8.2 Termination of the Trust and Final Distribution

The law places a limit on how long a noncharitable trust may continue. This constraint has come to be known as the *Rule Against Perpetuities* (hereinafter "the Rule"). As long as the Rule is not violated, the settlor is entitled to set forth in the governing instrument when and under what circumstances the trust shall terminate. If the settlor fails to do so, the trust shall terminate when its purposes are fulfilled. If the terms of the governing instrument are silent on what then happens to the trust property, the property shall pass back to the settlor or the settlor's estate upon a resulting trust.

§8.2.1 The Rule Against Perpetuities

No interest is good unless it must vest, if at all, not later than twenty-one years after some life in being at the creation of the interest.[1]

The Rule Against Perpetuities places a limit on how long certain types of trusts may continue. During the life of a trust (*i.e.,*

---

[26]Id. §427.

[27]*See generally* Leach, *supra* note 22, at 651-654; Bogert, Trusts and Trustees §213.

§8.2 [1]J. C. Gray, The Rule Against Perpetuities §201 (4th ed. 1942).

during the period when the trustee has legal title to the property), ascertained and unascertained beneficiaries and remaindermen have equitable interests in the trust property.[2] If during that time there is a condition which must be fulfilled before someone may acquire an equitable interest, that equitable interest is said to be a *contingent* one. (The condition of survivorship is perhaps the most common such condition precedent the trustee is likely to encounter today.) In the context of trusts, the Rule thus governs how long equitable contingent interests may remain outstanding before they must extinguish or be converted into vested interests (interests which are held by someone unconditionally).[3]

The Rule is against the remoteness of *vesting in interest*, not remoteness of *vesting in possession*.[4] To illustrate the difference between the two, let us assume A transfers property to B in trust for C for life, remainder to Mrs. Jones, who currently lives in Washington, D.C. From the time the trust is created Mrs. Jones's interest is *vested*, though not possessory. This is because at the time the trust is created, she is ascertained and during the life of C there is no event that will extinguish her interest. At the death of C, the trust property passes outright and free of trust either to Mrs. Jones or to her estate. In other words, Mrs. Jones then gets possession of the property, be she dead or alive.

On the other hand, were A to make a simple unconditional gift of the property outright and free of trust directly to Mrs. Jones, bypassing the trustee altogether, Mrs. Jones's interest at the time of transfer would be both *vested* and *possessory*. For purposes of the Rule, however, vesting only is what matters.

An exhaustive study of the Rule is beyond the scope of this book; moreover it would duplicate the efforts of others.[5] Rather, the trustee should use the guidelines that follow to assist in developing a methodology for ruling out Rule problems and for fram-

---

[2]*See generally* Bogert, Trusts and Trustees §181.
[3]Id.
[4]Id. §213.
[5]*See* id. §213 nn.1, 2 and accompanying text.

ing appropriate questions for counsel when such problems are encountered. Hopefully, the trustee will be able to confront the Rule efficiently and cost-effectively, with courage and with confidence.

It should first be made clear that if property becomes the subject of a charitable trust within the period of the Rule, such a trust may last forever.[6] Thus it is said that the Rule does not apply to charitable trusts.[7] Let us take as an example a scholarship trust fund for gifted and needy U.S. citizens. Each U.S. citizen, born and unborn, has a contingent equitable interest in the trust. The interests are contingent because certain conditions precedent — prior conditions as it were — must be satisfied before the citizen may receive a scholarship distribution from the trust. The conditions are that the citizen must be alive, gifted, needy, a scholar, a U.S. citizen, duly selected, and so forth. The beneficial interests are equitable not legal because legal title to the property is in the trustee. As a matter of public policy the use of the trust property for such a charitable purpose perpetually may be subject to such conditions.[8] Not so, however, with noncharitable trusts.

Under the common law, a contingent interest in a noncharitable trust must extinguish by vesting or otherwise within the period allowed by the Rule. That period is 21 years after the death of certain people who are alive at the time the contingent interest is created. These people are known as *measuring lives* or *lives in being*.[9] If at the time the interest is created one could conjure up a possible fact or circumstance — a worst case scenario as it were — that would cause a condition precedent to remain outstanding beyond the period of the Rule, there may be a common law Rule problem that the trustee will have to confront. At the very least,

---

[6]*See generally* 4A Scott on Trusts §365.

[7]*But see* Bogert, Trusts and Trustees §341.

[8]*See generally* id. §351.

[9]*See generally* Dukeminier, Perpetuities: The Measuring Lives, 85 Colum. L. Rev. 1648 (1985); Becker, A Methodology for Solving Perpetuities Problems Under the Common Law Rule: A Step by Step Process That Carefully Identifies All Testing Lives in Being, 67 Wash. U. L.Q. 949 (1989).

the trustee will have some analytical work to do as it is more than likely there are provisions in the governing trust instrument or somewhere in a state statute that will have some bearing on whether the trustee actually has a perpetuities problem with the trust.

How does one go about determining whether a particular contingent equitable interest violates the Rule in its classical form? First, determine when the contingent interests were created. Second, determine who the lives in being are. Third, determine who under the terms of the trust are to take vested interests. And finally, calculate whether such a vesting, under a worst-case scenario, could occur more than 21 years after the time when the last survivor of the lives in being dies. To illustrate the process and to expose uninitiated readers to the complexity and subtlety of the Rule's application, throughout this section the following hypothetical trust will be subjected to the four-step analysis:

A settlor transfers property inter vivos to a trustee. The settlor reserves an inter vivos right to the net income as well as a right of revocation. Upon the death of the settlor the trust converts to a discretionary trust. The provisions of the discretionary trust are that the trustee may apply income and invade principal for one or more of the settlor's grandchildren, whenever born, who are alive when a particular discretionary distribution from the trust is made. At the point in time after the death of the settlor when no grandchild of the settlor is alive and under the age of 30 years, the trust shall be held for the benefit of the youngest then-living great-grandchild of the settlor. That great-grandchild, if there is one, shall have a right to all the net income in all events as well as a general inter vivos power to appoint the trust property. Any property remaining in the trust at the death of that great-grandchild shall be paid to the executor of the great-grandchild's estate.

A time line of the trust would look like this:

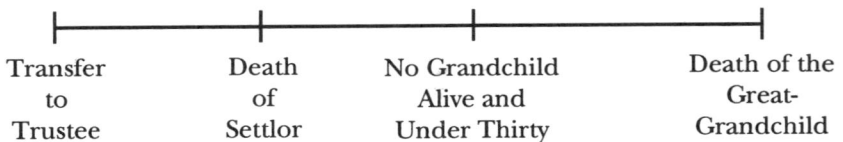

Transfer to Trustee	Death of Settlor	No Grandchild Alive and Under Thirty	Death of the Great-Grandchild

§8.2.1.1   The Creation of the Interest

It is self-evident that because a will speaks at death, a contingent equitable interest under a testamentary trust cannot be created before the testator dies. (Thus the testator can never be the life in being at the time of the creation of the testamentary trust.) With respect to any trust, whether testamentary or inter vivos, insofar as the Rule is concerned, contingent interests do not exist while a trust is revocable, that is, while there is an outstanding unexercised general inter vivos power to appoint the trust property.[10] Thus contingent interests are created at the time when a trust becomes irrevocable — a time which will not always coincide with when property is transferred to the trustee.

In our hypothetical trust, the equitable contingent interests of the grandchildren and great-grandchildren, born and unborn, are created at the death of the settlor when the reserved right of revocation (assuming it is never exercised) extinguishes. At that time certain of the settlor's issue receive equitable interests that are contingent upon survivorship and the trustee's exercise of discretion. During the lifetime of the settlor of our hypothetical trust, the settlor alone, as holder of the power, is deemed to hold unconditionally all the equitable interests and is deemed to possess a vested interest in the property. Thus, as the Rule is concerned with when vesting must occur, there cannot be a Rule violation until after the extinguishment, by the settlor's death or otherwise, of the power.

§8.2.1.2   The Worst Case Life in Being

It is unfortunate, but a mastery of the many nuances of worst case life in being identification takes good intuition and much practice.[11] By way of illustration, the worst case life in being in our hypothetical trust is the last survivor of the children of the settlor who were alive at the death of the settlor, assuming the reserved

---

[10]*See* Leach, Perpetuities in a Nutshell, 51 Harv. L. Rev. 638, 654 (1938).
[11]Id. at 641-642.

right of revocation — which is tantamount to a general power of appointment — is never exercised. Why must some child of the settlor be the life in being? Because, taking the period of gestation into account and ignoring, for purposes of the Rule, recent developments in the science of postmortem reproduction, the child cannot come into existence after the settlor's death, which is when the reserved right of revocation is extinguished and when the contingent interests are created. A child cannot be conceived from the grave.

Why is that child the worst case life in being? Because that child, after the death of all other lives in being (namely the settlor and the settlor's issue living at the time of the settlor's death) could then produce non-lives-in-being grandchildren of the settlor whose equitable interests during the discretionary phase of the trust are contingent and whose ages will govern the time when the remainder interests will ultimately vest in a great-grandchild.

What is the worst case? The worst case is that the only child of the settlor dies immediately after conceiving a grandchild of the settlor. At that point all lives in being at the death of the settlor are dead and vesting now must occur before the expiration of 21 years. Had another life in being been in existence at that time (for example, another child of the settlor), then the day of reckoning could have been postponed.

Professor Leach, with characteristic clarity and economy of language, went to the heart of the problem in his article entitled *Perpetuities in a Nutshell*, when he wrote that the lives in being "need not be mentioned in the instrument, need not be holders of previous estates, and need not be connected in any way with the property or the persons designated to take it."[12] In our hypothetical trust, the children of the settlor are neither mentioned nor holders of previous estates; yet they are lives in being for purposes of the Rule. The trustee wishing to learn the art of life in being identification would do well to begin by studying the representative measuring life illustrations in Part III of Professor Leach's article.[13]

---

[12]Id. at 641.
[13]Id. at 641-642.

§8.2.1.3   The Vesting of Interests Under Trusts

A trust beneficiary's interest is vested if the interest is not subject to a condition precedent such as survivorship.[14] When an ascertained person is entitled, whether dead or alive, to an ascertained portion of the trust property, the interest in that portion is vested. What the trustee may find difficult to grasp about the vesting aspect of the Rule is that an interest may vest in someone for purposes of the Rule; yet the person may not get the use of the interest before death.[15] It is the person's probate estate that will ultimately get the use of the property. The trustee cannot begin to understand the Rule without having solved the vesting riddle.[16]

In our hypothetical trust, the words *then living* make the interests of conceived and unconceived great-grandchildren contingent in part on their being born before and not dying before the trust terminates. These contingencies — or conditions precedent — will remain outstanding during that phase of the trust's life after the death of the settlor when there exists a grandchild of the settlor who is both alive and under the age of 30 years. The instrument provides that at the point in time after the settlor's death when no grandchild is alive and under the age of 30, someone is then either going to hold a vested remainder interest or a vested reversionary interest under a resulting trust. The remainder interests will then be vested for two reasons, of which either one is sufficient vesting for purposes of the Rule: (1) the subsequent death of the great-grandchild, if any, who met the implicit conditions of birth, survivorship, and age will not extinguish his or her interest, because in that event the trust property would merely find its way into the great-grandchild's probate estate; (2) the qualifying great-grandchild will be the holder of an inter vivos power of appointment which, for purposes of the Rule, is tantamount to the great-grandchild's possessing a vested interest in the

---

[14]*See* J. C. Gray, The Rule Against Perpetuities §§101-103 (4th ed. 1942).

[15]Id. at §102.

[16]The trustee may wish to consult chapter 3 of Thomas F. Bergin and Paul G. Haskell's Preface to Estates in Land and Future Interests (2d ed. 1984), which has a useful section on the "concept of vestedness." *See also* id. at 66-73.

207

trust property which is the subject of the power. If there is no great-grandchild around to take when there is no grandchild alive and under the age of 30, the property will pass to the settlor's probate estate upon a resulting trust, the reversionary interest having been vested in the settlor and the settlor's estate during the entire life of the trust.[17]

§8.2.1.4   A Possible Vesting Beyond the Period of the Common Law Rule

Applying the Rule to our hypothetical trust, we assume the settlor and all the settlor's descendants who were alive at the settlor's death have died, except for one child of the settlor. After the death of the settlor, that child produces a grandchild of the settlor. The child then dies when the grandchild is a day old. Now all lives in being are dead and we have a day-old non-life in being grandchild of the settlor. If we can conjure up only one scenario whereby there could be a vesting in someone later than a day after the grandchild's twenty-first birthday, we have a common law Rule violation. We can. Here is one such scenario: At the age of 25, the grandchild receives a discretionary distribution of income or principal from the trust. Here is another: The grandchild has a thirtieth birthday at which point the property vests in a non-life in being great-grandchild of the settlor. In both cases, property would vest in non-lives in being more than 21 years after the death of the life in being child of the settlor.

§8.2.1.5   Consequences of a Violation of the Common Law Rule

If an equitable contingent interest fails, it does not mean necessarily that the entire trust fails.[18] The tainted interests are

---

[17]*See* Gray, *supra* note 14, §327.1.

[18]*But see* Leach, *supra* note 10, at 1336 (if equitable contingent interest is an "integral part of the dispositive scheme," then entire trust may indeed fail).

constructively stricken from the instrument and the trustee will continue to administer any remaining equitable interests that may be in compliance with the Rule. In our hypothetical trust, for example, the provisions for the benefit of the settlor are valid because he had reserved to himself a right of revocation in the nature of a general inter vivos power of appointment which, for purposes of the Rule, is tantamount to retaining a vested interest in the trust property. If the instrument had provided that the settlor's children were to have beneficial interests in the discretionary trust, the trustee could continue to administer their interests as they would be lives in being. Unfortunately the instrument did not so provide. Therefore, effective immediately upon the death of the settlor — which is when the interests are created under our hypothetical trust — the contingent equitable interests of the settlor's grandchildren during the discretionary phase of the trust are deemed *nonexistent* because of the possibility of a discretionary distribution of income or principal to a non-life in being grandchild more than 21 years after the death of the last life in being child of the settlor. As vesting in a "then-living" grandchild may occur beyond the permissible period of the Rule, the remainder provision fails as well.

What are the consequences of these failures? The consequences are that upon the death of the settlor the trust stops — drops off into thin air as it were. By operation of law there are no more terms governing the disposition of income and principal. Thus the life of the trust has come to an end. The trustee, however, may not consume the property.[19] Rather the trustee, now holding the property upon a resulting trust,[20] must transfer title to the executor or administrator of the settlor's probate estate. The trust property will then follow the fortunes of the settlor's probate estate, passing either in accordance with the terms of the settlor's will or under the laws of intestacy.[21] Had the children of the settlor, along with the grandchildren, been permissible beneficia-

---

[19]*See* Restatement (Second) of Trusts §345 comment *i* (1959).
[20]*See generally* Bogert, Trusts and Trustees §468.
[21]Id.

ries during the discretionary phase of the trust, the life of the trust would have continued (for the benefit of the children only, however) until the death of the last life in being child of the settlor; then the trust would fail. Our hypothetical trust instrument, however, contained no such provision for the benefit of the settlor's children.

§8.2.1.6   The Perpetuities Savings Clause

Today, a trust instrument is likely to contain a so-called perpetuities savings clause that triggers the termination of the trust at a time certain, unless the trust in the ordinary course of things terminates at an earlier time.[22] This time certain provision is designed to trigger a vesting within the period of the common law Rule no matter what.[23] Most such clauses operate by providing for a termination in all events 21 years after the death of the last survivor of specified lives of being, at which point the property is distributed outright and free of trusts to remainderman specified in the savings clause.[24]

If such a provision were in the governing instrument of our hypothetical trust — perhaps providing for termination 21 years after the death of the last survivor of all issue of the settlor alive at the death of the settlor — then there is no way that a non-life in being might receive a discretionary distribution or a vested remainder interest more than 21 years after the death of the last survivor of all lives in being.

The lesson here is: *Check for a savings clause.* The trustee should be faulted — if not held liable — for allowing a perpetuities panic to build before someone discovers that there is a valid governing savings clause, particularly if the trust is charged for any legal and administrative expenses attributable to the nonfeasance.

---

[22]*See, e.g.,* Bogert, Trusts and Trustees §1046 (section VIII(k)).
[23]Id.
[24]Id.

§8.2.1.7   Perpetuities Legislation

Since the Second World War there have been waves of legislative initiatives designed to corral and mitigate the harshness of the Rule. It was Professor Leach who more than anyone else was responsible for setting things in motion when, in 1952, he published several law review articles calling for legislative modification of the Rule.[25] He suggested that the Rule be applied on the basis of events that actually happen and that offending provisions be reformed to approximate as near as possible the settlor's intent.[26] Whether the ensuing legislation has had or will have any social utility is a matter beyond the scope of this book. What is clear however is that these initiatives have added additional complexities to the Rule. Take for example the Uniform Statutory Rule Against Perpetuities[27] (USRAP), which has already been adopted in ten states.[28] It essentially grafts onto the common law Rule a 90-year wait-and-see provision and provides for judicial reformation in lieu of the imposition of a resulting trust. Thus even in a USRAP jurisdiction the trustee may not ignore the common law Rule. In our hypothetical trust, for example, the USRAP would allow discretionary distributions to the settlor's grandchildren for a 90-year period beginning with the settlor's death. The interest of a great-grandchild would be good if it were to vest within that period.

There is another lesson here for a trustee faced with a common law Rule violation: If a review of the governing instrument does not turn up a savings clause, do not forget to check for an applicable statute.

---

[25]Leach, Perpetuities: Staying the Slaughter of the Innocents, 68 L.Q. Rev. 35 (1952); Leach, Perpetuities in Perspective: Ending the Rule's Reign of Terror, 65 Harv. L. Rev. 721 (1952).

[26]Id.

[27]Uniform Statutory Rule Against Perpetuities, 8B U.L.A. 333 (1993).

[28]See generally Fellows, Testing Perpetuity Reforms: A Study of Perpetuity Cases 1984-1989, 25 Real Prop. Prob. & Tr. J. 597 (1991).

§8.2.2   *When the Trust May Be Terminated*

A trust, once established, ordinarily cannot be altered, amended, revoked or terminated in mid-course except pursuant to its own provisions. [29] Such a provision might take the form of a reserved right of revocation, a general power of appointment, a right to demand principal, or a right in the trustee to invade principal. Only in a few states is a trust revocable by the settlor unless there is express language in the governing instrument to the contrary. [30] The termination of a trust also may be achieved if all the equitable and all the legal interests have been merged in one person, [31] if its purposes are impossible of fulfillment, or if its purposes have been fully accomplished. [32] Some states have enacted statutes providing for the termination of small trusts. [33] In the United States, the coalescing of all *beneficial* interests in one person who is not the trustee ordinarily will not trigger a termination of the trust unless the purposes of the trust have been accomplished. [34] A trust may be cancelled because it was created through fraud or undue influence or mistake, [35] although cancellation perhaps belongs more in the category of annulment than termination.

§8.2.2.1   Mid-course Termination of the Irrevocable Trust

If all the beneficiaries including the remaindermen are in existence and of full age and legal capacity, may they (or in the case of a charitable trust, may the attorney general) collude with the

---

[29]*See generally* 4 Scott on Trusts §330.1.

[30]California and Texas are among these states. *See* id. §330.1 n.6 and accompanying text.

[31]*See generally* id. §341.

[32]*See generally* id. §335.

[33]*See generally* Committee on Formation, Administration, and Distribution of Trusts, Procedures for Terminating Small Trusts, 19 Real Prop. Prob. & Tr. J. 988 (1984).

[34]*See generally* 4 Scott on Trusts §337.

[35]*See generally* 4 Scott on Trusts §§333.1 (fraud), 333.3 (undue influence), 333.4 (mistake).

trustee to terminate an inter vivos trust even if its purposes have yet to be accomplished? Would the settlor or the settlor's estate have any standing to object? One could well imagine, for example, a situation whereby the spendthrift adult children of a settlor collude with the trustee to break the provisions of an income-only spendthrift trust that was established for their benefit by the parent.[36] Some commentators have argued that the settlor, as a matter of public policy, ought to have standing to compel the trustee faithfully to carry out the terms of his trust.[37] Others, most notably Professor Scott, would seem to disagree.[38]

In this day and age of enormous pressure on the elderly and the handicapped to divest themselves of their property, the trustee should exercise due diligence before accepting an irrevocable inter vivos trust. He should assure himself that he is neither buying a lawsuit nor expected to violate that trust.

§8.2.2.2   The Revocable Trust

The settlor of a trust may reserve a right of revocation.[39] Inherent in that right is the lesser right to amend the trust; inherent in the right to amend is the right to insert by amendment into the trust instrument a revocation provision. A legally incapacitated settlor cannot exercise a reserved right of revocation.[40] May, however, the settlor's agent, acting under a Durable Power of Attorney,[41] exercise it? In theory, yes, provided three conditions are met: (1) the applicable Durable Power of Attorney statute authorizes such an agency, (2) the Durable Power of Attorney under which the agent purports to act is either sufficiently broad or sufficiently precise to cover the purported act of revocation, and (3) the governing trust instrument itself contains a provision

---

[36]See 2A Scott on Trusts §151 ("It is held that even though the trust is a spendthrift trust, it can be terminated by the beneficiaries and the settlor if they all consent and are under no disability.").

[37]See §4.1.

[38]Id.

[39]See 4 Scott on Trusts §330.

[40]See generally id. §330 n.7 and accompanying text.

[41]Uniform Probate Code §5-501, 8 U.L.A. 513 (1984).

that authorizes revocation by proxy.[42] The trustee honors at his peril a revocation by proxy, unless all three conditions have been met. Close attention to matters of authority are warranted as well if the trustee is in receipt of an instrument of revocation submitted by the settlor's conservator or guardian.[43]

Suppose the governing trust instrument contains a revocation provision that *excludes* revocation by proxy. Would such a qualified revocation effectively foreclose revocation by a guardian or agent operating under a Durable Power of Attorney? Why not? Presumably it is the intention of the settlor that during periods of incapacity the trust be irrevocable and that the revocation provision be suspended so that there is no basis of authority on which the agent or guardian can act.[44] To the extent the agent or guardian is foreclosed from terminating an irrevocable trust created before incapacity, so too should it be foreclosed from terminating a trust where the power of revocation is suspended.

§8.2.3   Distribution Issues

The trustee who distributes the wrong amount or pays it to the wrong person must bear the loss. The cases which surcharge the trustee for making erroneous distribution are peculiarly distressing. It has been held that if the trustee pays the wrong person even under advice of counsel, the trustee will be obliged to refund the amount with interest. Particular care must be taken when a power of attorney or order for payment or assignment is presented. It is as dangerous to pay over to one whose interest has terminated as to pay over on an invalid assignment.

The trustee ought not to pay a minor's share to the minor or the minor's natural parent, lest the trustee be required to pay again when the minor comes of age. Payment should be made only to the minor's formally appointed guardian (which may of course

---

[42]*See* Kline v. Utah Dept. of Health, 776 P.2d 57 (Utah 1989).

[43]*See, e.g.,* In re Matter of Bo, 365 N.W.2d 847 (N.D. 1985).

[44]"Where the settlor reserves a power to revoke the trust under certain circumstances, he can revoke it only under those circumstances." 4 Scott on Trusts §330.8.

be the child's natural parent) or to someone informally appointed pursuant to the terms of a statute enacted to facilitate the distribution of trust property to minors.[45] A well-drafted trust instrument will make provision for retaining the minor's share in trust until the minor reaches the age of majority. Such a provision, however, is not helpful when small amounts are involved.

The fact that the trustee has been diligent or has taken advice will not be of any help when it comes to misdelivery. The trustee's only protection for misdelivery is if it were done under a court order obtained without fraud and with proper notice having been given to all interested parties.

Prior to making distributions the trustee should make certain that all taxes due with respect to the property have been paid, including income, estate and generation-skipping-transfer taxes. The trustee who distributes property needed to satisfy a tax obligation may be personally liable for all or a portion of the tax.[46] The key to an orderly and satisfactory settlement of the trust's tax obligations is timely coordination with the settlor's executor, the beneficiary, or the beneficiary's executor, as appropriate.

§8.3   The Transfer of Trust Property

When the trustee transfers trust property to a bona fide purchaser, title passes free of trust.[1] Such a transfer forecloses the beneficiary's rights against the transferee, though not necessarily against the trustee. Any rights the beneficiary may have against nonbeneficiary takers of the trust property, including those who fail to qualify as bona fide purchasers, are covered elsewhere in

---

[45]*See, e.g.,* Uniform Transfers to Minors Act, 8B U.L.A. 497 (1993).

[46]*See generally* Bogert, Trusts and Trustees §265 (income tax); Stephens et al., Federal Estate and Gift Taxation ¶8.02 (estate tax) and ¶12.03 (generation-skipping tax) (6th ed. 1991).

§8.3   [1]Restatement (Second) of Trusts §284 (1959); *see generally* 4 Scott on Trusts §284.

this handbook.[2] Recall, however, that a transferee only secures the protection and status afforded a bona fide purchaser if title to the property is obtained for value and without notice.

§8.3.1   The Trustee's Personal Creditors

As a general rule, an attachment of the trust property by the trustee's personal creditor is subject to the rights of the beneficiary.[3] The rationale is that the creditor does not pay value to the trust nor does the attachment give the creditor legal title. Certain attachments of real estate, however, may be exempted by statute from this general rule. Many states, for example, now have statutes subordinating the interest of the beneficiary to that of the trustee's personal creditor when the attached real estate is held in an unrecorded trust.[4] Thus it is of primary importance for the trustee of an inter vivos trust containing real estate to record the governing instrument; timely recording effectively deprives the personal creditor of the trustee any access to the trust's real estate. Under most such statutes, the attaching creditor who has no notice of an unrecorded trust of real estate will prevail over the beneficiary even though the creditor receives notice before taking the property on execution.[5] The statutes that give this unusual right do not ordinarily apply to personal property.[6]

§8.3.2   Purchasers for Value of Trust Property

In the case of real estate, the prospective purchaser ordinarily has notice that the property is held in trust since the instrument is a matter of record. The purchaser must then determine whether

---

[2]*See* §5.4.2.

[3]Restatement (Second) of Trusts §308 (1959); *see generally* 4 Scott on Trusts §308.

[4]*See* Restatement (Second) of Trusts §308 comment *b* (1959).

[5]*See generally* 4 Scott on Trusts §308.2.

[6]*See generally* Bogert, Trusts and Trustees §884.

the trustee has the power of sale.[7] If the trustee has that power, the transferee will take clear title even though the trustee thereafter misappropriates the proceeds.[8] In England and in many American jurisdictions the purchaser expressly is exempted by statute from monitoring the application of the purchase price.[9]

In the relatively few cases of unrecorded trusts of real estate and in nearly all cases of trusts of personal property, the first matter to be determined is whether the purchaser had notice of a trust's existence. There being no instrument of public record this question becomes one of fact. In the case of *real estate*, for example, the purchaser may be put on notice of the trust as a result of the explicit use of the word *trustee* in a previous deed,[10] material information communicated to the purchaser orally, or the existence of some peculiar circumstance, such as occupation of the property by a person who claims to have a beneficial interest in it.[11] In the case of *securities*, the word *trustee* appearing upon the face of the certificate is sufficient to put the purchaser to his inquiry not only as to the existence of the trust but also as to whether the proposed transfer is within the trustee's powers.[12]

The prospective purchaser who learns that a trust exists must demand to see the trust instrument to determine whether the proposed sale is authorized.[13]

§8.3.3 Pledgees of Trust Property

Let us assume that the trustee pledges trust property to secure the trustee's own personal obligation. What are the rights of the pledgee as against the beneficiary? The pledgee is in a critical

---

[7]*See* §3.5.3.
[8]*See generally* 4 Scott on Trusts §321.
[9]Id.
[10]*See generally* id. §297.3.
[11]Id.
[12]Id. However, under the Uniform Commercial Code, the issuer or its transfer agent registering a security for transfer is not bound to inquire into the trustee's power. U.C.C. §8-403 (1977); see also Uniform Act for Simplification of Fiduciary Security Transfers §2, 7B U.L.A. 689 (1958).
[13]Restatement (Second) of Trusts §297 comments *d, k-n* (1959).

position: He may be a bona fide purchaser and fully protected in his security rights or, if the circumstances are against him, he may be at the extreme opposite pole, in the position of colluding in a breach of trust with full responsibility to the beneficiary as a constructive trustee. Thus a person who in good faith lends money to the trust and accepts a pledge of trust property will be fully protected despite a subsequent misappropriation of the proceeds of the loan. [14] However, if the lender accepts a pledge of known trust property to secure what the lender knows to be the trustee's personal indebtedness, the lender colludes in a breach of the trustee's duty of loyalty. It should be noted that a pledge of stock would be put upon inquiry by the presence of the word *trustee* on the face of the certificate. [15]

§8.3.4 Banks Receiving Deposits from Trustees

A bank generally is not bound to see that the trustee properly administers the trust's bank account even when it has notice that the money belongs to the trust. [16] It would be impossible to conduct business under any other rule. Therefore, in cases where the trustee, apparently acting in the ordinary course of business, draws funds from the trust account and deposits them in his own account, or in situations where the trustee deposits a trust check in his own account, the bank is not in any way liable. [17] If, on the other hand, the trustee, in breach of trust, attempts to satisfy his personal obligation to the bank with trust funds, and the bank is on notice of the trust, then the bank must give up the funds. [18]

---

[14] Id. §284 comment *g*.
[15] *See generally* 4 Scott on Trusts §297.3.
[16] *See generally* id. §324; Restatement (Second) of Trusts §324 (1959).
[17] *See generally* 4 Scott on Trusts §324.3.
[18] *See generally* id. §324.4.

§8.3.5   Stock Transfer Agents

The stock transfer agent who is asked to effect transfer of a trust's shares in a corporation, and the corporation itself, are placed in an unpleasant position whenever the trustee is engaged in a wrongful assignment or sale of the shares. The underlying rule is that any person who knowingly assists in the wrongful disposition of the trust property is fully responsible.[19] This means that, in the absence of a statute, whenever the corporation or its transfer agent knows of the existence of a trust it must ascertain whether the trustee has the power of sale.[20] As the duty to ascertain the trustee's authority is placed upon the corporation, it or its agent would be justified in declining to make transfer unless the trustee supplies the certificates for inspection or produces other evidence showing a right to make the transfer. Most states have now adopted statutes relieving corporations and their transfer agents of the duty to investigate a trustee's authority to transfer securities unless they have actual knowledge of the lack thereof.[21]

§8.4   The Trustee's Compensation

The general rule now in the United States is that the trustee is entitled to reasonable compensation.[1] In some states the trustee's fees are set by statute,[2] and in others it is a matter of custom and practice. The prevailing practice in this country is to calculate the trustee's compensation on the basis of a fixed percentage of income and principal.[3] When the trustee is also coun-

---

[19]*See generally* Bogert, Trusts and Trustees §901.
[20]*See generally* Bogert, Trusts and Trustees §905.
[21]Id.
§8.4   [1]*See generally* 3A Scott on Trusts §242.
[2]*See generally* Bogert, Trusts and Trustees §975.
[3]Id.

sel to the trust, however, the practice of charging on a time basis for the legal work and on a percentage basis for the fiduciary responsibility can give the appearance that the trust is being double-billed. In this situation, it is probably better both for the attorney-trustee and the beneficiary if all compensation is time based.[4]

Table 8-1 is an analysis of the standard charge schedules of corporate trustees in Boston, New York, Miami, Chicago, and Los Angeles. A review of this representative sampling should assist the trustee in formulating a fee schedule that conforms to industry standards.

Table 8-1.   Standard Charge Schedules of Corporate Trustees

Principal	Boston	New York	Miami	Chicago	Los Angeles
1st 1 million	1.0%	1.0%	.86%	.8%	1.1%
1-3 million	.73%	1.0%	.55%	.55%	.7%
3-5 million	.65%	.75%	.35%	.5%	.5%
5-10 million	.5%	.5%	.3%	.3%	Quoted
> 10 million	.35%	.375%	.3%	Quoted	Quoted

The figures in Table 8-1, stated in July 1993, are percentages of principal. Many corporate trustees also have a base charge of approximately $2000.00 per trust. Some charges are based not only on the value of the principal but also on the amount of income earned.[5] For special service above and beyond the call of duty, the trustee may be entitled to extra compensation, but the matter is not without some controversy.[6] In recent years corporate fiduciaries have been the subject of class action suits for their compensation practices.[7]

---

[4]*See, e.g.,* Grimes v. Perkins School for the Blind, 22 Mass. App. Ct. 439 494 N.E.2d 406 (1986); *see* §6.1.3.3.

[5]*See generally* Bogert, Trusts and Trustees §975.

[6]*See generally* 3A Scott on Trusts §242.2.

[7]*See, e.g.,* Upp v. Mellon Bank, NA, 799 F. Supp. 540 (E.D. Pa. 1992), *reversed,* 994 F.2d 1039 (1993).

§8.5   Conflict of Laws

When a trust instrument is prepared and executed in one state and the trust itself is administered in another, what is a trustee to do if the laws of the two states are in conflict? Which state's law is to be applied? Much depends upon the issue. Laws may be contradictory when it comes to the validity of the trust itself;[1] the construction of its terms;[2] rules of administration;[3] or the rights, duties, and obligations of fiduciaries, beneficiaries, creditors, and others who may come in contact with the trust.[4] One state may recognize spendthrift trusts, the other may not;[5] one may have adopted the Uniform Statutory Rule Against Perpetuities, the other may not have done so;[6] in one state, a word such as *heirs* or *issue* might encompass illegitimates; in the other state it might not.[7] States will have differing approaches to compensation, apportionment, revocability, disposition in default and investing. Such inconveniences are the inevitable consequence of a federal system of government.

As a general rule, the question of which law applies in a particular situation is best left in the hands of the lawyer. A review of Professor Schoenblum's treatise on multistate and multinational estate planning[8] or the conflict of laws chapter in Professor's Scott's treatise on trusts[9] will reveal to the trustee just how subtle, complicated, and unsettled — how lacking in easy answers — this area of the law is. We offer here some rough rules of thumb which the trustee may find helpful when framing requests

---

§8.5 [1]*See generally* J. Schoenblum, Multistate and Multinational Estate Planning §17.01 (1982).

[2]Id. at §17.02.

[3]Id. at §§17.03-17.04.

[4]Id. at §17.05.

[5]*See* §5.3.4.3(c); Schoenblum, *supra* note 1, §17.07; 5A Scott on Trusts §§625-628, 660.

[6]*See* §8.2.1.7.

[7]*See* §5.2.

[8]Schoenblum, *supra* note 1.

[9]5A Scott on Trusts §§553-666 (ch. 14).

for legal opinions. However, a detailed treatment of the subject of conflict of laws — including which court will have jurisdiction over a trust with multistate contacts — is well beyond the scope of this handbook.

First, a trust that contains a single parcel of real estate is governed by the laws of the state in which the parcel is located.[10] Unfortunately, if the trust contains real estate located in more than one state, or both real estate and movables, no similarly simple rule covers such variations on the theme.[11]

Second, a trust containing only movables is governed by the laws of the state in which the trust is being administered.[12] There are many exceptions to this rule. For example, what if a testamentary trust is being administered in a state other than the state where the will was probated? Under those circumstances, the laws of the state of probate might govern.[13] Moreover, what is the state of administration? Where the trustee resides? Where the movables are located? Which movables?

Third, notwithstanding the first two rules, if a settlor provides that the laws of a particular state are to govern the administration of a trust and the construction of its terms, then the court will honor the provision as to moveables, except when to do so would violate the public policy of the state in which the trust is being administered.[14] A court having jurisdiction over a trust's administration, for example, would not enforce a spendthrift clause in a state which looks with disfavor on spendthrift trusts, even if the settlor's choice of law were that of some other state more favorably disposed towards such trusts.[15] In the absence of express language as to which state's laws shall apply, a court may well infer that the settlor of an inter vivos trust intended the laws of the settlor's domicile to apply, particularly if the governing instrument was

---

[10]*See generally* Schoenblum, *supra* note 1, §§17.01.1, 17.01.3, 17.02.1, 17.03.1; 5A Scott on Trusts §§648, 649, 652, 659; Restatement (Second) Conflict of Laws §§277-278 (1971).

[11]*See generally* 5A Scott on Trusts §§643-663.

[12]*See generally* Schoenblum, *supra* note 1, §§17.01.2, 17.01.4-5, 17.02.2, 17.03.2-3; 5A Scott on Trusts §§574, 592, 605-607.

[13]*See generally* Schoenblum, *supra*, §17.01.2 (1982); 5A Scott on Trusts §592.

[14]*See generally* Schoenblum, *supra*, §17.01.6.

[15]*See generally* id. §17.07.

prepared and signed there.[16] But what if the settlor changed domiciles after execution? Or there were more than one settlor? What if the settlor resided in one state, had the instrument prepared in another, and signed it in a third? Again, the trustee will find it difficult obtaining legal opinions free of qualification and hedging when the trust has contacts with more than one state.

We have touched briefly on the problems that arise when the settlor was domiciled in one state and the trust is administered in another. But more likely it is the *beneficiary* — not the settlor — who was domiciled in a state other than the administration state. This situation can bring with it its own set of conflict of laws issues (*e.g.*, when the settlor provides for distribution upon the death of a beneficiary to the beneficiary's "issue").[17] The word *issue* can mean one thing in the settlor's domicile and quite another thing in the beneficiary's. In the settlor's state it may include illegitimates; in the beneficiary's it may not. Which meaning applies? The better view seems to be the state where the instrument was prepared and signed, particularly if it was the settlor's domicile, unless the settlor had expressed a contrary intention in the governing instrument.[18] To some extent, it is a rule of administrative convenience: While a trust may have many beneficiaries in many different states, there is usually only one settlor. Moreover, it is reasonable to expect that the settlor and the drafting attorney were relying on the prevailing meaning of the word in the state of preparation and execution, particularly if it was the state of the settlor's domicile. Otherwise, the meaning of the word is held hostage to the migratory habits of the beneficiaries.

Suppose a settlor provides that upon the death of the beneficiary the trust property passes outright and free of trust to the beneficiary's heirs. If the term *heirs* refers to intestate takers, which intestacy law is being referred to, that of the beneficiary's domicile or that of the settlor's? Does *heirs* cover only those persons, if any, who *actually* inherited the beneficiary's property under the laws of intestacy or those persons who *would have* inherited

---

[16]*See generally* 5A Scott on Trusts §612.
[17]*See* §5.2.
[18]*See generally* 5A Scott on Trusts §578.

the property assuming the beneficiary had died intestate?[19] If the term imports the indicative, then the law of the beneficiary's domicile would of course govern; if the term imports the subjunctive, then perhaps the trustee must look to the intestacy law of the settlor's domicile. But to which version of the law? The one in effect when the trust was executed? The one in effect at the time of the beneficiary's death? A prospective trustee should think long and hard before accepting a trust which employs without elaboration the term *heirs*.[20]

A final word of advice: The prospective trustee should make sure that as many potential conflict of laws issues as possible are preempted in the governing instrument, and should be particularly wary of "boilerplate" language, especially if it causes unfamiliar laws to apply to the trust's administration and to the construction of its terms. The prospective trustee should know the rules of the game before the game starts.

§8.6   The Corporate Trustee

In most jurisdictions, a corporation needs governmental authority to engage in the business of acting as trustee.[1] The requirement is statutory, there being no common law impediment to a corporation per se engaging in such activity so long as it possesses the general authority to hold *property*.[2]

By statute, the Comptroller of the Currency is vested with the authority to grant a federal trust charter.[3] A corporation with

---

[19]*See generally* National Shawmut Bank v. Joy, 315 Mass. 457, 462-467, 53 N.E.2d 113, 117-120 (1944).

[20]M. Reutlinger, Wills, Trusts, and Estates: Essential Terms and Concepts 99-100 (1993); 5A Scott on Trusts §578.

§8.6 [1]*See generally* 2 Scott on Trusts §§96.3, 96.5; Bogert, Trusts and Trustees §131.

[2]*See generally* 2 Scott on Trusts §96.

[3]12 U.S.C. §92a(a) (1989).

federal trust powers will carry the official designation of a national bank, whether or not it is authorized to engage in commercial banking activities as well.[4] The authority to grant a state trust charter, more often than not, is vested by statute in a state's banking commissioner.[5] Corporations with state trust charters often carry the designation *trust company*. A granting authority, whether federal or state, usually is charged by statute with the responsibility of regulating how the grantee corporation then carries out its trust charter.

Whether a particular group of organizers should seek a federal or state trust charter is well beyond the scope of this handbook.[6] It will depend upon many things, including which statutory and regulatory scheme best accommodates the group's business objectives and expectations.[7] Chartering authorities, for example, will differ as to capital and surplus requirements. It should be noted, however, that no federal trust charter may be issued to a national bank operating in a state whose capital and surplus requirements for banks are *below* levels set for trust institutions chartered by that state.[8]

---

[4]*See* 12 C.F.R. §5.22(a)(2) (1992).

[5]*See generally* Bogert, Trusts and Trustees §§135, 136.

[6]For a discussion of choice of chartering authority, see Symons & White, Banking Law 63-69 (3d ed. 1991).

[7]See id. at 72-75 for a discussion of the factors which the Office of the Comptroller of the Currency considers in deciding whether to grant a federal charter.

Anyone interested in acquiring a national charter may obtain the Comptroller's Manual for Corporate Activities, a three-volume guidebook containing the policies, procedures, and forms used in the application process. The manual may be ordered by writing to the Comptroller of the Currency at the following address: Comptroller of the Currency, P.O. Box 10004, Chicago, IL 60673-0004. A ninety-dollar fee ($90), payable to the Comptroller of the Currency, should accompany the written request. For a listing of state statutes relating to the chartering of bank and trust companies, *see* M. P. Malloy, The Corporate Law of Banks; appendix, chart 2.1 (State Bank Charters: Requirements) and chart 2.2 (Availability of Trust Powers: State Requirements) (1988).

[8]12 U.S.C. §92a(i) (1989).

§8.7 Merger

The doctrine of merger is occasionally a trap for the unwary; more often it is invoked in situations where it is inapplicable. Thus the trustee needs to understand the concept if only to recognize when the doctrine is *not* a concern.

Merger is what happens when one person is given the entire legal interest and the entire beneficial interest in property.[1] In such a case there is no trust;[2] the person simply owns the property outright and free of trust, all interests having "merged" in that person.[3] Thus, the creditors, the spouse, and the taxing authorities might well have greater access to the property than would be the case were the property the subject of a viable trust.[4] If merger has occurred, at death the property passes in accordance with the terms of the person's will or by intestate succession, not in accordance with the terms of the instrument governing the purported trust.[5] Obviously if those who are mentioned in the trust instrument are different from those mentioned in the will, merger will benefit the latter. Merger may have consequences as well in the welfare eligibility and recoupment area.

But more often than not there is no merger. Let us assume a trust, *A* to *B* for *C* for life, then to *D.* If the same person is the sole trustee and the sole income beneficiary, and if upon death the property passes to the person's executor or administrator — in other words to the estate — then there is a merger. In other words, if *B, C,* and *D* are the same person, there is no trust — in fact there never was one. (Nowadays one seldom runs across instruments where an estate possesses the remainder interest, with the possible exception of nominee or realty trusts.[6] The

---

§8.7 [1] *See generally* 2 Scott on Trusts §99; Restatement (Second) of Trusts §99 (1959); Bogert, Trusts and Trustees §§129, 1003.

[2] 2 Scott on Trusts §99.

[3] Bogert, Trusts and Trustees §129 (rev. 2d ed. 1984).

[4] *See generally* 2 Scott on Trusts §99.

[5] Id.

[6] *See* §9.3.

property usually passes directly by purchase to someone's relatives.[7])

As one can see, not much need be done to prevent a merger of interests. The simple introduction of a cotrustee into the formula should avoid such a result.[8] Or if upon the death of *C* the property passes to the then-living issue of *C* rather than to *C*'s estate there is no merger. In this day and age, one has to work hard to back into a merger.

The trustee should always keep in mind that a right to revoke or the possession of a general inter vivos power of appointment is not what triggers a merger.[9] Thus if *A, B,* and *C* are the same but *D* is the *issue* of *B/C* living at the termination of the trust, then there is no merger even in the face of a reserved right of revocation or general inter vivos power of appointment in *B/C*. It is when *D* is the estate of *B/C* that merger comes about. The existence of a reserved right of revocation or general inter vivos power of appointment does not affect the situation one way or the other. With the revocable living trust now the core of most estate plans it is important that the trustee separate issues relating to merger from issues relating to powers of revocation and general inter vivos powers of appointment. These powers are technically personal rights of disposition, not interests in property.[10]

---

[7]*See generally* National Shawmut Bank v. Joy, 315 Mass. 457, 462-467, 53 N.E.2d 113, 117-120 (1944).

[8]*See, e.g.,* First Ala. Bank of Tuscaloosa v. Webb, 373 So. 2d 631 (Ala. 1979).

[9]*See Joy,* 315 Mass. at 469-478, 53 N.E.2d at 124-126.

[10]*See* id., 315 Mass. at 474, 53 N.E.2d 113 at 124.

CHAPTER *9*

Special Types of Trusts

§9.1   The Charitable Trust

A trust for a charitable purpose is exempt from the durational requirements of the Rule Against Perpetuities.[1] Thus contingent interests created under such trusts may remain outstanding for-

___

§9.1   [1]Regarding income accumulation see 4A Scott on Trusts §365, §401.9; Franklin Foundation v. Attorney General, 416 Mass. 483, 623 N.E.2d 1109 (1993) (involving a 200-year accumulation trust established under the will of Benjamin Franklin); *but see* Bogert, Trusts and Trustees §341.

229

ever. Although charitable trusts have been around for a long time, the trustee should be aware that trust law has yet to develop a workable definition of the term *charitable*.

§9.1.1 Charitable Purposes

A trust involving contingent interests may continue in perpetuity for a charitable purpose but not for a private purpose or for a political purpose.[2] Unfortunately it is not always easy to distinguish private and political trusts from charitable trusts.[3] Courts have traditionally looked to the purposes enumerated in the preamble of the English Statute of Charitable Uses for examples of purposes qualifying for the charitable exemption from the time limitations of the Rule Against Perpetuities.[4] These purposes include relief for the poor, maintenance of nonprofit hospitals and schools, and repair of bridges and roads.[5] When generalizing from the preamble's list, however, one has to be careful. For example, not all trusts whose purposes are the relief of poverty or the advancement of education are charitable trusts. A trust to keep the settlor's children off the welfare rolls is a private trust, although its purpose is the relief of poverty.[6] A trust for the dissemination of literature for or against rent control is a political trust although, as far as the settlor may be concerned, its purpose is the relief of poverty and the advancement of education.[7] A trust to support a hostel for the homeless, however, would fall well within the letter and spirit of the Statute of Charitable Uses.[8] When it comes to matters charitable, trustees should seek out objective criteria: What is charity to one may be politics to another.

[2]*See generally* 4A Scott on Trusts §§368, 374.6.
[3]*See generally* id.; Rounds, Social Investing, IOLTA, and the Law of Trusts, 22 Loy. U. Chi. L.J. 163, 178-181 (1990).
[4]*See generally* 4A Scott on Trusts §368.1.
[5]Id.; Bogert, Trusts and Trustees §§321, 362.
[6]4A Scott on Trusts §369.5.
[7]*See* Rounds, Social Investing, IOLTA, and the Law of Trusts, 22 Loy. U. Chi. L.J. 163, 179 (1990); *but see* Jackson v. Phillips, 96 Mass. (14 Allen) 539 (1867).
[8]See Rounds, *supra* note 7, 179 n.75 and accompanying text (1990); 4A Scott on Trusts §369.3.

A trustee who is unsure whether a particular activity is charitable should consider whether the activity is private or political before consulting the Statute of Charitable Uses. If it is neither then the chances are good that it is charitable. As a rule of thumb, a trust for the benefit of a named individual or of a class of beneficiaries ascertainable by their relationship to a named individual is a *private* trust (*e.g.*, a trust for the settlor's issue); a trust whose purpose is to influence the exercise of state power is a political trust[9] (*e.g.*, a trust for the purpose of influencing tax policy). Above all the trustee should not confuse Internal Revenue Code §501(c) criteria for tax exemption[10] with the criteria that have evolved over the years in a particular state for the charitable exemption from the time limitations of the Rule Against Perpetuities.

Trustees must strive in practice to maintain a clean separation between the political and the charitable. Boards of trustees of charitable trusts must resist the pressures to exploit for political purposes the enormous economic power which they control as stewards of the benefactions of others.[11]

§9.1.2   Standing to Enforce Charitable Trusts

It is in the nature of the typical charitable trust that its beneficiaries are so numerous and their interests under it so contingent and tangential that, as a practical matter, no beneficiary possesses a sufficient interest to seek its enforcement.[12] While each of us, for example, is a direct and indirect contingent beneficiary of endowed medical research, in essence it is all of us *collectively* — the *public*, as it were — who is the beneficiary. Thus for hundreds of years both in the United States and in England the "duty of main-

---

[9]Rounds, *supra* note 7, 179-180.

[10]*See generally* Bogert, Trusts and Trustees §362.

[11]The best endowed academic institution is Harvard with $5.48 billion, followed by the University of Texas with $3.65 billion. Frank, Wall St. J., July 26, 1993, at C1, col. 3.

[12]*See generally* 4A Scott on Trusts §391; Bogert, Trusts and Trustees §§411-417.

taining the rights of the public, and of a number of persons too indefinite to vindicate their own, has vested in the [state] and is exercised here, as in England through the attorney general."[13] This is a practical solution to the enforceability dilemma inherent in the charitable trust. The alternative — vesting everyone with standing to seek enforcement — would be intolerably chaotic and impractical.

But just because contingent beneficiaries of charitable trusts lack standing to seek enforcement, does it follow that others do as well? Let us assume that many years ago a number of grateful citizens contributed sums of money to a city for the purpose of erecting and maintaining a tomb and museum to house the remains and papers of a famous general. The tomb was built and the museum established. Now the tomb is in disrepair and the museum has been all but abandoned by the mayor, whose thoughts are on other matters. What about the currently living relatives of the general? Would they have standing to enjoin the city from neglecting its stewardship of the tomb and museum? Would those who contributed to the complex have standing in their capacities as settlors to seek enforcement of the trust? Must the welfare of the tomb and museum be dependent solely on the enforcement discretion of the attorney general who perhaps does not want to embarrass the mayor?

According to Professor Scott, persons having a special interest in the performance of a charitable trust can maintain a suit for its enforcement.[14] They however must show that their interest is not merely derived from their status as members of the general public. Thus the incumbent of an endowed chair at a medical research facility would have standing to seek enforcement of the endowment trust.[15] Rights of enforcement would also accrue to a minister entitled to income distributions from a clergy support trust.[16] Likewise a respectable argument could be made that the general's proximate relatives who are currently living would have

---

[13]Jackson v. Phillips, 96 Mass. (14 Allen) 539, 579 (1867).
[14]4A Scott on Trusts §391.
[15]*See* id.
[16]Id.

an interest in the proper maintenance of their ancestor's tomb and that this interest is sufficiently "special" to vest them with standing to seek enjoinment of its neglect.[17]

In any case, public oversight of charitable trusts by multi-tasked, overburdened, undersupported attorneys general is generally more apparent than actual.[18] Even if, as a practical matter, there is no one looking over the trustee's shoulder, the ethical trustee conscientiously carries out the intentions of the settlor-benefactor.

§9.1.3   Cy Pres

It is . . . well settled by decisions of the highest authority, that when a gift is made to trustees for a charitable purpose, the general nature of which is pointed out, and which is lawful and valid at the time [the transfer is made], and no intention is expressed to limit it to a particular institution or mode of application, and afterwards, either by change of circumstances the scheme of the [settlor] becomes impracticable, or by change of law becomes illegal, the fund, having once vested in the charity, does not go to the heirs at law as a resulting trust, but is to be applied by the court of chancery, in the exercise of its jurisdiction in equity, as near the [settlor's] particular directions as possible, to carry out his general charitable intent.[19]

In the event that circumstances make it impossible or impractical to carry out the specified purpose of a charitable trust, the doctrine of *cy pres*[20] may be available as an alternative to the imposition of a resulting trust in favor of the settlor or the settlor's estate. In other words, the doctrine of cy pres may provide an alternative to the trust's termination. If the court finds that a

---

[17]The matter of whether the settlor has standing to enforce the trust is covered in §4.1. *See generally* Rounds, Protections Afforded to Massachusetts' Ancient Burial Grounds, 73 Mass. L. Rev. 176, 180-182 (1988).

[18]*See generally* 4A Scott on Trusts §391.

[19]Jackson v. Phillips, 96 Mass. (14 Allen) 539, 580 (1867).

[20]*Cy Pres* is an Anglo-French phrase equivalent to the modern French *si près*, meaning "so near" or "as near." 4A Scott on Trusts §399. This abbreviated phrase was taken from *cy pres comme possible*, which meant "as near as possible." Bogert, Trusts and Trustees §431.

particular trust is cy pres-eligible, it will fashion an alternative scheme of disposition which closely approximates the specified unfeasible one. For a trust to be cy pres-eligible, however, the settlor must have manifested a "general charitable intent."[21]

The concept of cy pres is not particularly esoteric or radical. It essentially involves the textual search for any generalized intent on the part of the settlor which is independent of the specific circumstances of a given moment. As many charitable trusts are designed to continue forever, specific circumstances are bound to change. Institutions come and go; what was legal becomes illegal; problems are solved and new ones surface. Even if courts had not articulated the doctrine, a trustee, in the face of changed circumstances, would always have an obligation to ascertain whether the settlor's intent was general or specific and then to act accordingly. Thus a prospective trustee of a charitable trust would do well to insist that the settlor-benefactor spell out unambiguously whether the charitable intent is general or specific.

An example of judicial deference to reversionary interests[22] is illustrated in the events which gave rise to the Supreme Court case of *Evans v. Abney*.[23] The Court was asked to consider the constitutional implications of the administration and termination of a trust created under the 1911 will of U.S. Senator A. O. Bacon of Georgia. Pursuant to the terms of the will, property had been transferred in trust to the Senator's home city of Macon, Georgia for the creation of a whites-only public park. Following the Court's earlier decision in *Evans v. Newton*[24] (holding that the park could not continue to be operated on a racially discriminatory basis), a state court had ruled that the Senator's intention to provide a park for whites only was not of a general charitable nature. Accordingly it was held that the trust had failed and that the parkland and other

---

[21]*See generally* 4A Scott on Trusts §399; Bogert, Trusts and Trustees §436; Restatement (Second) of Trusts §399 (1959).

[22]*See, e.g.*, J. Gray, The Rule Against Perpetuities §§34, 41.1, 113, 113.1, 113.3, 327.1 (4th ed. 1942) (settlor of limited charitable purpose trust retains vested reversionary interest in trust property); National Shawmut Bank v. Joy, 315 Mass. 457, 462-469, 53 N.E.2d 113, 117-121 (1944) (failure of trust triggers resulting trust in favor of settlor or settlor's estate).

[23]396 U.S. 435 (1970).

[24]382 U.S. 296 (1966).

trust property associated with it must revert upon a resulting trust[25] to the Senator's estate. If, on the other hand, there had been a finding of general charitable intent, presumably the state court, invoking the cy pres doctrine, would have ordered the continued operation of the park on an integrated basis. Such a finding would have, for all intents and purposes, voided the equitable reversionary interests of those entitled to the Senator's estate.

As to the actual holding of *Abney*, the Court found that the state court's failure to find general charitable intent in the establishment of the trust did not constitute "state action" under Fourteenth Amendment analysis. Thus no federal constitutional grounds were found for extinguishing the private reversionary interests in favor of continued public operation of the park.

In *Ebitz v. Pioneer National Bank*,[26] the Massachusetts court interpreted the concept of general charitable intent more elastically than the Georgia court had in *Abney*. At issue was the provision of a testamentary trust established "to aid and assist worthy and ambitious young men to acquire a legal education."[27] The will was executed in 1963 and allowed in 1970. The plaintiffs were female law students who made timely applications to the trustee for assistance from the fund which were rejected on the ground that the testator had intended males, not females, to be beneficiaries of his largesse. The trial judge held that "[t]o exclude females as possible recipients of financial assistance from a trust fund established for the purpose of assisting qualified students interested in the pursuit of a legal education would constitute an unreasonable and arbitrary exclusion."[28] He then speculated that the enforcement of such a provision might be unconstitutional. With that he ruled that the term "young men" meant "young men and young women." The trustee appealed. The trial judge was upheld on appeal by the Massachusetts Supreme Judicial Court, which

---

[25]*See generally* §§4.1.1, 8.2.1.5 (discussing the resulting trust).

[26]372 Mass. 207, 361 N.E.2d 225 (1977).

[27]Id. at 209, 361 N.E.2d at 226.

[28]Id. at 212, 361 N.E.2d at 228 (Quirico, J., dissenting) (quoting trial court's holding).

found the reference to "young men" ambiguous in the context of the entire instrument.

In dissent, Justice Quirico wrote: "Surely it is not the law that a testator or donor may not bestow the benefit of his own funds on a class of persons of one sex to the exclusion of persons of a similar class but of the opposite sex, if that is his stated intention."[29] Citing *Abney* he suggested that the case was not "clouded" by any constitutional question.

The expansive approach to general charitable intent exemplified by *Ebitz* is contrasted by the approach taken by the Montana court in *In re Will of Cram*.[30] At issue was a testamentary trust that provided for cash stipends to young males certified by the Future Farmers of America of Montana and the 4-H Club of Montana to be of good character, in need of financial assistance, and interested in the sheep raising business. The two organizations had links to the state educational system. In response to an equal protection challenge to those provisions of the trust that were gender exclusive, the Montana lower court modified the trust to remove any state involvement in the mechanics of the grantee selection process. On appeal, the actions of the lower court were affirmed.

The settlor clearly intended to discriminate, that is, to benefit young males to the exclusion of young females. However, the trust as modified involved no state action.

> A private person has the right to dispose of his money or property as he wishes and in so doing may lawfully discriminate in regard to the beneficiaries of his largess without offending the Equal Protection Clause as long as the State and its instrumentalities are not involved, and unless the trust is unlawful, private trusts are to be encouraged.[31]

As *Abney, Ebitz,* and *Cram* suggest, there is yet no judicial consensus as to the elasticity and limits of general charitable intent. Thus the trustee, when faced with a charitable trust whose

[29]Id. at 213, 361 N.E.2d at 228.
[30]606 P.2d 145 (Mont. 1980).
[31]Id. at 150.

purposes cannot be carried out, is well advised to place the matter of what is to be done next in the hands of the appropriate court by way of a cy pres petition.

§9.2   Trusts for Deferring Taxation of Income

Employee benefit plans and IRAs essentially are arrangements for deferring the taxation of income. Many such arrangements call for the holding of assets in trust.

§9.2.1   The Employee Benefit Trust

When an employer in the United States establishes a retirement "plan" for its employees it is usually of the "qualified" variety. If it is a *qualified plan*, the employer can take its contributions to the plan as a tax deduction.[1] Under certain circumstances, contributions by or on behalf of an employee are not taxed as income to the employee at the time the contributions are made.[2] Taxation on income generated by plan assets may also be deferred.[3] Plan distributions at retirement or at some other time, on the other hand, may have tax consequences.[4] For a plan to be qualified it must meet certain requirements set forth in the Internal Revenue Code and elsewhere.[5] Congress, by means of the Employee Retirement Income Security Act of 1974 (ERISA), articulated a comprehensive federal statutory framework for the design and administration of qualified plans.[6]

---

§9.2   [1]*See generally* Bogert, Trusts and Trustees §§255, 270.20.
[2]Id.
[3]Id.
[4]*See generally* Bogert, Trusts and Trustees §264.7.
[5]*See generally* id. §255.
[6]Id.

With the exception of so-called *insured plans*, for a plan to be qualified it must have associated with it a trust that serves as a receptacle for the plan's assets. While ERISA requires that the trust contain certain provisions if the plan is to be qualified, state law governs what constitutes a valid trust.[7] Thus, legal issues associated with an employee benefit trust might well be brought to a state court for adjudication.[8] Unfortunately the establishment of a plan often requires a consortium of actuaries, pension lawyers, tax lawyers, labor lawyers, human resource lawyers, and SEC lawyers in order to determine what property may enter the trust. The common law trust lawyers, that is, those who are familiar with the common law rules applicable once property finds its way into the hands of a trustee, are left out of the process altogether. Moreover, most if asked would prefer not to get involved.

When confronted with an employee benefit trust, the trustee should first assess its common law terms. Most likely it will be a trust with several trustees. Depending upon the type of plan, it could have many settlors (the employees and the employer), many beneficiaries (perhaps retirees entitled to annuitized payments) and many remaindermen (employees and retirees and the postmortem designees of employees and retirees). Some beneficiaries and remaindermen are likely to have vested interests and some to have interests that are partially vested and partially contingent upon length of time with the employer.[9] Depending upon the type of plan, some beneficiaries and remaindermen (perhaps certain retirees) may well have rights of withdrawal in the nature of general inter vivos powers of appointment. The employer may have either an equitable contingent remainder or a vested reversionary interest in trust assets to the extent they are not needed to fund benefits. Each employee is probably entitled to complete the dispositive terms with respect to that employee's interest in the trust. (This is accomplished by the filling out of a beneficiary designation form supplied by the employer's human resources department.) The

[7]Id.
[8]Id.
[9]Id.

governing instrument is likely to provide that income generated by the trust assets be periodically added to principal.

Once the trust is looked at in common law terms (that is to say, once the governing trust document is analyzed to determine in what respects it requires a *deviation* from the common law), the trustee and trust counsel should then turn to ERISA to determine in what respects federal trust law alters and embellishes the common law trust principles discussed in this handbook. They will be surprised to discover that ERISA has codified some long-standing common law trust principles; but, contrary to what they may have heard, the federal gloss has added little that would alarm the conscientious and ethical trustee of an old-fashioned private trust.

Insofar as the trustee is concerned, ERISA has codified and embellished the duty of loyalty by creating a thicket of prohibited transactions.[10] Still, it amounts to little more than an elaborate codification of the common law prohibition against self-dealing by trust fiduciaries.[11] The "Prudent Man Rule" of investment as it applies to employee benefit trusts has been altered by ERISA so that it might better be called the *Federal Prudent Expert Rule*.[12] Again, this is not a particularly radical development as it is unlikely that the common law would have long tolerated an amateur standard for investing the massive aggregation of wealth lodged in the nation's employee benefit trusts. ERISA has also limited the common law rights of a beneficiary's creditors to reach employee benefit trust assets.[13] It has put certain nontrustees on the hot seat — particularly investment managers — by imposing on them fiduciary status. Finally, the area of allocation of fiduciary responsibilities has been elaborated and codified.[14]

Of all ERISA's codifications, the allocation of fiduciary responsibility may be perhaps the most perplexing. Many troubling common law questions lurk behind the codification. For example,

---

[10]Id.

[11]Id.

[12]Id.

[13]ERISA §1056(d)(1); I.R.C. §401(a)(13). (For an employee benefit plan to be qualified, an employee's interest in its associated trust may not be assigned or alienated.)

[14]*See generally* Bogert, Trusts and Trustees §255.

if the governing instrument allocates investment responsibility to an investment manager, what common law oversight obligations remain back with trustee? To what extent have the allocation of responsibility provisions of ERISA altered the common law principles of cofiduciary liability?

The beneficiary designation form is completed by an employee usually without legal advice and usually at the human resources office. It is by means of the form that the terms of the employee benefit trust applicable to that employee are completed and that the link is made between the employee benefit trust and the employee's own estate plan. More wealth is likely to transfer pursuant to the terms of the form than pursuant to the terms of the employee's will,[15] yet much more attention and thought is likely to have gone into the drawing of the will than the filling out of the form. In any case it is in the interests of all parties that the terms of the beneficiary designation form cover all contingencies and be unambiguous.

§9.2.2   The IRA Trust

An Individual Retirement Plan[16] (commonly known as an IRA) may offer some income tax deferral opportunities for individuals. Associated with a particular IRA may be a trust which serves as a receptacle for an individual's contributions.[17] With the possible exception of a SEP IRA,[18] the trust is essentially a common law revocable inter vivos trust.

In order for an IRA to qualify as such, the Internal Revenue Code requires that the trustee of any associated trust be a bank, a thrift institution, an insurance company, a brokerage firm, or any

---

[15]*See generally* Langbein, The Nonprobate Revolution and the Future of the Law of Succession, 97 Harv. L. Rev. 1108 (1984).

[16]*See generally* I.R.C. §408.

[17]Id.

[18]In a Simplified Employee Pension IRA, the employee establishes the arrangement and the employer participates in its funding and administration. I.R.C. §408(k).

other person who demonstrates to the IRS that he or she will administer the account in a manner consistent with the requirements of the law.[19] It should be noted that by these provisions the Internal Revenue Code is not bestowing trust powers on such institutions or otherwise preempting state law[20] — it is merely laying down requirements that must be met if an individual is to enjoy the tax deferral advantages of an IRA.

One requirement for tax deferral is that the IRA trustee may not invest trust assets in works of art, rugs, antiques, metals, gems, stamps, coins, or other items of tangible personal property specified by the IRS.[21] Amounts invested in such "collectibles" are treated for tax purposes as distributions to the individual.[22] However, gold or silver coins issued by the U.S. government or any type of coin issued under the laws of any state will not be considered collectibles.[23] An interest in a portion of a gold coin portfolio is not considered a collectible.[24]

It is a common misconception that under federal law, an IRA trust affords the same protection from creditors as a trust associated with a qualified employee benefit plan. A qualified plan is established under §401 of the Code. To be sure, that section has an antialienation requirement which appears to preempt state property law. An IRA on the other hand is established under §408 of the Code, a section which contains no such antialienation provision. Thus the trustee should first look to see if an applicable state statute speaks to the rights of creditors in the IRA context. If there is no such statute, then the assets in an IRA trust likely would be reachable by the taxpayer's creditors. This is because in an ever-increasing number of jurisdictions assets held in a common law inter vivos trust are reachable by creditors of the settlor-beneficiary.[25]

---

[19]*See* I.R.C. §408(a)(2).
[20]*See* id. §408(h).
[21]*See* id. §408(m).
[22]Id.
[23]Id. §408(m)(3).
[24]Id. §408(m)(3)(A); *see also* Priv. Ltr. Rul. 89-40-067 (July 12, 1989).
[25]*See* §5.3.3.1.

§9.3   Trusts That Resemble Corporations

A trust can be employed to facilitate the management of certain property and to make it readily divisible and transferable.[1] Let us assume, for example, that the owner of an apartment building wishes over a period of time to give it and the land on which it sits to his grandchildren. He might transfer the land and building to a trustee and take back 100 certificates each representing a one-percent fully vested beneficial interest in the trust. As time goes by he parcels out the certificates to his grandchildren. The nominee trust, the realty trust, the Massachusetts business trust, the voting trust, the investment trust (trusteed mutual fund), the Real Estate Investment Trust, and the Illinois Land Trust are variations on this theme.[2]

The key to the arrangement is that the trustee has the title and the beneficiaries have fully vested beneficial interests. Thus, in theory, the inter vivos or postmortem transfer of a certificate of beneficial interest ought not to trigger public filings at the registry of deeds or a cumbersome subdividing of the underlying asset. Thus the arrangement may offer a measure of confidentiality and convenience of management in the face of fractured ownership. Under the governing instrument the management responsibilities of the trustee may be intense (*e.g.*, the voting trust) or virtually nonexistent (*e.g.*, the nominee trust).

Because these trusts look more like corporations than trusts, the certificates of vested beneficial interests, as a matter of state property law, tend to behave like stock certificates. If a certificate holder dies, the certificate is likely to end up either in holder's estate or in a marital deduction or family trust established under an instrument that the holder executed while alive.

These corporate-like trust arrangements raise a number of tax and securities regulation issues which are well beyond the

---

§9.3   [1] *See generally* Bogert, Trusts and Trustees §§247-252.
[2] Id.

scope of this handbook.[3] There is also, however, the issue of limited liability which deserves at least a mention here. It is a matter of paramount concern to all parties, trustees and beneficiaries alike. Do the certificate owners as the equitable owners and the trustee as the legal owner of the land and building enjoy limited liability as they might if the land and building were inside a corporation?[4] What about the general rule that the beneficiary incurs no liabilities arising inherently out of his beneficial ownership, except for taxes?[5] Would such a rule apply to these corporate-like trust arrangements? Unfortunately it is impossible to generalize with respect to these issues. It depends upon the facts and circumstances and the jurisdiction.[6] Thus the first thing that the prospective trustee of a corporate-like trust arrangement should do is ascertain to what extent (if at all) the liability of the parties is limited. A discussion of the alternatives and countermeasures available to the trustee in the face of unlimited liability however is beyond the scope of this handbook.

Finally the authors over the years have encountered a number of instances where attorneys, particular conveyancers, have attempted to fashion a nominee or realty trust form into a viable private revocable inter vivos trust instrument. They do this by making the interest of beneficiaries contingent upon such events as survivorship. Usually the modified instruments are awash in ambiguities and gaps, that is to say, contingencies unprovided for. The best approach is to keep the corporate-like trust instrument separate from the private inter vivos trust instrument. It is the latter which should contain the contingent provisions, such as those which relate to generational succession and the unborn and

---

[3]For a brief summary of the federal income tax treatment of corporate-like trusts, see Bogert, Trusts and Trustees §§270.30-270.40; for matters relating to securities regulation, see generally L. Loss & J. Seligman, Securities Regulation (3d ed. 1993). *See also* Problems of Fiduciaries Under the Securities Laws, 20 Real Prop. Prob. & Tr. J. 503 (1985).

[4]*See generally* Bogert, Trusts and Trustees §247. *See* §7.3.

[5]*See generally* Bogert, Trusts and Trustees §247; *supra* §5.6.

[6]Id.

unascertained. Moreover there is no reason why the latter may not contain as an asset beneficial interests in the former.

§9.4   Commingled Trust Funds

As a general rule, the trustee may not commingle the assets of one trust with the assets of other trusts, absent express authority in the governing instrument. This common law prohibition generally does not apply to the common trust fund and IOLTA arrangements.

§9.4.1   The Common Trust Fund

The *common trust fund* is a special type of corporate-like trust arrangement which, because of §584 of the Internal Revenue Code, is available as a practical matter only to banks and their fiduciary customers. In theory it allows for cost-efficient, diversified administration of small accounts. It works this way: The bank executes a declaration of trust or plan for the purpose of serving as trustee of a common trust fund. The specifications are set forth in a state statute[1] and in federal regulations.[2] The arrangement is then available exclusively for the collective investment and reinvestment of moneys contributed to the fund by the bank in its capacity as trustee of other trusts and as executor and administrator of estates. The bank's guardianships may also participate. Essentially a participating entity, such as a trust, purchases a

---

§9.4 [1]Thirty-five states and the District of Columbia have adopted the Uniform Common Trust Fund Act, 7 U.L.A. 401 (1985). The remaining states have enacted some form of common trust fund enabling legislation. *See* 3 Scott on Trusts §227.9 n.26. *See generally* Bogert, Trusts and Trustees §677.

[2]12 C.F.R. §9.18 (1992) permits, where not in contravention of local law, a national bank acting as fiduciary to collectively invest funds in a common trust fund maintained by the bank, so long as the fund meets the requirements set forth in §9.18. *See generally* Bogert, Trusts and Trustees §677.

beneficial interest in a trusteed basket of securities — a piece of another trust. One can see the similarity between the common trust fund and the corporate-like trust arrangements mentioned in §9.3.

In the 1930s there had been concern that a common trust fund would be taxed as an association.[3] If that were the case, the common trust fund would have no economic utility, because with each participating fiduciary account being subject in any case to tax on income attributable to its participations in the fund, participation in a common trust fund would have effectively generated a double tax. Beginning in 1936 these road blocks were removed. In that year the precursor to §584[4] was enacted into law removing the threat of federal income taxation at the fund level.

In recent years the hot issue associated with the common trust fund has been whether banks should be allowed to commingle their investment management agency accounts. This would effectively give banks the authority to market participations in their common trust funds to the public in competition with mutual fund participations. So far banks have been unsuccessful in acquiring this authority.[5]

To reiterate, because of §584 there is no economic advantage for anyone other than a bank to operate a common trust fund. A nonbank trustee who wishes to afford his small trusts the diversification that comes with commingling must look to the mutual fund. It should be kept in mind, however, that the common law prohibits the commingling of the assets of multiple trusts and the delegation by fiduciaries of investment discretion.[6]

---

[3]*See* Brooklyn Trust Co. v. Commissioner, 80 F.2d 865 (2d Cir. 1936), *cert. denied*, 298 U.S. 659 (1936) (composite fund taxable as an association); Bogert, Trusts and Trustees §677.

[4]Federal Revenue Act of 1936 §169, 26 U.S.C.A. §169 (1936). *See generally* Bogert, Trusts and Trustees §677.

[5]*See* Investment Co. Inst. v. Camp, 401 U.S. 617 (1971); *see generally* Bogert, Trusts and Trustees §677.

[6]*See* §§6.1.4, 6.2.1.

§9.4.2   IOLTA Trusts

With the exception of Indiana, all states and the District of Columbia have adopted either by statute or judicial fiat IOLTA programs.[7] *IOLTA* stands for "Interest on Lawyers Trust Accounts." Under an IOLTA scheme, a lawyer is either authorized or compelled under threat of license suspension to commingle or pool unproductive nominal and short-term client funds that the lawyer holds in trust. The income generated by the pool is then remitted to designated charitable and professional entities. It is expected that by 1995 the aggregate amount of income generated by IOLTA nationwide since 1978 will be in the range of one billion dollars. One court has ruled that common law trust principles are not applicable to IOLTA.[8] The constitutionality of IOLTA is currently under challenge in the Fifth Circuit.[9]

§9.5   Quasi-trusts and Hybrids

Certain arrangements are trusts in substance but not in form. The *charitable corporation* is a classic example. Some hybrid arrangements, such as the custodial IRA, have the characteristics of both the trust and the agency. The Massachusetts Supreme Judicial Court has ruled that the Boston Common is held by the City of Boston upon a quasi-trust.[1]

---

[7]*See* Rounds, Social Investing, IOLTA, and the Law of Trusts, 22 Loy. U. Chi. L.J. 163, 173-174 (1990).

[8]"We are not convinced that the deposit of clients' funds into IOLTA accounts transforms a lawyer's fiduciary obligation to clients into a formal trust with the reserved right to control the beneficial use of the funds as claimed by the plaintiffs." Washington Legal Found. v. Massachusetts Bar Found., 993 F.2d 962, 974 (1st Cir. 1993); *but see* Ritchie et al., Decedents' Estates and Trusts 1318 (8th ed. 1993) ("funds received by a lawyer on behalf of a client are held in trust for the client").

[9]Washington Legal Found. v. Texas Equal Access to Justice Found., No. 94-CA-081JN (W.D. Tex. Feb. 7, 1994).

§9.5   [1]Codman v. Crocker, 203 Mass. 146, 150, 89 N.E.2d 177, 178 (1909).

§9.5.1   The Charitable Corporation

Is a gift of property to a charitable corporation a transfer in trust? Is the corporation a trustee of the property such that its governing body is subject to all the common law duties and obligations of a trustee? Professor Scott, while acknowledging some technical differences between the charitable trust and the charitable corporation, on balance finds them more similar than dissimilar.[2] Certainly if the gift is restricted the governing body should segregate the property and behave as ethical fiduciaries with respect to it. Above all they should carry out the lawful intentions of the transferor, and the attorney general and the courts should see to it that they do.

The realities of the situation are different however with respect to unrestricted gifts to a charitable corporation. Implicit in the gift is that the property will be used only for the legitimate expressed charitable purposes of the corporation. As a practical matter, however, the ultimate use of that particular gift may be impossible to monitor, particularly if it has been commingled with the general assets of the corporation or used for its general support. The governing body has a fiduciary duty to benefactors of unrestricted gifts to see to it that the corporation cleaves to the letter and spirit of the corporation's charitable purposes. Whether that obligation is enforceable or not is another matter.[3] If the governing body expects to so deviate it should segregate all benefactions and conduct its deviations with other funds.

Enforceability and fiduciary obligation are key elements of the trust. With respect to an unrestricted gift to a charitable corporation, the former element may well be lacking. Thus benefactors interested in enforceability may want to shun the charitable corporation in favor of making gifts to a charitable trust where the parties are more legally defined and where their rights and obligations more legally settled.[4]

[2] 4A Scott on Trusts §348.1.
[3] *See* Fishman, The Development of Nonprofit Corporation Law and an Agenda for Reform, 34 Emory L.J. 617, 668-671 (1985).
[4] *See* Karst, The Efficiency of the Charitable Dollar: An Unfulfilled State Responsibility, 73 Harv. L. Rev. 433, 435 (1960).

§9.5.2   The City, the States, or the United States as Trustee

While the United States of America and the states, counties, and municipalities within it in theory may have common law or statutory authority to hold property in trust, the absence of the key element of credible enforceability makes such trusteeships something other than of the common law variety.[5] The practical, political, and legal realities are that a state attorney general, even if so inclined, would find it very difficult to effect a judicial removal of a governmental entity as trustee of a particular trust.[6] Thus to the extent political influence and press oversight[7] are the only viable means of enforcing such arrangements, a discussion of the nature of those arrangements falls outside the scope of this handbook.

§9.5.3   Cemeteries and Parks

Cemetery land is usually held by a municipality or other governmental entity, a cemetery corporation, or a religious organization. Occasionally one will come across a cemetery situated within the borders of a privately owned parcel. Is a trust impressed upon such land? It would seem that some kind of trust is associated with cemetery land and there are some cases to that effect.[8] In the face of the common law rights of persons to visit, honor, and protect the graves of their deceased relatives, it is clear that those in control of cemetery land do not have untrammeled rights to ex-

---

[5]*See, e.g.*, Probe Hits US Funding of Indian Trust Funds, Boston Globe, April 4, 1992, at 5 (Bureau of Indian Affairs accused of decades of mismanagement of trusts).

[6]*See* Karst, The Efficiency of the Charitable Dollar: An Unfulfilled State Responsibility, 73 Harv. L. Rev. 433, 478-479 (1960).

[7]*See, e.g.*, McGrory, Criticism Over Fund Draws Flynn Response, Boston Globe, Jan. 5, 1992, at 26 (trust administered by city of Boston becomes a center of controversy as a result of negative publicity).

[8]See Rounds, Protections Afforded to Massachusetts' Ancient Burial Grounds, 73 Mass. L. Rev. 176, 180 n.118 (1988); *see, e.g.*, Sanford v. Vinal, 28 Mass. App. Ct. 476, 552 N.E.2d 579 (1990).

ploit and alienate the land.[9] On the other hand, as a matter of classic trust law it is not always clear to whom the burden of responsibility runs. In the case of a cemetery corporation it is clear that an affirmative burden runs to the governing body; with respect to a cemetery situated on private property, the owner of the property's fiduciary responsibilities may be passive, such as merely to leave the cemetery undisturbed and to allow others onto the land at reasonable times to visit, honor, and protect the gravesites.[10] The law of trusts has been an underutilized weapon in the battle to protect cemeteries, particularly historic cemeteries.

The legal status of parkland is also somewhat ambiguous. Much depends upon how the land came to be a park. If the land was set aside pursuant to the terms of someone's will, then it may well be held upon a charitable trust,[11] although, as in the case of governmental trusts in general, the trust's enforceability may exist more in theory than in reality. If the governmental entity had carved out the parkland from public land or had taken the land by eminent domain, then the arrangement looks less like a trust. One court, however, has held that the Boston Common is held by the City of Boston upon a quasi-trust.[12] The law of trusts has been an underutilized weapon not only in historic preservation battles but also in battles for open space.

§9.5.4   Custodial IRAs

In form a custodial IRA administered by a bank or mutual fund is an investment management agency relationship between the custodian and the person establishing the IRA.[13] If the arrangement were in substance a common law agency, then it would terminate upon the death of the customer. The result then would be that all funds subject to the arrangement would pass to the customer's estate, notwithstanding any provisions of a bene-

[9]See Rounds, *supra* note 8, at 180-182.
[10]Id. at 183-184, 188.
[11]See *generally* Bogert, Trusts and Trustees §322.
[12]Codman v. Crocker, 203 Mass. 146, 150, 89 N.E. 177, 178 (1909).
[13]See I.R.C. §408(h).

ficiary form to the contrary. Most states, however, now have statutes on their books anticipating this problem.[14] The statutes provide that the terms of custodial IRA beneficiary designation forms shall be honored notwithstanding the failure of such forms to comply with the Statute of Wills.[15] Thus by virtue of these statutes an IRA custodian begins to look very much like a common law trustee, particularly during the period between when the taxpayer dies and when the balance in the account is distributed.

§9.5.5   The Totten Trust

When *A* opens a savings account in the name of *C* and retains control of the account, courts are inclined to find that the arrangement is essentially a revocable living trust with *A* being both the trustee and the holder of a reserved right of revocation.[16] Some jurisdictions require that upon the death of *A* the money be paid to *A*'s estate, unless notice of the arrangement is given to *C* during *A*'s lifetime.[17] The validity of the standard revocable inter vivos trust, however, is not contingent upon notice being given to post-mortem beneficiaries.

§9.6   False Trusts

The public should be aware that just because an arrangement is described in trust-like terms, it does not necessarily have the

---

[14]*See* Bogert, Trusts and Trustees §255 n.11 (final footnote of section) and accompanying text.

[15]Id.

[16]*See* 1A Scott on Trusts §58.1 n.3; *see also* In re Matter of Totten, 179 N.Y. 112, 71 N.E. 748 (1904).

[17]*See* Annot., Gift or Trust by Deposit in Bank in Another's Name or in Depositor's Own Name in Trust for Another, as Affected by Lack of Knowledge on Part of Such Other Person, 157 A.L.R. 925 (1945).

requisite elements of a trust. Phrases like *cash surrender value* or *internal build-up* do not make an insurance contract a trust. Nor is the Social Security Trust Fund a trust fund.

§9.6.1   Insurance

Although many insurance products are structured or marketed to look like trusts, they are *contracts*, not trusts.[1] In spite of provisions for separate accounts and yields pegged to market performance, the insurance company does not segregate the premium as a trustee would;[2] rather the premium is commingled with the general assets of an insurance company and in exchange the insurance customer receives the company's promise to pay a certain amount, at a certain time, subject to the happening of certain events.

§9.6.2   Agency Arrangements

Powers of attorney (including Durable Powers of Attorney), investment management agency accounts, and escrow agency accounts are not trusts.[3] With some common law and statutory exceptions,[4] under none of these arrangements does title to the subject property pass to the agent.[5] Upon the death of a principal, any property that is a subject of the agency must pass to the principal's estate. This of course need not happen under a trust arrangement.

---

§9.6   [1]*See generally* 1 Scott on Trusts §14; *see also* Uhlman v. New York Life Ins. Co., 109 N.Y. 421, 17 N.E. 363 (1888).

[2]A trust is not to be confused with insurance company reserves, which are sums of money an insurer is required to set aside to insure the solvency of the company. Arrow Trucking Co. v. Continental Ins. Co., 465 So. 2d 691, 696 (La. 1985).

[3]1 Scott on Trusts §§8-8.1.

[4]*See* id. §8 n.6; *see also* Restatement (Second) of Agency §14B comment *e* (1957).

[5]1 Scott on Trusts §8.

§9.6.3   Legislative Budget Items Couched in Trust Terms

It has become a practice of politicians to employ trust terminology to promote various governmental programs.[6] A case in point is the so-called Social Security Trust Fund,[7] although many state legislatures are developing similar schemes for "dedicating" tax revenues. The Social Security Trust Fund is a budget item; it is not a common law trust of the type which is the subject of this handbook. To be sure, the concept may impose enforceable contractual obligations on the United States and concomitantly bestow certain property rights on certain taxpayers. A taxpayer, however, could not successfully in a judicial forum invoke principles of trust law to prevent a congressional raid on the fund.

---

[6]See I.R.C. §9501 ("Black Lung Disability Trust Fund"); §9502 ("Airport and Airway Trust Fund"); §9503 ("Highway Trust Fund"); §9504 ("Aquatic Resources Trust Fund"); §9505 ("Harbor Maintenance Trust Fund"); §9506 ("Inland Waterways Trust Fund"); §9507 ("Hazardous Substance Superfund"); §9508 ("Leaking Underground Storage Tank Trust Fund"); §9509 ("Oil Spill Liability Trust Fund"); §9510 ("Vaccine Injury Compensation Trust Fund"); §9511 ("National Recreational Trails Trust Fund"); Exec. Order No. 12858 ("Deficit Reduction Fund," more commonly referred to as the Clinton Deficit Reduction Trust Fund). With respect to the Clinton Deficit Reduction Trust Fund see generally Mitchell, . . . and Marred by Trust Fund Gimmick, Wall St. J., August 5, 1993, at A12.

[7]See generally W. Shore, Social Security: The Fraud in Your Future 3-15 (1975).

TABLE OF CASES

Table of Cases

TABLE OF RESTATEMENTS

Table of Restatements

TABLE OF UNIFORM ACTS

References are to sections.

INDEX

Index

Assignability of equitable interest, 5.3.2, 5.3.3.3, 6.1.2

Assignment of equitable interest, 5.3.2, 8.2.3

Attachment of equitable interest
generally, 5.3.3
beneficiary's interest, 5.3.3.2
settlor's interest, 5.3.3.1
by trustee's personal creditors, 8.3.1

Attorney. *See also* Compensation of trustee; Loyalty, duty of
conflicts of interest, 3.2.2, 6.1.3.3, 7.2.6, 8.4
fiduciary liability insurance 3.5.4.2, 7.2.5
IOLTA, 6.1.3.4, 9.4.2

Attorney general
consumer protection, 7.3.3.1
enforcement of charitable trusts, 4.1, 4.1.2, 5.1, 9.1.2, 9.5.2
reporting, 6.3

Attorneys' fees, 6.2.4.4

Bank as trustee
generally, 3.2.4
authority, 3.1, 8.6
brokerage facilities, 6.1.3.4
common trust funds, 6.2.1, 9.4.1
Comptroller of the Currency, 8.6
compensation, 8.4
conflicts of interest, 6.1.3
consumer protection, 7.2.3.5(a)
deposits by trustees, 8.3.4
inside information, 6.1.3.4
IRAs, 9.2.2
loans to trust, 3.5.3.2
mutual funds, 6.1.3.4
nominees, 3.5.3.2(e)
officers liability, 7.2.9
Regulation 9, 3.1, 6.2.1
reporting obligations, 6.3.3
soft dollars, 6.1.3.4
trust company, 8.6

Bankruptcy and ERISA
antialienation requirements, 5.3.3.3(d)

Benefactor. *See* Settlor

Beneficial interest
as property, 5.3

Index

Bond
allocation of income, 6.2.4.1
amortization of income, 6.2.4.3
as investment, 6.2.2.1
safekeeping of, 6.2.1

Bond, trustee's, 3.4.1, 7.2.3.6, 7.2.4

Borrowing
by trustee from trust, 6.1.3.1, 6.1.3.2, 7.2.1
by trust from third parties, 3.5.3.2(c)
by trust from trustee, 3.5.3.2(j), 6.1.3.1

Breach of fiduciary duty. *See* Breach of trust

Breach of trust. *See also* Duties of trustee; Liability
abandonment, 3.4.3
absolute liability, 7.1
acquiescence in, 7.2.4
causal connection with injury, 7.1
calculation of damages, 7.2.3.2
churning, 3.2.3
cotrustee, 6.1.4
commingling, 6.2.1, 9.4.1
conflict of interest, 6.1.3.2-6.1.3.4, 7.1, 7.2.1, 7.2.6, 7.2.8, 8.3.4
concealment, 7.2.4
condonation, 7.2.4
constructive trust as remedy for, 3.3
delegation, 6.1.4, 9.4.1
defunding, 2.3
delay in selling imprudent investment, 7.2.3.2
dilatory administration, 5.4.1.2
discharge by beneficiary, 5.5, 7.2.7
earmark, failure to, 7.1
exculpatory provision, 7.2.6
expectation interest of settlor, 4.1.2
imprudence, 7.2.2
inefficiency, 5.4.1.2
insuring against, 7.2.5
intentional breach, 7.1, 7.2.1, 7.2.8
IOLTA, 6.1.3.4, 9.4.2
loyalty, duty of, 6.1.3.2-6.1.3.4, 7.1, 7.2.1, 7.2.6, 7.2.8, 8.3.4
misdelivery, 7.1, 8.2.3
negligence, 7.1, 7.2.2
participation in, 7.2.4
pledging, 8.3.3
predecessor, 6.2.1, 7.2.4
punitive damages, 7.2.3.3
remedies of beneficiary, 5.4.1.5, 7.2.3
remedies of settlor, 4.1, 4.1.2

Index

Conflict of interest
  attorney, 3.2.2, 6.1.3.3, 7.2.6, 8.4
  bank, 6.1.3.3
  broker, 3.2.3, 6.1.3.3
  family member, 3.2.5
  remedies, 7.2.3
  trustee, 6.1.3

Conflict of laws, 8.5

Consequential damages, 7.3.3.1, 7.2.3.2

Constructive trust, 2.3, 3.3, 5.4.2, 8.3.3

Consumer protection actions
  attorney general, 7.3.3.1
  beneficiaries as consumers, 7.2.3.5(a)
  settlor as consumer, 7.2.3.4(a)
  treble damages, 7.2.3.5, 7.2.3.5(a)

Contingent equitable interests
  generally, 3.5.1, 5.3.1, 8.2.1.1, 8.2.1.3
  creditor accessibility, 5.3.3
  employee benefit trust, 9.2.1
  Medicaid eligibility and recoupment, 5.3.5
  Rule Against Perpetuities, 8.2.1, 8.2.1.1
  spousal accessibility, 5.3.4

Contract
  distinguished from trust, 3.5.1
  exoneration, 3.5.2.3
  limitation of liability, 7.3.2, 9.3
  liability of trustee, 3.5.4.1, 7.3, 7.3.1
  as property of trust, 2.2.1, 2.2.2
  reimbursement, 3.5.2.3
  trustee's authority to, 3.5.3.1, 3.5.3.1(d)

Conveyance of trust property
  at termination, 3.5.1
  by trustee, 3.5.2.2

Corporate fiduciary. *See* Bank

Corporate trustee. *See* Bank

Corporation
  authority to act as trustee, 3.1, 8.6
  as beneficiary, 5.1
  charitable, 9.5.1

Corpus. *See* Property requirement

Cotrustee
  liability, 6.1.4, 7.2.4, 7.3.1
  merger, 8.7

Index

Index

Durable Power of Attorney, 2.1.1, 3.4.1, 8.2.2.2, 9.6.2. *See also*
   Agency; Agent

Duties of trustee
   to account, 6.1.5
   acquire all property due trust, 6.2, 6.2.1
   collect from predecessor, 6.2.1
   collect insurance proceeds, 6.2.1
   competence, 6.1.1
   control trust property, 6.2.1
   confidentiality, 6.2.3
   defend trust, 6.2.1
   earmark, 3.5.3.2(e), 6.2.1, 7.1, 7.2.1
   enforce claims, 6.2.1
   efficiency, 5.4.1.2
   keep and render accounts, 6.1.5.2
   litigation, duty to defend, 6.2.1
   litigation, duty to bring suit, 6.2.1
   impartiality, 6.2.5
   inflation, protect against, 6.2.1, 6.2.2.1, 6.2.2.2
   information, 6.1.5.1
   insure trust property, 6.2.1
   invest, 6.2.2
   litigate, 6.2.1
   loyalty, 5.5, 6.1.3, 6.2.3
   make property productive, 6.2, 6.2.2
   of personal attention, 6.1.4
   promptness, 5.4.1.2
   protect trust property, 6.2.1
   proxies, to vote, 3.5.3.1(e)
   prudence, 6.1.1
   remaindermen, 3.5.3.1(b)
   segregate, 6.2.1
   separate income from principal, 6.2.4
   settlor, 4.1.1, 4.1.2, 4.2, 6.1.2
   sovereign, 6.3, 7.3.4
   subscription rights, 6.2.1
   succession, 3.3
   supervise agents, 6.1.4
   supervise cotrustees, 6.1.4
   terms of trust, 6.1.2

Earmark, duty to, 3.5.3.2(e), 6.2.1, 7.1, 7.2.1

Embezzlement, 2.3, 7.3.4.2

Employee benefit plan. *See* Employee benefit trust

273

Index

Index

Index

IRA trust
generally, 9.2.2
creditors, 9.2.2
filings, 6.3.1
investments, permissible, 9.2.2
SEP, 9.2.2
1099-R, 6.3.1

Irrevocability, 4.1-4.2, 8.1, 8.2.1.1, 8.2.2.1-8.2.2.2

Issue, defined, 5.2

Joint estate and powers of cotrustees, 3.4.4.1, 3.4.4.2

Jurisdiction. *See* Conflict of laws

K-1, 6.3.1

Laches, 5.5

Land, power to sell, 3.5.3.1(a)

Lease, power to, 3.5.3.1, 3.5.3.1(b), 3.5.3.2(b)

Leasehold investments, 6.2.2.1

Legal interest
generally, 3.5.1
merger, 8.7

Legal list, 6.2.2.1

Legal title of trust property, 2.1, 3.5.1

Lending. *See* Borrowing

Liability
limited, of trusts resembling corporations, 9.3
of beneficiary, 6.6, 9.3
personal liability of trustee, 3.5.4.1, 7.1, 7.2.9
of trustee to beneficiary, 7.2
of trustee to nonbeneficiaries, 7.3
of trustee to settlor, 4.1.1, 4.1.2
of trustee to sovereign, 7.3.4
of trust officer, 3.5.4.2, 7.2.9

Life in being, 8.2.1, 8.2.1.2, 8.2.1.4, 8.2.1.5

Life interest. *See* Beneficiary

Limited charitable intent/purpose. *See* Cy pres

Index

Index

Property, trustee's right to exchange, 3.5.3.1(a)

Proxies, voting, 3.5.3.1, 3.5.3.1(e), 6.1.4

Prudent, duty to be, 6.1, 6.1.1

Prudent Expert Rule, 9.2.1

Prudent Investor Rule, 6.1.4, 6.2.2.1, 3.5.3.2(i)

Prudent Man Rule, 3.5.3.1(a), 3.5.3.2(i), 6.2, 6.2.2, 6.2.2.1, 6.2.2.2, 6.2.5

Public policy
conflict of laws, 8.5
exculpatory provisions, 7.2.6

Punitive damages, 7.2.3.3

Purpose of trust. *See* Intent of settlor

Qualified employee benefit trust, 9.2.1

Quarries, 6.2.4.3

Quasi-trusts, 9.5, 9.5.3

Racketeering statutes. *See* RICO

Real estate
bona fide purchaser, 8.3.2
conflict of laws, 8.5
leasing, 3.5.3.1(b)
possession, right to, 3.5.2.1
recording, 8.3.1, 8.3.2
REIT, 9.3
sale, power of, 3.5.3.1(a)

Real Estate Investment Trust. *See* REIT

Realty trust, 2.1.1, 5.3.1, 5.3.2, 5.6, 9.3

Receiver, 7.2.3.4

Recording, 8.3.1, 7.3.2

Registration (deeds). *See* Recording

Registration (SEC), 7.3.3.3, 7.3.4.2

Regulation 9 (Reg 9), 3.1, 6.2.1

REIT, 9.3

Reimbursement, 3.5.2, 3.5.2.3, 6.1.3, 7.3, 7.3.4.1

Index

Index

Index